Y0-BQE-418

Yankee Revenooer

DEDICATION

To my wife, Myrtle Weathers Kearins, and all the moons over Carolina whose silvery radiance has guided me as beacons among the firelights and shadows of a thousand forest floors.

YANKEE REVENOOER

Jack J. Kearins

Moore Publishing Company
Durham, North Carolina

N.C.
351.7
K

YANKEE REVENOOER Copyright © 1969 by Moore Publishing Company, Durham, North Carolina. All rights reserved. Printed in the United States.

Library of Congress Catalog Number: 70-79094.

c.2

INTRODUCTION

by

Mrs. Reva Rothrock

Former United States Commissioner, Raleigh, North Carolina

It is a privilege to introduce John Kearins and his book YANKEE REVENOOER. The author skillfully shares personal experiences with the reader in a humanely interesting and humorous way with malice toward none.

It is the story of a dream come true for a boy and a man who considers himself most fortunate for having been able to do those things in life he wanted to do. If John claims any distinction between himself and his fellow man it is in that he considers himself "a lucky guy," because he had always wanted to be a revenooer, and became one, and because he wanted to write a book about revenooering and wrote one. YANKEE REVENOOER is a most fitting title.

John was born in Lawrence, Massachusetts, lived in New York in his youth, went to Washington, back to New York, and then to Raleigh, North Carolina where he has been married to Myrtle Weathers of Panther Branch, North Carolina and Washington, D.C.

I first met John while I was serving as United States Commissioner at Raleigh, North Carolina, where many of the cases before me were related to moonshining violation of the federal liquor laws. John was the senior revenooer stationed at Raleigh, and his friends called him "Race."

When it came to the point of establishing the proper amount of bond to be set for a prisoner's appearance in court John was always in agreement on the lowest possible figure. He never hesitated to speak up in a good man's behalf. He held freedom to be man's greatest possession and was most careful not to jeopardize it. His no's and yes's were equally as loud in any given testimony. I know of none who violated his trust in them.

The duties of the United States Commissioner are to hold hearing, find cause, or no cause, to set bond and bind over the offender for trial in Federal District Court. Since the complaint is the foundation for issuance of a warrant there must be shown probable cause that a crime has been committed and that the person, or persons, for whom the warrant is sought, has committed it. The federal officer who makes an arrest must take the accused person without unnecessary delay to the nearest available U.S. Commissioner. It is a rare case when accused moonshiners do not agree with the reports of U.S. Alcohol and Tobacco Tax Investigators, a tribute to the diligence and patience of the revenue officers.

The traditions of the office of U.S. Commissioner in the southern states do not suggest regular office hours or days of the week on which to work. It is not at all unusual to receive a phone call at home during late night hours and on Saturdays, Sundays, and holidays, from a revenooer with moonshiners in custody.

There is something bordering the patriotic sense in approaching an A&TT office late at night and seeing the lights burning bright inside. The same lights you knew had burned bright in the early morning hours as well.

A stranger might have a hard time in distinguishing the officers from the moonshiners. All of them might be well bearded, tired looking, and dressed in rough clothing, and there is an easy going dialogue in effect which does not suggest of culprit and captor, or perpetrator and apprehender. They are men among men.

Through the atmosphere of the room always comes the odor of moonshine or mash from the men's clothing.

A woman commissioner learns forthwith and forevermore to knock loud and clear before entering such a place. Hats are removed, and all men stand. Where loudness and levity had reigned there begins a strange quiet and a new seriousness. The revenooers and their fellow men are at the fingerprinting and photographing equipment. The typewriter keys fly, and there is an audible reflection from one of the moonshiners as to how he was caught and by whom he had been reported. Serious business is at hand. It is the time of the accused being faced by his accuser.

YANKEE REVENOOER is not a legendary book about legendary

characters by a legendary revenooer. It is of reality of men and God's creatures, of the ones who dwelt fleetingly in the many immediate worlds John Kearins has known.

It is readily apparent that in that world full of shadows in which he lived John eagerly sought the sunshine in all of it; and yet he was willing to accept the shadows when they came, no matter how dark they were. As the old proverb states: "In the mud and scum of things. . .something always, always sings."

John told me of a birthday card he received from his mother on his twenty first birthday. He said that he memorized it and carried it in his wallet for a number of years. It went like this:

"As you travel along life's happy road,
With always a song in your heart,
May you find your truest happiness,
In having done a good man's part."

Mrs. Reva Rothrock
Raleigh, North Carolina
January, 1969.

YANKEE REVENOOER

FOREWORD

While this book is not a who, what, when, where and why of alcoholic beverages I feel that it will be helpful to the reader for me to include some brief comment and history of such.

Moonshine is non–taxpaid distilled spirits in the United States. It has been called by many names. Some are: Blockade, Bootleg, Booze, Corn, Kickapoo Juice, King Corn, King Kong, Panther Juice, Tiger Sweat, White Mule and White Lightning.

Moonshine is made by almost as many recipes as there are manufacturers, and there are manufacturers, and there are plenty.

Licensed Beverage Industries, Inc., in a booklet distributed by the National Council Against Illegal Liquor set forth reported still seizures in 1956 as totaling 25,608.

In 1965 the total number of illicit still seizures is listed as 19,391. These figures include seizures by Federal Agents, and State and Local Agents combined.

Moonshine basically is a product of distilled fermented mash made from sugar, yeast, cornmeal, hog feed or other readily obtainable grains combined and mixed with water.

This is contained in a fermenter which is usually a barrel or box. It is fermented for a period of time set by the whims and fancies of the individual manufacturer. His convenience, taste, and smell are usually his guides.

Many factors should be taken into consideration. These are largely ignored in cellar, and creek–side operations with home made stills.

Haste is the most important accomplishment for the moonshine distiller. Sanitation, and the niceties of all other cooking arts are ignored in favor of haste. Haste permits the last dollar in value to be squeezed from a run before the clarion cry "The Revenooers are

Coming" signals the end of production. The dollar is the highlight of moonshine enterprise. Some even say that moonshine is made to sell, not to drink.

The lowest priced legally manufactured whiskey is far superior to the best, and most painstakingly made moonshine in spite of all legends, claims, and hopes otherwise of the manufacturer.

It is a criminal offense to manufacture moonshine, as it also is to sell it, possess it, or traffic in it in any manner. Regulations on the manufacture and sale of beverages containing alcohol go back an astounding number of years.

Wine making in temperate climates is synonymous with the development of man's earliest culture. Beer making, in the northern lands which were too cold for the growing of grapes, was an early art which dates back almost to earliest civilization there.

In the year 2000 B.C., the code of King Hammurabi of Babylonia called for the death sentence of wine sellers who permitted unruly persons on their premises. This was probably the first official ruling relating to alcoholic beverages.

A chronology of significant dates and events relating to the history and taxation of alcoholic beverages, in part, is as follows:

1260 A.D.–The Arabians drank a distilled beverage called Aqua Vitae. (Water of Life). Later the Arabs taught the Spaniards to make it. Subsequently the Spaniards made their process of manufacture known to Irish monks. England had in effect a tax on distilled spirits. The Irish and Scotch people evaded the tax and operated small stills in their homes and in neighboring hills. These same Irish and Scotch people, when they came to America, brought their knowledge of distilling to the colonies.

1625–America's first saloon opened in Boston.

1633–Massachusetts first required a permit for the sale of liquor.

1637–The first brewery was built in Massachusetts.

1643–Connecticut required a license for sale of wines and liquors.

1700–Rum was being made in Massachusetts and Rhode Island from molasses shipped from the West Indies. Rum was the first coin in the commerce of slavery. Prime slaves were purchased for a few gallons of rum.

1760–The Irish and Scotch peoples from the highlands brought to America their knowledge and ability to make whiskey. They continued them in mountainous areas of Southern Pennsylvania and

Kentucky which was then a part of Virginia. (Kentucky did not become a state until 1792).

1783–Bourbon whiskey distilled from corn came into being. Bourbon County, Kentucky, was a vast area. Kentucky itself was in Virginia and known as Kentucky County.

1791–Whiskey act of March 3, 1791. Tax at 54 cents per gallon capacity was levied on stills and a tax of 7 cents per gallon on whiskey was imposed on production.

1792–Whiskey was being sold in Pennsylvania at 25 cents per gallon which could not have been done if the taxes were paid.

1794–The Whiskey Rebellion. Seven thousand persons led by Albert Gallatin, (later Secretary of the Treasury) and others, protested the whiskey tax at Parkinson's Ferry, Pennsylvania. The Governor of Pennsylvania refused to call out the State militia to cope with the situation. President Washington called in 15,000 militia from other States. A compromise agreement was reached between the protesting citizens and their government. Many were charged with liquor law violations and the cost to the Government was $1,500,000. However, the authority of the Federal Government was thereby established in such matters.

1802–April 6th. Abolishment of taxes on the liquor industry was proclaimed by President Jefferson who called it the "Infernal" excise system.

1814–September. Congress placed additional taxes on distilled spirits and on the right to retail spirituous liquors.

1817–Act of December 23rd. Congress abolished all taxes on distillers and distilled spirits. No further Internal Taxes were imposed for 43 years. Average price for whiskey was 14.4 cents per gallon in Ohio.

1861–August 5th. Congress passed a bill providing for Internal Taxations.

1862–July 1st. Congress passed the act which is the basis for our present tax system. This Act imposed taxes on a number of items including distilled spirits, fermented liquors and beer. The office of Commissioner of Internal Revenue was also created.

1863–Office of Deputy Commissioner of Internal Revenue was created and three "detectives" were hired for the "protection of the revenue."

1863–The tax on distilled spirits was twenty cents per gallon.

1865–Distilled spirits were taxed at $1.50 per gallon.

1866–Distilled spirits were taxed at $2.00 per gallon.

1868–July 20th. Congress passed an act providing for stamp taxes on liquor and tobacco. Taxes then were at 1000 percent of original cost.

1864 to 1875–This was the period of activity of the "Whiskey Rings" composed of distillers, politicians and Revenue Agents who worked together to defraud the Government.

1875–"Whiskey Rings" smashed. Loss to Government from such combines was estimated at from two–hundred million to one billion dollars.

1883–Taxes repealed on all commodities except distilled spirits, fermented liquor and tobacco. Internal Revenue collections from these items supplied the bulk of the money needed by the Treasury until 1914.

1914–Income Tax Law passed under 16th amendment. Taxes were increased on beer, wines, champagne and similar products.

1917–August 10th. Act passed which prohibited the manufacture of distilled spirits for beverage purposes from grains, cereals, fruit, and food products.

1918–November 21st. Act passed which prohibited the manufacture of fermented malt liquors and wines from grains, cereals, fruit and food products after May 1, 1919. The same Act prohibited the sale of distilled spirits, malt liquors, and wines for beverage purposes after June 30, 1919.

All of these acts were consolidated in Title 1, of the National Prohibition Act which became the start of the prohibition era which remained until 1933.

1919–January 29th. The 18th Amendment to the constitution was ratified. The Amendment stated: "The manufacture, sale, or transportation of intoxicating liquors within, the importation thereof into, or the exportation thereof from the United States and all territory subject to the jurisdiction thereof for beverage purposes is hereby prohibited." The Amendment was to be effective one year from date of ratification.

1919–December. The Prohibition Unit was set up in the Bureau of Internal Revenue to combat the illegal liquor traffic.

1925–3700 employees engaged in narcotics and prohibition enforcement by the Government. 77,000 arrested for liquor law violations. $11,200,000 valuation placed on property seized. 7 agents killed. 39 injured in the performance of their duties.

January 16th, 1920, to May 9, 1934. 85 agents killed by gunfire. 41 additional agents killed from other occupational hazards. 96 agents wounded. 128 assaulted. 191 injured by violators.

1933–December 5th. Congress adopted the 21st Amendment, providing for repeal of the 18th Amendment.

1934–May 10th. Alcohol Tax Unit organized within the Internal Revenue Bureau providing for inspection and enforcement.

May 10, 1934 to March 1, 1965. 13 investigators killed by gunfire. 17 killed and 502 injured in automobile accidents while on duty. 617 assaulted by violators. 107 injured by violators resisting arrest, and 30 wounded by gunfire from violators.

November, 1951. Alcohol and Tobacco Tax Division envolved from Alcohol Tax Unit.

1964–During fiscal year taxes on alcohol products amounted to more than three and one–half billion dollars. Taxes on distilled spirits in 1964 by the Federal Government were in the amount of $10.50 per proof gallon.

1965–Federal Revenues on alcoholic beverages were $3,879,648,164. State revenues were $1,660,567,934. Local Revenues were: $171,942,919. Total public revenues on alcoholic beverages were: $5,712,159,017.

ONE

ON GROWING UP

That big, black boat, rocking and scraping against the sea wall, that summer in 1930, carried a hidden cargo which was unknown to anyone, not even me. Somewhere in its stinking innards there were forces abroad in all those smashed liquors, and they were shaping my destiny.

When I came to know it I was older and far away from wherever that boat was. It may have been on the bottom of the ocean or engaged in smuggling along remote and alien coastlines.

I can see it all now as it was before me on that hot prohibition summer afternoon. It began in Battery Park, New York, where Manhattan dips its feet into the sea, and where, not far from shore those great, moving, soul–stirring pictures of a New Yorker's New York Skyline are made.

The spectators, standing near the boat, expressed curiosity about it in any given number of languages. Someone said, "It's one of them mind sweepers." To me it was a boat returned from a voyage, awesome and mysterious. I had to know more, somehow, some way.

It was just a bit to starboard of the outbound Staten Island Ferry starting point. It was on a hot Sunday afternoon.

Four of us, boys about fifteen years of age, were gazing intently at a big black boat which, for some reason or other, was an object of curiosity to a number of bystanders.

We worked our way forward in the crowd. I heard someone else say, in a tone suggesting authority, that the boat had been converted for the business of smuggling whiskey. We soon learned that the boat had been seized for "rum–running" violations of the Federal Prohibition Laws, and that it had been captured by a Revenue Cutter crew.

The boat bore obvious bullet scars and smelled peculiarly akin to what I had come to recognize as "drunkards breath."

Even to me, a tenderfoot completely, in my knowledge of boats, there was something obvious about the boat which suggested grace and speed at full throttle.

It had been brought to harbor that morning a fireman said. A balloon peddler said that it had almost escaped. A guy who was on the same "el" train with us coming downtown, said that the skipper of the boat had been killed and buried at sea.

One guy said that the boat was merely a fishing boat and that people were too darned curious. I looked for the customary gear such as I had seen at Fulton's Market, and at the Bronx River sports fisherman's pier, and it had none.

My imagination was stirred by all the salty lingo going on about me, and I hitched up my white–duck pants, tucked my white middy shirt under my belt, and wished that I had worn my sailor cap so that then I might say something, and someone would listen to me. . . .in my imaginary personal uniform of the sea.

I had to be content with daydreaming, and I struck a pose which I had once seen the skipper of the coastwise steamer "Lexington" take while he was docking at Christopher Street.

All of my nautical experience had taken place in two round trips from Providence, Rhode Island to New York, but in those early years that was something of the sea and ships, and I relived the best moments of both trips. I looked straight ahead as though I was seeing things along the sea wall that nobody else could.

I saw them, and the shifting of the crowd did not bother me or block my view.

I saw a Revenue Cutter deck beneath my feet, and I felt the wheel in my hand on the bridge. I saw a dark night and rolling seas the dim silhouette of a rum–runner, painted black. I saw the St. Elmo's fire alongside.

My ship was in full commission with the terse admonition I gave myself, "Captain John Kearins Commanding." Everyone has to start somewhere.

It was such ideas of youth which make firemen, policemen,

political figures and presidents.

It was because of such, and other things that I had that day become enthused with the field of Revenuersmanship.

I was just starting with life itself and I had a long way to go.

Before we get to Revenuering all the way, let me beam you in on the biggest preliminaries of all; the wonderments I found in learning and knowing people. Since we all have such chores, I will tell you in this chapter of my own ways in that.

Let me tell you how it came about that I was at the sea wall at the Battery that day. In this lies the fact that what real simple things are to a youngster, are not always known by grownups.

For the teenager, next year is an eternity away, and nothing is everyday or commonplace.

There are people who say that there is naught to do for the younger people in any big city. They said the same thing when I went to New York from Lawrence, Massachusetts in 1929.

I was thirteen years old then and was what some people called a gang–gatherer. It did not take me long to hook up with a gang. The name of the gang was always changing and we were Rovers, Ramblers, Eagles, Hawks, and when one guy took to studying Spanish we went over to the glittering entity of "The El Dorado Boys." This, to us, suggested class, and we thought it fitted our station in life, and our vanity, in those girl–conscious moments we were beginning to have.

I learned how to play stickball, one–a–cat, how to shoot crap and play poker for pennies. I learned how to snitch mickeys which is what we called potatoes. We roasted the mickeys over an open fire on a place called Cow's Hill.

Cow's Hill was a massive rock vein which challenged the most enterprising builders, and it stood its ground while the adjacent premises became a series of apartment complexes.

The gang was always in pow–wow while we cooked the mickeys.

We gathered around the fire, usually just after nightfall, and made our plans and aired our gripes.

We talked about cops and crooks mostly.

To us, guys who played with goils were sissies.

We never talked about goils to any extent. We talked of cats, dogs, horses, and people, as we saw them.

We told stories of new kinds, and we laughed at jokes which were not funny to us because of their humor but because of some hidden, unidentifiable meaning of which we knew nil.

We added new words to our vocabulary. We combed our hair. We found new games to play. We brushed our teeth without having to be told, and went to the movies at night instead of on Saturday afternoons.

The movies we watched were usually about gangsters, well–dressed, slick looking, fast talking ones. Edward G. Robinson, and James Cagney, and George Raft guys were for real with us. Cowboys and Indians, and Aesop's Fables, became kid stuff, and we began to understand the meaning of wisecracks, and jokes which the vaudeville actors told. We actually looked at and understood the Pathe News.

For a while we remained with Cow's Hill, and we varied our mickey suppers with roasted corn and store bought hamburgers from the nickel burger places which looked to us like little ceramic fortresses that were springing up everywhere. More and more we favored sitting down to eat on a revolving stool rather than standing up in the dim light of Cow's Hill or at best, stretched full length on the ground propped on one elbow.

At first not many women or girls sat in those places to eat, and when a copiously endowed man with oversized buttocks sat on a stool we poked each other and giggled behind his back at the overlapping flesh.

We deserted Cow's Hill for the lore of the bull pen.

We took to hanging around the big guys most of whom were going to college. We talked of being the reason people who sold penny chewing gum and nickel hamburgers could create large corporations. Volume was responsible for Henry Ford and Walter Chrysler becoming millionaires. We didn't know any millionaires so we filed such information away in our minds for future reference.

It was great to listen to the big guys describe their adventures with possessive, bold, beautiful women everywhere they went. Those lies they told about intimate contacts with good–looking, well stacked gals on the subway, to and from school, were the spiciest. When they finished a tale it was not something from the BMT or the Interborough Rapid Transit System, but it was straight from the Baghdad express decorated with soft lights, silk lingerie, and sweet music. There were no champions though. It happened to one and to all.

One of the big guys would razz another unmercifully, and then would improve upon a more unlikely story.

Sometimes they would draw together in a tight circle, apart from us, and we could hear parts of the conversation like "dis broad and dat babe," and "everybody was crocked," and "I told my bootlegger dis and I told him dat, my personal Moonshiner, dat is."

Once I knocked a little round metal box out of the hand of one of the big guys who was showing it around in a circle. I retrieved it and ran away with it and the younger guys followed. We looked at it up on an apartment house roof. On the cover it said: "Three Merry Widows," and "Agnes, Mabel and Becky." "Price one dollar." We opened the box and laughed and one of us said, "Those damlittle babies, playing with girls balloons." Agnes, Mabel and Becky must be some kind of balloon champions." One kid took the box home with him. When he blew up one of the balloons that night his old man cuffed him, and he told his father that I had given them to him. The old man shook his fist at me every time I saw him after that. To make it worse the big guy I snatched the box from caught up with me later and proceeded to teach me a lesson. Being too stupid to learn I became the first "young guy" to whip one of the "big guys." I grew bold and stood right there with them when they talked, and soon they accepted me.

We gave each other nicknames. Mine was "Borston" which meant "Boston," because I came from near there and said things like "cawfee," and "park" and "bottle" the way folks up in Massachusetts did.

I didn't object to my nickname. It was pretty good considering that we had a "Nutsy," a "Booby," and the usual "Polack" and "Dutch," and those kinds of names.

No one seemed to mind his nickname. We were all together in rebelling though, when someone else said it in the wrong way.

Summarily, we were feeling our oats. We moved into other gang territory. We went there with stick ball bats, which were really broom sticks, and nobody bothered us. We assimilated with other gangs. We were ready for anything.

The ball teams all over New York provided us with a tidy little source of income for our summertime needs. We'd put up a "kitty" and bet it on our own team a couple or few times a week, and by hustling, playing hard, and winning, we split it umpteen ways. I pitched, caught, and played in the outfield. I held a long bat, or close to the top, and I took roundhouse swings by stepping forward to meet the ball. One day I stepped a bit prematurely and took a fastball dead in the groin while I was off balance. They put in a substitute to take the walk for me, and I was out of the game. After that I concentrated on the spaces between the opposing team in the field, and was satisfied to shorten up on my grip, and to pull and push, and get the ball into the empty places.

One year like that we were real close, and after that because of school ties, studying and other things, we couldn't even put together a baseball team anymore.

On Saturdays and Sundays we took to roaming by subway and elevated trains, roller skates, and we split into a special group of four.

Our immediate gang then became Red, Dutch, Swede and Boston.

Roller skating on the mall in Central Park was an up and coming thing. The layout of the park had the rich people living on three sides, nearly, and the poor people living on the other side. When it came to skating in the park the mall was a place for everybody.

An Irish longshoreman told me once that he went there to watch the "Swells" and their ladies on roller skates. After that I had a whale of a time pretending to myself that I was a "Swell" and that my girl from South Bronx, was my lady.

I rolled my "R's" and I stood a little straighter when I skated as though I were the personal student of somebody famous in the roller skating world.

I did it all so good, I thought one day, as I was taking my skates off. A very effiminate looking man approached me and we had a dialogue. My girl was taking it all in, and for a while she kept quiet as we spoke.

He began the conversation. "You are a very accomplished skater, my dear fellow."

"There's nothing to it."

"But there is. Just everybody can't do it. At least not with the correct sway and body grace, which you seem to have acquired.

"Timing."

"More to it than that, my dear, dear young fellow."

"My teacher is responsible."

"Who is that?"

"Monsieur Lucien."

"Himself."

"None other."

"Bravo."

"A sterling teacher, Monseiur Lucien," I said, rolling about three "n's" all together at the end.

"Terribly demanding, I hear."

"Exactly."

"Your companion, did she too study under Luciennn?"

"Mademoisselle Luciennn."

"Do you like girls?"

"What else is there?"

"Have you ever done, ah, er, uh, certain things with a man?"

My lady spoiled everything right then and there for all of my lofty talk, and gentle manners. She said to the man, "Hey, you queer or something?"

We got up and left, and if she said it once that day she said it ten times, "Mind you, a goddam queer right there in the park in broad daylight." I had to find out what she was talking about. I asked the big guys and they laughed at me and told me all about it.

I never did ask the girl how she knew about those things, and I wasn't going to, after the way the big guys had their fun over it at my expense.

I did tell the others in my gang about it and we discussed it a bit and promptly forgot about it.

The next day I saw my "certain" friend's picture in the paper, posing with a group of Broadway chorus girls. The guy was identified as a dance director, and I was more confused than ever. To me it was sort of like a meatpacker being a vegetarian. It didn't make sense.

All the "Swells" and their ladies wore shoe skates, or shoes with wheels attached. The women wore white ones and the men wore black ones. Those kinds of skates had wooden wheels.

Like I said, my shoes had telltale signs. My skates had "Union Hardware" imprinted on them, and they sold for about a dollar and a half per pair. New wheel replacements cost fifteen cents each. We called such skates "Ball Barriens" to distinguish them from the seventy–five cents a pair "kid skates" that had sleeve bearings. "Ball Barriens" for us meant the Cadillac of the trade. High kid shoes and wooden wheels were for the rich, so they were out for us.

Adult roller skating on the mall became a passing fad, and we shifted our skating arena to the public streets uptown and the Bronx Park Zoo area.

To get to Bronx Park we skated all the way. We took the routes where the roadway was not of cobblestone paving.

We went up to the Park mostly on Saturdays because we found that hitching on to the trucks and wagons was an added attraction to skating.

On Sunday there were few commercial vehicles abroad.

When we would hang on to the back of a wagon or truck, the driver did not know that we were there. We would take positions where we would be concealed from his view. The solid tires on some of the trucks helped to keep the driver unaware of an added burden to his machine.

Some of the wagon drivers saw us and ignored us. These were mostly peddlers who perhaps found some company in our attachment to their tailgates.

Sometimes a wagon driver would drive us away with a rifle–like crack of his whip. A few have touched me, and my friends, too. We just took it and reached out for the next wagon tailgate that came along.

A few times some rookie cop would appear from nowhere and let one of us have it with the business end of his nightstick.

No one ever got hurt, and if we got mad it was because we didn't see the cop coming, and a nose–thumbing helped things along and sent us on our way with dispatch.

At the park, Dutch was always the most animated and fascinated one of us all. He would display it by making spontaneous exclamations, of whatever he was thinking about, right then in front of the other spectators at the cages or exhibits.

It was Dutch who first observed some foolish antics on the part of monkeys. Once he had been watching some monkeys for a while, and we left him there. When he joined us he said that some guy told him that at certain times of the month for women that monkeys could tell what was happening and that it made them rambunctious.

Once Dutch told an animal out loud that it ought to be ashamed of itself and called the animal's conduct to everyone's attention.

Another time he asked publicly of a keeper how he mated the giraffes. The keeper was tactful and said, "They mate themselves."

Dutch came back with the remark that it was a good thing that the giraffes were not head high all over.

Swede, whenever he separated from us, would be certain to be somewhere engaged in conversation with adults about politics, the state of the union, Veteran's pensions and any news of the day.

Once though, Swede got into some adult conversation with a scoutmaster and his girlfriend. It was a dilly! The scoutmaster was about thirty or so in our minds. He was neat enough in appearance with his hair combed back and parted in the middle. It was blonde, and too long for those days. He was of average height and build and had what I recall as almost powder blue eyes. He also had the slightest suggestion of a moustache. I guess it was waxed, but then I thought it was shiny from spittle at the thin tapered ends.

When the guy spoke he gave me the impression that he was uptown, or poor man's Bohemian, and not too worldly wise in his philosophy. He said things as though he imagined them rather than having had experienced them. He knew a little about everything, it seemed to me, but not too much about anything but sex maybe. He certainly did love to talk about it.

He was a change rattler, too.

He twirled that moustache while he jingled change with one hand, and then he would abruptly switch at some imagined point for punctuation of his sentences and start jingling with the other hand.

The guy spoke of higher mountains than the highest, roping, branding, mating and womanizing. It was as though he was a rootin' tootin' sexy cowboy bent on a roundup of all vices for himself.

He grinned readily whenever he completed a sentence. He was a woman-hound through and through, and he spoke connatatively about the figures six and nine, and he drew pictures in the sand for us which told deep dark secrets about the figures six and nine.

Much later, in 1967, I heard about the State of New Jersey officials changing the number of route 69 to number 231 or something that because of the legends of number 69 and because of the pilfering of the highway signs for some sort of room trophy by students and fanciers of those numerical designations.

Not long ago I heard that the whole theme had been carried to 34½, 138, etc. out in California by aspiring devotees of addition, subtraction, multiplication and division and things.

By now no doubt it has been computerized and probably is

approaching a science in status. I hate to think of square roots.

My guy demonstrated the whole thing right there in the Bronx Park Zoological Gardens with the mechanization of his forefinger in the sand for us. We had the added visual aid of his girlfriend standing right there on duty and agreeing all the while as the moving finger wrote.

That gal had an eye for figures and a figure for eyes.

I wondered almost aloud where in hell a guy met a gal like that. It was strictly down–behind–the–barn stuff in the vernacular of the day. We knew it and so did they. There was one thing in my mind and that was that those two had studied their arithmetic better than I had. I was curious about the gal's total score and how she graded herself, but I was still a million miles away from it all right there.

I had the guy figured as a Bronx bred cowhand and as a chief scout for the Grand Concourse bicycle beaver–patrol.

Kids played Beaver by strolling in front of women seated on park benches in warm weather. At last reports I understand that air–conditioning has made it almost obsolete, for the viewer and the viewee. Only boys played it. The bicycle was the answer to quantity viewing. The pill will eventually assassinate it. The only reason I mention the thing is because of its historical significance.

That day Swede was more animated than I had ever seen him. He was a tiger endeavoring to get a first hand demonstration right there of something which is not usually a spectator sport.

I was blowing hot and cold, and if it had all been in these medically conscious times I might have thought I was having a heart attack, even if it was sort of pleasant at that.

The dialogue for a while went something like this:

"How about you two just sort of showing us right here? Nobody ever comes here."

"I'd have to be awfully sure before we went ahead with it."

"Hell, nobody'd see you."

"How old are you Swede?"

"Twenty–one."

Swede would have told him that he had voted for Abraham Lincoln if that was what the guy wanted to hear.

The rest of us didn't want to hear anything like that, and I think I was the one who said "Let's go," and nobody needed any urging. Swede did stay to get the guy's address which was not too far from the park, and he joined us up near the big bird cages.

Red didn't seem to get any sort of kick from the whole deal and was quiet as usual.

Dutch said, "She feels soft as hell."

I recall him skating behind her while the guy was drawing his sixes and nines in the sand.

I shuddered to think of the possible fates of that pair if they had carried on like they did with some gangs not too far from where we lived. Those guys were fond of gang banging, as they described one of their livelier arts.

I didn't say much about the girl here because she impressed me as being a willing companion to the guy in anything he said, wanted, or did. I did have to tell you what kind of a guy he was so you would know the whole set up. Everyone knows at least one guy like that.

Things happened fast, as they always do, at that time of life in the city, and the country too. Through all of it my hopes never strayed too far from my ambition to one day chase rum runners far and wide.

TWO

NEW LIFE AND LEVITY

I started my apprenticeship. I began the long odyssey of the journeyman revenooer that was to lead me through official places, tenements, and forests and the association with all the creatures of my worlds therein.

I left Pennsylvania Station about midnight in the latter part of February, 1935. I took the Washington express. It was pulled part way by the new electrical drive system that was still under construction. My car was occupied by a number of construction workers employed on the main line at various points.

I watched the snow covered world of winter and the lights of cities and towns we passed through. It meant only to me that thousands of people were out there asleep. I wasn't sleepy at all. I thought of home and I missed it already. I wondered what Washington would be like.

Where was the Mason–Dixon line? Was Baltimore farther south than Washington? Did Washington people talk with a southern accent? I felt deeply absorbed in those reflections, and I recollected from my earliest days of geography and answered my own questions. I dozed off.

I heard the conductor coming through the train and he roared out a challenge and a statement at the same time. What he said was, "Philleradelphier," and "Barrod Street Station." He sounded like a boxing match referee with a booming, resonant voice. Everybody on that train knew where we were right then. It made me feel as though I were in the first round for my own quest of revenooering championship of the world.

The wheels of the train were cheering me on with their echoing "DA–DA–DA–DA" as the rail sections met the wheels time after time.

At the next station a couple of husky construction workers boarded the train. The younger one sat next to me and the older man sat in the seat in front of us and he promptly went to sleep.

I said hi to the young guy as he sat down and I moved closer to the window to give him more room.

"You with the Pennsy?"

"No. I'm with the government."

"What department you in?"

"Don't know yet. Just reporting. Got a Civil Service appointment." I was loving the sound of my own words.

"Glad to know you. Always did want to meet a government man besides a mail carrier. That's all I ever knew around home with the government."

He had on work clothes. He continued, "You're gonna be a white collar man too I suppose."

"Oh sure."

"That's good. I never had a chance at it. I like what I have and hope it don't peter out too quick. It's steady and the work keeps me in shape."

"How far are you going?"

"To Wilmington. I ride back and forth on the train every day. Takes a lot of my time traveling and the further down we go the further we are away from home. When we get near Baltimore and Washington, I'll have to take a room down there."

At Wilmington he woke up Pop and said, "Pop, this is Johnny, a friend of mine with the government." Pop took my hand in his and it felt like a catcher's mitt. He said, "Glad to meet a government man. You with the FBI?"

"Don't know. Gotta get an assignment." I beamed all over and half thought to myself of the Dillinger movie I had seen, and the FBI, and the revenooers. The other half of my thought was, Gees, and this is only the beginning. Wow.

"Washington, here I come," I spoke to myself not quite audibly. I leaned my elbow on the window sill and looked the way I thought a FBI man or a revenooer man should. I gave what I thought was an official goodby wave to Earl and Pop up at the front of the car, waiting for the train to stop.

The conductor came down through the car shouting. No, he hollered it. "Whilminggtunn, Whilminggtunn, Dellawayerr."

I can still hear it just the way he said it. It was beautiful to me in the early morning on my first official U.S. government job reporting day. It was sort of like he was punctuating the first sentence of my official life with all the significance and emphasis he could give it. That was exactly what he was doing to me too. That guy was a traveling man's conductor and a railroad man's conductor. I was feeling that I was in my own back yard instead of grinding the miles away from it, sensation by sensation.

I heard the same conductor a couple of years later on a northbound trip. I caught his voice as he came through the cars through the clackety–clack noises of the wheels and the swoosh of the wind when he opened the door to my car. I thought he was better even that time, and that he should be, because he was in about the second paragraph of my officialdom instead of the first sentence.

At Baltimore another conductor announced. It came out like "Ballimer Merlin." We were off the electricity and on to steam. We had made faster time with the electric engine up front. The choo–choo did better in spelling out new and far away places to me.

The choo–choos always had something all their own when they started up with that first running down of steam. It sounded like a bunch of firecrackers trying to out fire each other, and then it quit in a hurry and the train began to move. It was that way to me that morning at Wilmington.

Some of the choo–choo drivers could play that whistle and make it mourn a lonesome all its own up there at the front of the train. They played another kind of song as the train went around a curve and it was different if you were sitting back in the last car. It was even more lonesome then. That old whistle got things to hopping in all rooms of the houses along the rail routes. You have heard the story of the farmer with the big family and how he blamed it on the Cannonball Express, or Freight number 84, for coming along at an hour of the morning when it was too early to get up and too late to go back to sleep.

I was thinking about those things that morning on my way to Washington. I guess it was so that I wouldn't feel myself getting further and further from home.

I got ready but good when I heard the guy coming down through the train hollering "Warrshinggtonn, Dee See."

I could see the lighter grays of morn painting the horizon for the day's work ahead for both of us. It was truly a new horizon in my life and I looked at it good.

I saw the powerful lights of Washington yards making the steam from the standing locomotives look like cotton puffs hanging in the half night, half day of dawn.

The pullman cars and their patrons were asleep in the shadows.

The conductor was echoing his "Warrshinggton," "Warrshinggton" through the train as though he were trying to call George from over on the other side of the Delaware.

Gosh! Then I saw it, the big white dome. I saw it for the first time. I knew all at once how folks who had been abroad for eons felt when they saw the Statue of Liberty as they were inbound from overseas.

It tickled and it chilled.

I turned away to paint that instant indelibly in my mind. I turned back to see it again, all of it that I could see from my point of view.

I looked to the side and saw half–consciously the brook and valley names on the sleeping cars alongside.

I looked again toward the Capitol and I wondered if all Americans felt as American as I did right then.

I wished that Ma could have been there with me so she could see it all that very moment, and feel it and hear it sing its sunrise service to me. For the first time I felt the pangs of homesickness prodding me with doubt about the wisdom of what I was doing. My suitcase seemed heavier as I got off the train. I wondered how long it would be before I got home again. I smelled the coffee brewing in the station restaurant. I went in and had a cup.

I felt better after the coffee. I took in all the little things which travelers, porters, waitresses and railroad men did in a big station in an important place. I think I was waiting to see Washington at its very best outside. I wanted to see it out there before me in the light of a full golden sunrise. To see it that way for my very first time. I wanted to get the same feeling from seeing all of it that I had felt when I saw the Capitol dome. I wanted all of the best that a new and important day could produce for me. I wanted to sing God's praises.

I didn't get into a cab in the taxi line. I went out in front of the station to look. I stood there looking for about twenty minutes. I liked what I saw, Washington, D. C., U.S.A.

A taxi was swinging around to enter the cab line and he slowed down in front of me and stopped. I got in and gave him the name of a hotel where I wanted to stay. He drove me around in a tight circle to a point across the plaza and let me out. The meter said 20 cents. I gave him a half dollar and told him to keep the 150 percent tip. He thanked me, and I felt like a big shot and was ready to take the day head on. Life sings like that sometimes.

I went into the hotel lobby and asked for the manager. I had a note for him from a friend of his who was a friend of our family. The manager was asleep. I registered and left the note with the clerk. I went up to my room with a bellhop. I tipped him and dismissed him. I sat down on the bed and looked out at the Capitol some more. I fell asleep and awakened when I heard someone at the door It was the manager.

He greeted me heartily and bade me to tarry for his hospitality. He asked me to have breakfast with him after I cleaned up and shaved and dressed for the day. It wasn't a bad start at all. I was thinking that I would have to use my middle initial in my official signatures. The name on the envelope of introduction to the manager stated formally enough for me, Mr. J. C. Dekletermayer, Mgr. That was not the manager's real name, of course, but the Mr. J. C. was sort of impressive to my notion.

No hotel manager was ever nicer than J. C. He introduced me to the hostess in charge of the domelight room where we ate. He picked up my check and signed it and everything was for free. He called me "Jawn" and he did everything just right to show me a genuine welcome mat. He gave me a very reasonable weekly rate and said, "I hope that you will be with us here at Washington for a good while." I wondered what Reverend Raymond had written in the note that I had given to the manager. It had to be good, but good.

I caught the way he said "at Washington" instead of "in Washington." While it's just a matter of prepositions grammatically, it is bigger than that, and more official sounding. It makes whatever is said more emphatic and more concerned to say "at Washington." At puts Washington more in the hub of things national than in does.

I found the administration building without difficulty.

I had a busy day and filled out forms, and took a physical examination that was abeaut. I went through all the details which personnel mysteries seem to afford. I wound up the official day in the Internal Revenue Building where I had to report for the physical. I wasn't to work there though, doggone it. I was to work in the Department of Agriculture.

I didn't go back to my hotel right away. I was in the Internal Revenue Building, at Washington, and I wanted to browse around and maybe see and talk to some revenooers.

I didn't find any walking around. In fact, I didn't even see one character with high boots on or a gun in a shoulder holster. Shucks, I didn't even see a guy with a beard and suspenders like he might have been an old timer at Revenooering. I thought that "Bureau of Internal Revenue" sounded more governmenty than anything else.

I was disappointed and decided on a change of scenery. I reached down into my overcoat pocket and pulled out the other four letters of introduction I had been given before I left New York.

I looked at the name and address on the first letter envelope and walked uptown to the business district. It wasn't far and in a few minutes I was entering an exclusive beauty parlor. It had a fancy name. I inquired for a lady who operated the salon. She came out in a minute or so and greeted me most kindly and graciously. I was alert, like a government employee should be, and polite and courteous in keeping with my position at Washington.

She was related to my recommendor. She was terribly busy I could see, but she said, "I am Adelle. Meet my sister Cecily," and I did. We made plans to have dinner at the Shoreham that night, the three of us.

Closing time was not far off so I stayed at the salon and read magazines and looked at the gals coming and going through the place. Time passed quickly enough.

Adelle called for her car and someone brought it over. It was a La Salle and the black paint job was waxed all hollow. Adelle climbed behind the wheel and Cecily sat beside her. I got in the back seat and took hold of the handstrap and sat back, wishing my old gang could see me now. The car smelled new, and the perfume from those two ladies made everything seem rich and at Washington–like.

The gals were maybe from forty to fifty and not many years apart in their respective ages; they were good looking and wore expensive dresses, and each had a fur coat that I guessed was mink. I didn't know anything about fur then, but anyhow they were nice coats.

We had a nice meal, and I was thankful that one thing that Ma and my sisters had insisted on was good manners at the table. I knew the score there, like holding the chair for the ladies, getting up and down, and the hardware utility involved in eating in nice places. As Washington went, I had a job down near the bottom of the totem pole, but that night I acted and was treated as if I were junior adminstrative assistant to the President of the United States. (Franklin D. Roosevelt)

The ladies dropped me off at my hotel around ten o'clock after leaving the restaurant and going by their house for a little while. They insisted on paying for my dinner. When we went by their house I was glad I had let them. They were loaded with dough.

I sacked out in a hurry when I reached my room, but not before I sat there looking at the Capitol all lit up. I couldn't get over it.

Everyone was nice to me when I reported for work in the administration building of the Agriculture Department. I was introduced all around, and I met people whose names I had seen in the papers back in New York. People seemed to be more friendly to me than anywhere else I'd been and I returned the friendship forthwith.

A nice young Jewish guy from Brooklyn was designated to show me about and teach me the ropes. He was a good one. We had a dialogue going in a short time. I had his uncle for a Bronx Home News customer years ago, it turned out. He had been in Washington for about a month and that made him an old timer. That's the way you think at that age. Since we had so much in common from the olden days we had real rapport. I had supper with him at his boarding house. I arranged to move there within the next two weeks.

The boarding house lady was a real old woman over seventy at the minimum. She was a FFV, which means First Families of Virginia. She talked in a southern accent without the drawl. She said hoose for house, and aboot for about, like I said goils for girls when I wanted to be real New Yorkese.

I met Southern fried chicken that night, and string beans cooked a long time in boiled country ham juices. I tried hot biscuits, collards, black–eyed peas and sweet potato pie. I knew that if I burped from all of it there would have to be a southern accent there.

Ma talked of the yankees she had met, Engineers in World War I,

Civil Engineers building governmental structures, and in fact she said, "The Germans would have loved to hear some of those conversations back '17 and '18 right there at that table."

"Son, I've got just the room you need upstairs. Looks out on the front side, has a fireplace, a nice writing desk, go up and look at it. Veronica, come here show this Yankee the front room Mr. Helfering is moving from." I liked Veronica and I would have followed her anywhere. She showed me the room. She lived in the next room. I took the room. It was all of $28.00 per month including three meals a day except on Sunday when there were only two served, breakfast and supper.

I ate supper every night there until I moved in. The next Saturday afternoon, Veronica, or Vonnie, as she had asked me to call her, took me for a drive all over Washington. We had supper and danced at Chimney Villa, over in Virginia. We got along great. Vonnie's car was just like mine. I couldn't wait to get up to New York and bring it down.

I thought that everyone who goes to Washington to take a government job should have it as good as me. I still had three letters to go as introductions to folks at Washington.

Vonnie and I went way uptown one Sunday afternoon and I presented my third introductory letter to a newspaper man and his family. We had dinner with them. I introduced Vonnie as my girl. They were great and we had a swell time.

The fourth letter was to a guy in the telephone company. I went to see him with a Brooklyn buddy of mine a few Sundays later. It was the day before payday, and we were both broke. We had a nice meal there about two o'clock and another about seven. They had turkey and served us a couple of beers apiece, and it couldn't have happened to a pair of more deserving and appreciative guys.

The fifth letter was to a guy on some YMCA committee, but I didn't use it. I was afraid that he would want me to stay there, and I was too settled and content to move and YMCA did not spell GIRLS at all.

Vonnie went to New York with me on the train when I went up to get my car. I introduced her to Ma and my family. They enjoyed her Southern accent. We drove down to the Holland Tunnel enroute to Washington. We had stopped in midtown, and I showed her the sights along Broadway. She was from Charleston, South Carolina, and she had never been to New York. We had a swell trip back too.

At night I loved to sit down and write letters to just about everyone I knew in New York, and to some of my relatives elsewhere. I got snacks from the icebox while I wrote.

At the office things were swell, and if I didn't finish my daily chores I stayed after work and completed them. The boss was considerate and affable, and the job was easy. What else could there be?

I swapped tales with guys from Oklahoma, Oregon, Buffalo, New York, Broken Bend and the Dakotas. They came from all points of the compass to Washington.

We had an office "Fishing Club." We would go up on weekends to a place called "The Gooses" up Chesapeake way, and hire a power boat. We caught bluefish and croakers galore each trip.

I played golf after work at Hain's Point and other places. We had an office softball league and I was a catcher. We won the league championship.

We had bull sessions at the office and at the boarding house. Some guys were more full of bull than others. One guy, Buddrow, would relate of his experience in the world of commerce and government in building things. His experience as he had said it, amounted to a total of thirty–eight years the way a guy from Alabama and I figured it up. Buddrow was twenty–three years and two weeks old at the time. He got sore when we reminded him of that fact. We said that he was in one hell of a hurry to get things over and done with. He called us traitors to his cause, and said that it was guys like me and Alabama who got the war between the states started anyhow.

For emphasis, he called me General Grant and the other fellow General Lee. We told him that he should call us Ulysses and Robert E. Because we were members of the same household and didn't stand on formalities.

Some girls were there when we told him that, and they thought we had a smooth line of chatter going. So did we. Buddrow pouted and wouldn't join the crowd going out to a party that night. While we were at the party he took his revenge.

He put an egg in the overcoat pocket of Robert E. He squeezed the egg for a better mess.

He put an egg in one of my shoes with the shell intact. I was laughing about the overcoat pocket egg–treatment. I didn't know about my shoe at that time.

I decided to take a couple of pairs of shoes down for a shine a week later. The shine boy stuck his hand into one shoe real quickly and broke the egg. He charge me two bits to clean the shoes when normally it should have been a dime. The guys there in the barber shop kidded me. One guy wanted to know if there were hen nests in my bed. Another said that I "must have a hell of a lot of chickens or shoes one," when the chickens had to use my shoes to lay their eggs in.

I said, "They know a nice clean place to lay an egg."

Robert E. Lee and I were planning our revenge. We double dated one night out at Hain's point. We saw a guy catch an eel in the Potomac. He didn't know what to do with it. We did.

General Lee had a washpail in the trunk of his car. We filled the pail with water and put the eel in it. We hurried home. We went to an unused bathroom on the ground floor at the back of the house. We closed the door after putting the eel into the bath tub with plenty of water. We wanted him nice and slippery. We took the girls up to a barbecue place and thence home. We had a whale of a time planning what we would do with the eel and old Buddrow, the experiencer.

About dawn the next morning the general and I had early reveille and got our eel. We took it to Buddrow's room.

For that one accomplishment in the snoring line, old Buddrow could have claimed a championship when we entered the room. We looked at Buddrow and almost changed our mind in that which we were about to do. He looked so peaceful and innocent of wrong-doing, just lying there snoring so heavily, rhythmically and whistling too.

When he had said that he was a champion hog caller in the Ozarks it may have been that he was telling the truth.

We took the eel from the pail. I raised the bottom of Buddrow's sheet and General Lee gently placed the eel about knee high alongside Buddrow. We sneaked back to our rooms and had longer to wait than we had anticipated.

Now I will grant you that a hog caller from the Ozarks must have a powerful voice. No hog from the Ozark country ever heard the kind of shouting we heard coming from peaceable Buddrow's room.

Even for a man with such vast experiences and adventures as he; a two pound dripping wet, icy–slippery eel can be a true surprise when it is discovered in one's own bed.

What followed the discovery of eelicus sleepycus was not unlike perhaps a surprise night attack upon a thousand troops at Gettysburg for the real General Lee and General Grant.

It was even worse to see the source of the noise standing there with a chair in his hand, shouting "snake" as loud as he could. It was worse to see that Buddrow wasn't wearing the conventional sort of bedgear for his age and the times.

The rascal was a night gown wearer, wearing an honest to goodness, bottomless, full length shirt, flannel outfit. Real snake bait.

The others in the house, terrified and completely wide awake, were standing around in whatever they had worn to bed.

As General Lee said to me of it later, "Ulysses, we might have gotten away with it if it hadn't been for that goldarned night gown." Gees, it was awful; and him standing there in his old shimmy saying a snake was licking him in bed "with a tongue that long." Robert E. held both arms at full length.

We couldn't hold a straight face knowing what we did. Ma was standing down at the bottom of the stairs with a butcher knife in her hand. She was saying, "Shush Child, it's nuthin' but a little bitty old snake anyhow, probably someone's hoose pet."

I looked up the staircase to the third floor landing. I looked straight into a vast expanse of lingerie and skin and bones. Maizie was there and all wide open at the bottom. Maizie was skinny as hell I'd always thought, but not that skinny.

"Can I call the police?"

What General Robert E. Lee and General Ulysses S. Grant needed then the least, was the police.

I said, "Hell no. Don't call anyone." I looked at Ma with her knife in striking position. I looked back up at Maizie to see if she was maybe a little fatter than she seemed to be the last time. She wasn't. I looked at Buddrow, and I looked at General Lee. No, emphatically we did not need the police but we would have them there if we did not do something fast. If we didn't, all of us would be arrested for indecent exposure and loud and unreasonable behavior.

If I had to be arrested I would prefer it be because of other more dignified forms of personal conduct.

"General Lee." I said, "We will advance upon the enemy and destroy him forthwith."

We ran into Buddrow's room and slammed the door locked. We looked at each other and laughed. Through the transom we could hear Buddrow continue to say, "The son–of–a–bitch was licking me too with a tongue that long."

"We got him," I shouted toward the transom. "Look and see if you have any snake bites or fang marks. The dern thing is a pit viper, not a hoose viper."

We went out the window and via the porch roof to the yard.

We were in our pajamas and got scratched a little from the porch column vines, but not much. Then we made our big mistake. We flipped the eel onto the front seat of Buddrow's car. We left it there and eased back to the house. We hoped that Ma would not come at us with the butcher knife before she knew who we were.

Buddrow believed that the snake was there all right, that we had gotten rid of it, and that we might have put it there. He didn't even dream that it was an eel. We figured he should have smelled it if nothing else.

I told General Robert E. about Maizie, and when we got upstairs he looked up at Maizie and turned to me, and said, "Goddam, General Grant, we put the eel in the wrong bed."

Buddrow found the eel in his car and then he knew. He was hurt deeply. Our revenge was such that he vowed to Ma that he would never spend another night under the same roof with us. Ma said later that he was all dignity and wounds. He said that he would never spend another night in a bedroom that had snakes that go around licking folks while they are sleeping. That was before he found the eel. Ma said that he had left owing a month's rent. She said it was too bad that it wasn't a boa constrictor instead of an eel. She laughed and said, "The fool, bless his heart, would have thought it was a whale instead."

One joker on the first floor was mad as a wet hen when he found out about it. He had slept through it all. "Gol ding it dern it I'd of give my weddin' suit to of have seen that fool an' that great big old eel asleepin' in the bed."

I stayed at Ma's place for over a year. I moved after Vonnie had transferred to Charleston to the Navy yard there. Vonnie and I had some great times that summer.

Once nice Sunday afternoon we took Ma down to her farm in Virginia. It was a big place and her son looked after things there.

Ma's son, Wilburt had some riding horses, and Vonnie and I would ride for miles while Ma and Wilburt discussed their affairs.

On the way home I would take Ma and Vonnie to dinner at a place where they really specialized in Southern fried chicken. The place was a farmhouse and had been an old inn many years before. Vonnie and I would still be wearing our riding clothes then and Ma as usual, had worn a black straw hat with pink and blue flowers. The flowers stuck too far up over the hat and they would bob about when Ma talked or ate.

I transferred from the Department of Agriculture to the Internal Revenue Bureau. I had an acute yen to get onto the path of the revenooer.

The Agriculture Department people were great to work with, but I had a job to get and I wasn't to be discouraged.

I moved further up town in the northwest section. I had apartments with two different guys. They got married. I decided to get an apartment of my own.

THREE

THE GREAT NORTH WEST

My first very own apartment was in the northwest section of Washington. One's own apartment was sort of a status symbol with me and not a gathering place for harem–like activities. Neither was it a watering place. It was a place to live and to live to one's own taste and by one's own means. It was as something of an independence to me. I came and went as I pleased and I did not have to await the beckonings and whims of others on a partnership basis.

I picked out a nice sounding address and I set out to obtain a place there. It was easy. There were several vacancies, and I picked one up high with a good view. I picked one with two bedrooms. I hated the efficiency type of apartment which had cost almost as much to rent in time and effort to furnish as a full one roomer; and a two roomer was not too far removed from that economically. I'm talking about then, not about now, for those who would compare notes. I had a few moolas in the bank to buy furniture, and a deceased uncle had helped me.

Every gal who heard about me getting that apartment, whether it was from me or somebody else, wanted to give free, semi–professional advice on how to furnish it. I received some swell suggestions that way, and I followed them, with good results.

The best thing I did was to go to a nice, but not the highest priced place and walk up to a guy who looked old enough to know what he was doing from constant exposure to such problems as I was having. I relied on the house's reputation, which was A–1 for the quality and fair price in what I was about to buy. It was a brand name place in the same spirit of the brand name label. I wanted a fair deal and wanted them to have a fair profit. I wanted quality in the amount of my cost.

I picked out this guy over near some sofas he was showing to a prospective customer. I hung around looking until he finished with her. He was about fifty–five I guess. I walked over to him and tossed the whole thing in his lap.

"I've got a free thousand to spend," I said. "I want to furnish a two bedroom apartment. I want the best deal and I want your advice on what to buy. I want straight goods all the way. If I don't like it when you are finished I will haunt you. The deal is yours on a man to man, no curves basis."

As it turned out I picked out a gem of a feller and salesman too. He knew furniture and knew it well. Before he sold me a thing he made a phone call. He put me on the phone and I talked with the guy on the other end. He had let the salesman do his choosing for him and he had come out fine, he said. He also said that he had a nice piano that he would let go reasonably if I was interested in one. I was. I got his address. He said he would go home then and meet me and the salesman there if we cared to. We did. We went.

I wish I had that piano now. I bought it for almost a song. No pun intended. I liked the guy's apartment decor, and I told the salesman that he could pick out and itemize things for me. We went to my apartment and he measured and took notes. He knew what he was doing.

When I left the guy for the day, he said, "I'll work on that tomorrow and call you at the office to let you know what I can do. I can stretch some in your favor here and there and throw in some extras."

He called me that afternoon and said, "Johnny, I'm throwing in a free radio, a kitchen set, and a lady davenport chair, a toaster, a couple of lamps." I was amazed and quipped, "Will the lamps have bulbs in them?"

When he said seriously, "Oh, yes, Johnny." I said, "Hurry up, before you change your mind." We made the deal.

Plenty of places in those days threw in some extras on quantity purchases of furniture. I liked what that salesman picked out. He picked each piece because it fitted a certain place in my apartment. Guys like that are the most reasonable, and best to deal with in the long run. If you can find them, that is.

I felt like a prosperous rancher with what he might call "a nice spread" to designate what he owned.

I made a real boo boo. It wasn't until the first night there that I realized that I had completely forgotten to buy bed linens. I let what I did have go when my last apartment mate and I split up. I slept on top of the pretty pink bed cover in one of the bedrooms. I took the blue spread from the other bed and used it for a blanket.

I really enjoyed that place. The only thing I never did like about it was the telephone location. I'd have a party here and there, and some joker from the other side of the United States would use my phone to call an old drinkin' buddy or some babe who grew prettier with every ounce of whiskey he consumed. Once I had a bill for $36.00 that some jerk rolled up. It took me a year to get it out of him. I would never have known who made the call except that he was the only one there from a place called Tacoma, Washington. The phone was in my bedroom. A guy at a party there could close the door and phone, phone, phone.

On the other hand, when it came to phone callers, there was one babe who went with a friend of mine who had the real "itis" when she had a cocktail or a highball. She would get there and pester the hell out of everybody there whenever the phone rang. It seemed that she was always expecting a call "from out west," or a telegram, or a cablegram from the continent. I would be on the phone talking to someone who she'd never know, and she would interrupt me and ask me if it was for her from St. Louis, or St. Paul. I would reply that it was the Angel Gabriel that I was talking to; not really that, but something like it. My friend said that she was divorced from her husband for that reason. She would ask him the same things at the damndest times, he said. She wasn't the only gal who had to go continental or intercontinental phonewise that I've ever seen. They drive me nuts because they can't be completely in one place at one time. You know what I mean. They look at the divided attention thing like it was alive.

All my friends liked my new apartment though, and we really had some good times. We had some mighty nice people there.

It fitted in the Washington scene too. Pulchritude, and pleasant, sensible company were in abundance there in Washington with the women–to–men ratio being as high as it was. I will elaborate on that some.

They said there were ten women to every man in Washington. I am inclined to think that that figure is an exaggeration. I would think that it would have been more like six to one.

Public dance halls were not allowed to operate. Something better than that was as far as I was concerned. There were private dancing instruction clubs. You paid a down fee of five or ten dollars for lessons and became a member. I joined one which must have had ten girl members for each boy member. It was nice.

On Saturday night the big dance for the members would be held. The charge would be about 75 cents for men and 50 cents for women. The instructors would be there, and they were good and would point out weak points in dancing techniques to the members.

It was a great place to meet girls. Once in a while I went there with a girl, but that was rare. Stagging was the accepted way to attend.

For a tall guy those places were the mostest. Washington had an abundance of men well under six feet. I was six one. There was an overflow of tall girls, and I just loved it. I got along with them beautifully. One of the most beautiful girls I have ever seen was six feet, four inches tall.

Once I bet a guy five bucks that I could leave my apartment and be back in less than an hour with a girl I had never seen before that night. It was on a Saturday night around seven o'clock. It was the night of a dance at the dancing school ballroom.

I raced up to the place and paid my admission to the dance. I looked around for a partner. I spotted a gal about six feet, two inches in her stocking feet. I asked her to dance with me. A waltz was playing and she was great as she glided along. We chit–chatted about nil as people will do. She was from California, she said.

I told her that a few friends were coming over to my place and that I would be delighted if she would join us. She accepted. Her name was Jane and she was nice looking and well built. I told her that my name was John, but I didn't go into how some people always called me Jack, and how it was a common situation back East to be known by either name.

She seemed just a bit apprehensive about me being in such a hurry to get back. I told her that I would explain it all to her later. She seemed satisfied and slipped a little closer to me on the car seat. She shifted gears while I depressed and released the clutch pedal. We were synchronizing nicely.

We hadn't set up any conditions about telling the girl what we were up to. I figured in the spirit of the thing that I should not tell her until after we got to the apartment.

The whole thing had started that night when I chided Baxter for not being able to dance. I coaxed him a few times to consider taking dancing lessons but he wouldn't follow through on it. He didn't know many girls, and didn't know how to begin a conversation with one without difficulty. He had the old city–boy idea, the way I had it for a while, that only sissies played with goils. I recovered nicely from my opinion at the right time. I had started playing with goils when we changed our gang name to "The El Dorado Boys" in keeping with our newfound culture.

I was trying to convince Baxter that night that he could really meet some girls if he were able to dance. He was six three and about two hundred pounds. He was nicer looking than I was, and had a better job. He was a couple of years older than I was too. He got me going that night when he said, "What do I say to them to start a conversation?"

"Baxter, you big little boy. As big as you are and as educated as you are you still haven't learned how to say words to a gal who's just dying to meet you and talk to you in the first place?"

"Aw hell, Jack."

"Fix me a highball Jack. I want to sit down and think the whole thing out. In the first place I don't think it's as easy as you make out it is."

"Do you mean the dancing or the talk with the girls?"

"I mean the talk with the girls while you are dancing with them."

"Look, Baxter, you're dancing with your arms all over her. Right?"

"Right."

"You've got your face poked right into hers. Right?"

"I guess so."

"Whaddya mean, you guess so. I'm telling you that you have."

"I'm so tall. It would be just my luck to have to dance with a girl a foot shorter than I am."

"Nuts. I'll bet you five bucks that I could go out right now and be back with a girl from the dancing school that I've never seen before."

"Right now?"

"Hell, no. It'll take me forty minutes to go there and back."

"I'll bet you can't have one back here in an hour."

I looked at my watch.

"I'll take that bet, Baxter. If I do though, you'd better join a dancing class."

The light in the elevator was a bright one. It was more than illuminating. It was enlightening when I looked at Jane. I had caught and captured a real doll in a mere fifty–five minutes.

I rang the bell instead of using a key, so that Jane wouldn't think that I was a wolfey heading with her into his lair. She would at least know that someone else was included in the night's plans.

When Baxter answered the door he had the funniest look on his face. I think that he was hoping that I didn't have a girl with me and that he was glad that I did have one.

Baxter was glad indeed. He paid the bet without hesitation, but he had a sneaking suspicion that I had merely obtained the services of a girl friend. He asked her a few questions and was satisfied that I had done exactly what I had said I would do.

Baxter said, "Jane, how long have you known Jack?"

"Who's Jack?"

"He is."

"He is? He told me that his name was John. What is this, John?" And so I said, "Some people call me Jack and some call me John. I allude to myself as both, but I'm really the same guy."

"I've heard of that, but you had me going for a minute."

"You hurt my feelings Jane. Now let me tell you what my big hurry was about in getting you here."

"Okay. John–Jack."

"Fix me a drink, and tell me what it is all about. Baxter,let's us dance while he makes the fixin's."

"Er, ahh, ha , ha, I don't dance."

"You're kidding. Everybody dances."

"I'm nobody."

I went out to the kitchen and fixed the drinks. I kept one ear tuned to what was being said in the living room. The radio was playing "Harbor Lights." Outside of that all was quiet.

When I went back into the living room "I'm in the Mood for Love" was playing. I nearly dropped my cocktails. Baxter and Jane were doing not too badly at dancing. I watched and waited until they had finished. I handed them a drink each.

"Okay Baxter. Up with the fiver."

I knew that Baxter had told Jane about what we had done, and how it was that she was there. Jane seemed a bit cool and Baxter was beaming.

Baxter gave me the five dollars. Jane said, "I hope you're proud, smartypuss."

I was waiting for her to say, "I hope my cocktail doesn't contain a Mickey Finn." I felt like a procurer.

Baxter eased things a bit when he said, "By the way, Jack, I've decided to take dancing lessons."

"Just now?"

"Yeah, just now."

"That's great." I was elated. "How'd you do it, Jane?"

"Do what?"

"Get him to take dancing lessons."

"I didn't have anything to do with it. I just said that I would help him to learn to dance."

"Baxter, you're a girl stealer. I go out of the room to fix you both a drink and when I get back you're dating and making plans to go dancing and making happy times without me." I laughed and told them that they made a nice looking couple.

It could have been worse. I could have come back empty handed. I had brought back a real beauty, and that was a tonic to my ego. She was a good sport, and I proved my point. Best of all, I had Baxter all set to take dancing lessons. They really hit it off. Both made so much of the fact that they were tall and that made it nice. I began to feel like I was a midget at six one.

We sipped our drinks and I got up and played "Carolina Moon" on the piano, and they tried dancing to that.

I said, "I've got five bucks burning a hole in my pocket. Let's go over to Chimney Villa and spend it."

From Jane, "The three of us?"

"No. The four of us."

Baxter said, "How do you figure four?"

Jane spoke up, "You probably are counting on getting another girl the way you got me, I suppose. Only this time it'll probably be in thirty minutes."

"Less than that." I looked at the phone and smiled.

Jane said, "Let's take him over, Baxter. I'll take two and a half's worth."

I kept looking at the phone. I was planting the seed to grow into ideas in their heads that I would have to do some phoning around.

"Give me five minutes and I'll have one here."

"Ha, ha, don't forget to explain the John–Jack thing."

"Wait a minute Jack. You say that you can get one here in five minutes. Do you mean one you know or don't know?"

"One I don't know."

"It's 8:42. Let's get on with it. Right now."

I looked toward the phone and said, "Do I hear you right?"

"You heard what he said, Jane."

"Okay it's 8:43. I'll be back by 8:48, win or lose."

I walked over to the door and went across the hall to an apartment where four girls lived. I left my door unlocked. I rang the doorbell. "Hi," I said to the girl who answered the door. She was all of four feet, nine inches tall.

"Hi. You're 7–C, aren't you?"

"Yeah. John–Jack is what my name is 7–A."

"Won't you come in?"

"Is whatchamacallit home?"

"No, I'm here by myself."

"What are you doing this very minute?"

"Sitting at home waiting for the phone to ring for someone to ask me for a date."

"Mind if I ask you for one by ringing your doorbell instead?"

"You work fast."

"Faster than fast. We gotta be back in my apartment and leave with the others pronto. They're ready to go."

She was real game. She was almost tiny and moved fast. We were back at my apartment in time but without much to spare. Baxter was goggle eyed when we walked in. Jane said, "I don't believe it. I don't believe it. I love it, I love it."

I didn't know if it was because I'd gotten another girl on the same kind of conditions that I'd gotten her, or if she was elated that she would be with Baxter. I think it was a little of both.

I had forgotten to get the girl's name, and when introductions were in order I hesitated at her name. Jane was quick to speak up,

"Now don't tell me that you don't know the girl's name?"

She said it real cute like, and I knew that she was fishing. The girl came to my rescue. She said, "No, I don't believe he does. He just met me a couple of minutes ago. My name is Wilma. Baxter spoke up and said, "Aren't you sure it wasn't five minutes ago?"

"Baxter, you're a riot," Wilma said. "What difference would three minutes make?"

"A lot with that guy. He makes ten bucks an hour in his spare time."

Wilma said, "I like rich guys." She moved next to me and nudged me. She looked up and then over at Jane and Baxter. "What big people. The three of you must be twenty feet long." Jane laughed and hugged Baxter happily and hard, and said, "You bet we are. I'm ten feet tall myself."

I held up five fingers at Jane and Baxter.

Jane said, "Come out to the kitchen with me Wilma. I've got something to tell you."

I heard them laughing and Baxter said, "Seven–fifty isn't a bad price to pay to meet a million–dollar baby. I'll pay you Jane's part too."

The girls came back and I said to Baxter, "Let's go into the bathroom. There's something I want to tell you."

"Baxter, you are not learning well at all. Let Jane pay her part. We'll spend it together anyway. The day's lesson is that you figure you are getting a bargain at ten bucks. Isn't that right?"

"Yeah."

"Look at it this way. She thinks that she is getting a hell of a lot too, for $2.50. She wants to pay that. She really does. It gives her a little independence. She needs it. She's been a good sport. Some gals would think they'd been taken under the circumstances of tonight."

"Do you think away ahead like that all the time you are talking to girls?"

"I like them so I pay attention to what I am thinking and saying while I'm around them. There's your clue. Quit thinking about the girls themselves and pay attention to your thoughts. Your mind will take care of the rest and turn it into speech for you."

"What do you think of Wilma?"

"A swell kid. Too short for me to date too much. She has three peacherinos for roommates. One of 'em about five–eleven in her stocking feet. I've seen her at the mailbox downstairs."

When we greeted the girls in the living room, Wilma said, "Hey John–Jack, you ought to meet Louise. She's five eleven." I turned to Baxter and said, "See what I mean?"

More than a few odd incidents evolved around the over supply of women in Washington. One little gem of narration was a result of that.

The man was over near Union Station one day and a panhandler approached him. "My good man. Could you be so kind as to give me a quarter for food and lodging. I'm hungry and I just got here riding the rods from Joisey."

"A good looking fellow like you ought to be ashamed of himself to have to beg money from others."

"It's just temporary. I'm down on my luck."

"Fella, if you're going to be here in Washington for any time at all you should know that there are ten women to every man here."

"I got no money. I can't date girls."

"That's what you think. You don't need money. Plenty of women here would like to take care of things for you for some attention in return. Do what I tell you now, and you will see that I am right."

"Yes sir. I surely will."

"Here's a couple of bucks. Get your clothes cleaned and a bath and haircut before you do anything."

"I certainly will. Gee, thanks, mister."

"All that you have to do is to go way out on 16th Street. Go way out. There are plenty of apartments out there with women living in them. Lonely women. Knock on any door that looks good to you. If a lady answers it, just turn on your charm and keep talking. Tell the lady your problems of hunger and lodging."

The tramp followed the man's instructions. He looked in a mirror and was pleased at what he saw. He blessed his benefactor inwardly. He hoped that some day he would be in a position to repay the man handsomely for his kindness. He set out on the bus for northwest 16th Street.

Up on 16th St.,he knocked on an apartment house door. A good looking woman answered. He turned on the personality but good.

"Good evening, M'am."

"Good evening. What may I do for you?"

"Well, I'm down on my fortune temporarily. I lost my job and I am—er—ahh—excuse me M'am. I am not used to asking favors."

"Oh you poor dear man. You're hungry."

"Worse than that, M'am. I'm starved."

"Come inside and let me fix you something to eat."

"Thank you. Thank you M'am."

"Call me Heloise. I hope that you enjoyed your steak. How about another glass of wine? Let me get one of my husband's cigars for you. Why not stay here? He won't be back for a couple of weeks."

"Well M'am, I hate to impose on your good nature."

"Oh Alfred, don't talk like that. After all, we are both human beings and a bit lonesome too. Do stay a while, Al."

"Oh I guess I could all right, not having any ties or anything like that."

"Have another glass of wine, honey. It's Chester's favorite brand."

"I believe I will, Helly."

"Oh Al!"

Al was thinking of how it had been his lucky day. That guy at the station sure knew the ropes. He was darn lucky he met him. If he hadn't he might be sleeping on a park bench, hungry and cold.

"These sure are nice clothes, honey. Fit me to a "T.""

"Glad you like them, sugar, Chester does have good taste in clothes."

"Al, honey, let's eat up at the Shoreham tonight."

"Can't be any better than the Willard or the Mayflower. If it is, I just don't don't want to eat myself to death there."

"The roast beef is great there Al. You'd love it."

"Good Helly. I hope they have a good wine cellar too."

Al did little jobs around the house like hanging curtains and washing windows. They got along beautifully. Al's appreciation was not lost on Heloise. She strived to please him at every turn. They talked uneasily about Chester's return home. They fringed on the topic of running away together. No, that would not do. Hell, Al would have to go to work. They must find a way. They must. They must not separate. That would be awful indeed.

It was Heloise who thought of the solution.

"Why not stay, and when he comes back I will tell him that you are my cousin Alfred from Illinois and you can stay as long as you like. Chester is a dear and will understand."

"Come here Helly. Sit on my lap. I've got a kiss for you, darling.

You are so smart and so lovely and charming."

"Oh Al. Isn't it wonderful. We can have so much fun during the daytime when Chester is at work. Oh Al, you sweet dear."

In due time the husband returned. She introduced Al to her husband as Cousin Alfred, from Chicago.

The husband was very friendly and shook hands. He excused himself while he went into the bedroom to unpack. He reviewed the events of his trip. A nice glass of sherry would go good later.

He paused to reflect. He bolted out of the bedroom and confronted Alfred. He said, "You ungrateful louse. Didn't I tell you to go WAY OUT on 16th Street."

I guess that perhaps the busiest overground rapid transit system in the world, in the mid–thirties, considering area and population, would be the city of Washington facilities operated by the D.C. Transit System.

Tokens were used as fare payment. They could be purchased cheaper in quantity. A weekly pass, good on all lines in the District sold for a dollar. The company operated street cars and buses.

Many people who had cars found that it was simpler and less costly to purchase a weekly transit rider's pass than to drive. As a result, the vehicles were crowded to capacity during the reporting and dismissal hours of the government offices.

I knew two thrift–minded guys who worked different shifts. They utilitzed one pass both for business and pleasure trips. They really got their money's worth.

The bus service was good. Schedules were frequent and on time. The conductors came from all over the nation, just as did the average government workers living in Washington.

Some weeks I drove to work and others I rode on a pass. One way suited me as well as the other. Gas retailed for 11 cents a gallon. The bus ride afforded me an opportunity to observe all sorts of characters at their sleepiest and most tired times; on their way to and from work. Guys could meet gals in depression days in the oddest of ways. One of the favorite stories at that time might be related thusly. A detective told it to me.

"I had an experience on a bus, and off the same bus, that was a corker in human behavior. One winter morning I boarded the 16th St. bus at the corner of "R" St. N.W. I wasn't any smarter or dopier myself than the other passengers for that time and place. Usually though I do wake up more alert than most people I know.

I had to stand up that morning. The suburban riders had all the seats getting on at the start of the run.

That particular morning tested every form of ingenuity and patience I had, just because I tried to be at that hour of morning a friend to mankind at the side of the road.

I didn't mean to complicate things when I told the guy I was standing next to, that his fly was open, at the "Q" Street stop. I just didn't want the guy to make a fool of himself the way he was and do something like walking into the office innocently whistling "I'm in the Mood for Love," or "Why not Take all of Me." It could make a fellow a laughing stock.

It made it worse too because the fellow was older, and more serious looking than I was, and probably had a more responsible position. He was one of those nice pipe–smokers

I would not have noticed what had happened if the fellow had not been wearing one of those thick, homemade sweaters under his suit coat. Most everybody had on overcoats or fur coats.

The sweater was too small and whoever knitted it must not have seen him for a long time before they started their knitting. Anyhow, he was pulling the sweater down underneath his suit coat and sort of jostled me a bit while he was doing it. Naturally I looked to see what was happening and I could not help seeing his fly open. It was gapped pretty wide and I wanted to laugh like hell. I didn't though, and I sympathized with him so I told him in a whisper, "Hey Mac, your fly is open."

There are some people that will say that it takes a nervy joker to tell a guy something like that in a public place. I think that it takes a certain amount of integrity and discretion to apprise a person that sort of predicament.

When I whispered to that otherwise happy creature, I did it so softly that the woman right in front of him in the fur coat did not hear me.

I felt for that fellow right then and there because of the Mount Vernon incident I experienced years before at the swimming pool. It was at Mount Vernon, New York.

I will not go into that except to say that I thought when I came from the shower room to the pool in my newest style baggy swim trunks that I was hot stuff. I really strutted out of there. I walked almost the full length of the pool up to the diving board almost.

I excused myself past about five guys older than I was, and one of them hollered real loud at me and told me of my condition. I didn't wait to thank him. I just bellywhoppered into the pool. It was a long time before I went back to that pool. That fellow was really uncouth and I didn't want to be like him. That is why I whispered so quietly to the fellow on the bus and motioned downward with my thumb so that he would ascertain his unintentional situation as calmly as possible.

The man whispered back to me, "Thanks feller." He was flushed in the face a little and tried to be nonchalant. He looked straight ahead, and not down at what he was doing so that he would not be conspicuous. I looked the other way on purpose so that I would not attract attention to him. We were both doing the best we could.

I felt the guy nudging me the way it feels when a fish is playing around nibbling and tugging on the end of a fish hook before he latches on to the bait. I turned slowly toward him. He was pointing downward with his thumb.

I looked and saw that awful predicament that had happened to him because of my whispering and because he forgot to zip up his trousers before he got on the bus. I looked up and into his eyes. You should have seen them. No, you should not have, believe me.

That sight reminded me of something else down there near where the United Nations is now in New York. They had what they called an abattoir which was really a slaughter house.

They had one old sheep with a bell tied around his neck. He was a real rogue in sheep's clothing. He got the young sheep to follow him right up to the pearly gates of sheephood. When they all got up there the old muttonhead turned around and walked back for some more pedestrian sheep. The other sheep stayed there at the P.G. for sheephood until some guy with a sledgehammer or knife did them in. I looked into the eyes of some of those sheep before and after their demise and they were sad and not pretty at all.

My fellow bus rider's eyes were sad and not pretty at all. He was very emotionally disturbed and I was determined to help him in his plight. I tapped the woman in front of him lightly.

She must have thought she knew me. She turned and said, "Hi." I smiled, and she smiled back and turned away. I tapped her a little harder on the shoulder and when she turned, I put my mouth close to her ear and started to whisper. She turned sharply around and away from me and muttered something about Romeos on a bus at that hour of the morning. I didn't give up though. I just kept quiet and thought.

It was about reporting time that morning down where we were, not too far from the Veteran's Administration Building. It was pure peril to drive a car near there at reporting time on account of that bell they had going off. It was a signal to be inside the building forthwith or forever lose a day's leave or pay.

Sometimes that bell appeared to me to be like the bell that old abattoir sheep had tied around his neck except that it was a thousand times louder. It had a canceling out effect too except that it was official and scared the hell out of the folks who worked there if they weren't at least fifteen minutes early.

I used to pull my car over to the curb when it was time for that bell to ring if I was within five blocks of the place. The scurrying of V.A. pedestrians was like old time movie rushes. I'd hate to run over one of the poor devils.

I heard that a big shot in the outfit was responsible for it. It wasn't a dignified thing at all and put bad thoughts into people's head. One girl I knew who worked there said that she would rather commit adultery than be late; and that is not the proper attitude to have about business or pleasure.

It is not good for a working girl to wake up late one morning and because of penalties for tardiness arrive confused at the office with one brown shoe and one black shoe, or maybe forget to wear a slip, or bra.

I looked at my watch again and figured that I had better act fast. I was all business on account of the time. I thought that lady might have worked at Veteran's Administration and go shooting off the bus like a rocket. She would be defurred on the back side of her skunk coat.

The guy had a chunk of skunk snarled in his zipper, and the guy who had done the zipping couldn't make a decision at all. He was just standing there getting ready to bleed, around the eyes or ears, waiting for the crisis to pass.

I winked at him to give him confidence, and tapped the woman on the shoulder. She was about thirty five, nice looking, and had on a pretty fair grade of perfume. She liked me, too, I gathered from the way she smiled. I was all business.

I would have felt better if there had been time for introductions all around, but like I said there was that V.A. thing to be considered.

"Miss. You're in trouble. Be calm. It's only that the guy standing in back of you has his zipper caught in your fur coat."

"What? Tell him to unzip it."

"Er-ahh-ha-ha, it isn't that easy ma'm. The mechanism will not function that way."

"I could feel him back there. I thought he was getting fresh. I thought that you were tapping me on the shoulder. What did he open his zipper for in the first place? Tell him to take his coat off then and unzip."

"Madame, it is his trousers zipper that is the offender."

"Mister, are you crazy or something? Or are you a zipper inspector?"

"Don't blame me, lady. I'm just trying to be a good citizen and a friend to fellow man."

I had to do something fast. I was already wondering if the bell had been sabotaged the night before by disgruntled employees. I went up to the bus driver and told him what had happened.

"He was no help. No help at all. He listened and said, "No kiddin'." He broke out into a fit of laughter. He turned back to look but the bus was so crowded he couldn't see the situation. He roared again and said, "Wait till I tell this to the guys at the garage."

I acted. I pressed the stop button when I got back to the unhappy pair. I motioned for them to follow me. They did.

At the bus stop I knew we had to act fast to avoid gathering a crowd. I came up with a command.

"Take your coat off, lady."

She took it off.

"Wrap it around you, Buster."

He wrapped the coat around him, and I said to them, "Let's walk into that hotel lobby like we're all drunk and have been out all night. Stagger!"

We paraded into the lobby. We wobbled past the desk clerk and I led them to a fire door at the rear of the lobby. We sobered up and I said to the woman. "Stay here. We're going to unleash the skunk."

Inside the fire door I told the guy to take his pants off. He did. He was wearing long drawers, the kind with the back door. I laughed like hell. I wondered if his union suit was a one piecer or a two piecer. He held that skunk like it was alive.

I pulled at the zipper, up and down, and sideways. It defied all my efforts. He tried and failed. We cussed.

From the other side of the door. "Are you alright in there?" I think that she wanted to assure herself that we hadn't gone up over the roof and away with her fur coat.

"Yeah," I said.

"Don't come in, Miss." Gees, I thought, that guy is proper, proper, proper. He's afraid that gal will see him in his union suit, and the fur coat couldn't be that bad.

I took out my pocket knife. My resolution was simple. A seventy–five cent zipper against a couple of hundred dollars worth of fur coat. The zipper had to go. I cut it along the edge neatly and nicely. I looked at the guy. He was solemn. He was pulling down that tight little sweater as though he was trying to get it to hide his backside.

I handed him the trousers. He was most unhappy. The tears began to roll. His voice quivered and he muttered unintelligibly. He was beginning to get mad.

I opened the door and gave the gal her coat. She inspected it and smiled. She was happy to have it back intact. She thanked me and said, "I know you from someplace."

"You sure do. The 16th Street bus. Do you remember the time we were out drunk all night and wound up in the hotel lobby?" "I'll never forget it." Neither will I.

I went to the fire door and opened it. The guy was sitting on the stairs. He was terribly upset. I had to caution him.

I said, "It could have been worse. You might have gotten arrested for indecent exposure."

"Mister," he sobbed, "I'm not worried about my trousers."

"Well what in hell are you crying about?"

"Don't you hear that bell?"

"Yeah."

"Well I work down there at the Veterans Administration, and I haven't got a days leave left of any kind."

My friend's little story is, of course, an exaggeration in some ways and in others it is entirely plausible. It is; however, something of the time called the mid–thirties, and of a place called North West Washington, D.C.

FOUR

FROM REVENUER TO REVENOOER

When you ask someone in an Internal Revenue Service office for information or assistance with your taxes, the person to whom you talk is what is known as a Revenuer. When you have contact with Alcohol Tax Investigators then you are talking with Revenooers.

It is not only a matter of pronunciation. It is a matter of duties and a history of those duties. The pronunciation Revenooer (with the two o's) stems from the Gaelic and Celtic manner of speech. The Gaels and the Celts were the early distillers in America insofar as great numbers is concerned.

In 1863, three detectives were employed by the Internal Revenue to protect the revenue. There were no income taxes levied by the Federal government until 1914.

The Irish and Scotch pronunciations favored "Revenoo" in referring to the revenue. Hence the Revenooer, the enforcer of the liquor laws.

The cry, "The revenooers are coming" was heard more and more as a spontaneous flight force for those engaged in illicit distilling in the Southern Highlands and elsewhere.

The entity "Revenooer" has held through the years and can still be heard in many places.

I was a revenuer before I became a revenooer. I was one of not very many to do that.

On sunny days, the guys or gals in the revenue offices think how lucky the guy down the hall is. To be out there in the field, with the birds, the bees, the flowers, and acting the revenooer.

On snowy, rainy, stormy nights and foggy ones too, they are apt to say, "Lo the poor revenooer."

Most people wouldn't have the revenooer's job for a gift. They wouldn't like it if they didn't like creatures of all kinds, and people too, at their best and worst.

It's not the best paying job in the service. It does better all the time insofar as salary goes, and like so many other jobs the paper work increases all the time.

Before you get to the meaty paperwork as a journeyman or revenooer who has finished his apprenticeship in the trade, you have to get with nature and people. You have to develop and use the five senses as you have never used them before. You have to get out there with it, with the mash, and the moonshiner.

You frequent places like creek banks, darkened cellars, swamps, hills, woods, and towns. You ride dirt roads, paths, highways and alleys. You ride them the same way the guy in front of you does if you are in pursuit.

I have those things in mind when I think of the Journeyman revenooer.

I worked for a few years in the Income Tax Unit at Washington. Part of the time I was confined to a desk, and I would catch myself dreaming of the outdoors and adventure in an official Alcohol Tax Unit car. I was too young then to get into the A.T.U., but I was a lot older than when I had first thought about getting in.

I didn't stay at a desk very long. I was assigned to find lost documents and to keep a check on important papers in pending cases and their whereabouts during phases of investigation.

I would go all over the building in my work. Sometimes I would "look in" on the A.T.U. officers, and offices as sort of a personal preliminary job orientation process. To get the hang of things, was the way I figured it in my determined attitude for the future. I guess I was hoping that something might rub off on me. I didn't know what. I wanted to be commissioned as an Investigator.

I liked the job I had and I liked to work in Internal Revenue. I had a lot of friends there. I was happy in my work and I would have stayed there with good success if I didn't have that call back there in my mind, which had been echoing itself for a long, long time.

One day I was talking with the Chief of Enforcement for the Alcohol Tax Unit. He was a big man, and he had known all the phases of moonshining on the scene. He had been out there with it.

One noon time I was near his office and I strolled in. He asked me if I had eaten lunch. I had not. We went to lunch together. Niether of us ate heavy lunches so we stopped at a snacking place to avoid the crowds at lunch.

I asked him this and I asked him that. He knew that I had the fever, and told me that there were some vacancies to be filled in A.T.U.

The chief hit me with both barrels. It took me a week to recover.

"Have you thought about switching over to A.T.U.?"

"Not more than twenty–four hours a day, seven days a week."

"Let's go back to the office and get to work on the application and forms. Write me a formal request for transfer."

I filled out the forms and a couple of days later I went on vacation for two weeks.

When I returned to Washington I looked at the mail which had accumulated for me. I found the one I was looking for. The return address was "Bureau of Internal Revenue, Office of Commissioner." Guy Helvering, a great man, was the Commissioner.

I opened the letter as quickly as I could. I saw the castles floating in the air in front of me. I was really excited. I was directed to report for duty on the next Monday, four days hence, to the Investigator in Charge, Alcohol Tax Unit, Southern District of New York, Federal Building, 641 Washington Street, New York City.

I hurried down to the office and told the news. Everyone congratulated me on obtaining the job I had always wanted.

I found a couple of empty cardboard boxes, packed my personal effects from my desk and said goodbys.

I went back home to get things ready there. I was still on leave. The weekend was at hand and I had plenty to do.

The ride north to New York was vivid and filled with contemplation. I felt great all along the trip. I watched passing cars and wondered if any carried moonshine. I looked at cars in front of me to note the level of their rear springs. In those days that was a pretty good way to tell if a car was loaded. That's what they said.

When I reported, I was the youngest Investigator in the southern New York District. To me the whole thing was not work no matter what detail I might be assigned. I craved action. In some ways I figured it as playing cops and robbers for pay.

I talked with some of the other investigators while I was

undergoing fingerprinting and the general first day requirements. I enjoyed what they had to say and they seemed to think that I would have no difficulty in doing the job. I had been mentally conditioned in my attitude toward the job for a long, long time.

When one man came over and said, "I'd like you to work Raw Materials with me up in Harlem." I said that I would love it. When another came over and asked me if I would like to join his team, I said yes to that too.

The latter man put out some real bait for me. He took off his straw hat, felt inside the lining, and pulled out two shiny sheets of paper, with addresses on them, and showed them to me. He said that they were the addresses of moonshine stills.

I read the addresses and knew right where both buildings were situated. They were tenement houses up in Harlem. I recognized one address as a building where some years before I had an old Irish woman for a newspaper customer. I recalled that she lived on the third floor.

I recalled that the house was one which had in my news carrier days smelled of what I thought was bath tub gin.

"That place has been a whiskey house for years. A whiskey house is a place with adjacent rooftops on a level plane with the building. The janitor knows everything that is going on, too."

"Sure, I'll be glad to get on your team. Hell, I don't have anything to say where I will work. I haven't even been sworn in yet. I have no gun, no badge or black–jack. I'll have to see what the boss has to say."

It wasn't easy. I wasn't ready yet. The investigator in charge said that he knew how I felt, rarin' to go, but certain established practices had to be adhered to.

I was to read the manual and report forms, books on criminal law, searches and seizures and cautious words on the use of firearms. There was plenty there for me to learn and I read the books as though they were detective story magazines. Time passed quickly enough, and it was not as though I was in quarantine from the action in the field.

I read actual case reports which had been written in Indiana, South Carolina, and New York. I just about memorized each one and it stimulated me greatly.

I had my own mental images of the places mentioned such as

Hammond, Indiana, Calumet City, Illinois, and Florence, South Carolina.

I read with an enduring diligence, and my boss told me to take a break now and then. I talked with the older investigators and had coffee across the street with them. I was gaining an insight into the requirements of the job. Things were getting better all the time.

One afternoon I rode up to Mount Vernon, Westchester County, with the assistant chief. I had a great day. The A. C. was driving a gray Pontiac two door car and the back end sat up high because of overloaded springs. He said that the car had been seized with alky and forfeited for official use.

He answered thoughtfully all the questions that I asked him. When we arrived at New Rochelle, he interviewed a couple about sugar purchases, and I was a witness in all of it.

He told me many things about the job. The whole afternoon was a pure joy and really my first venture at work out there with the people.

I was curious about the things I heard of prohibition.

Joe, the assistant chief, told me what a great guy the chief was, and how he had met the challenges of prohibition and was one of the most trusted agents the government had. I had heard some things when I was a kid that bewildered me when I learned that the police would do nothing about them. It made me feel good to learn that someone had been about who would do something about it.

Once as a kid I had seen a policeman up in the Bronx watching a panel truck unloading beer barrels across the sidewalk. They were rolled down a chute affair to the basement area beneath a cider stube (cider bar). A man told me that he would give me a quarter if I ran up close to the cop and shouted "Buckerbarrel." I didn't know it but I was hollering "a buck a barrel," which meant the amount the cop would be paid for the district police kitty.

The cop didn't chase me. He was too busy in keeping tally on the number of barrels or kegs going into the cider stube. He threw his nightstick at me and left it lying in the street until he finished his bookkeeping. He missed me.

Once, near where I was going to school, I heard the kids talking mysteriously about a big warehouse building down the block. One kid said, "That's where Schultz got a brewery."

Sometimes in those prohibition times, I watched guys playing around with big cars, tagging bumpers, and riding close. They said that they were alky cars and could run close together at high speeds.

I was wondering about the facts of life, so to speak, in my new work. The chief called me in to his office one afternoon. I sat across from him at his desk. He made me feel real comfortable and at ease. I knew then that some enlightenment on a lot of things was forthcoming. I felt like a young 'un called in before his pa to hear the facts of contemporary life.

"John, what do you think about this kind of work that you are starting out in?"

"I think it will be great when I can get over to the East Side and up to Harlem."

"You have plenty of time for that."

"I guess so."

"Let's talk about a few things in this job. I'm sure that there are things which you want to know about. I want you to know about them too. I want to give them to you straight from the shoulder and the heart."

"Thank you."

"Let's talk about arresting people."

"Certainly."

"John, you must be firm in this work. You must be reasonable and never lose your head, no matter what. Never, never take a chance on arresting or convicting an innocent man. Do not hesitate or consider production as paramount or what anyone else thinks. You must make your own decisions and sometimes in a flash."

"I would rather see ten guilty men go free than one innocent man be convicted. I'll put that in writing if you want me to do so."

"No sir, I don't need it in writing." I was impressed. Not many bosses consider things like that.

"Moonshining is a big business, John. There are people in it who, if you give them the slightest encouragement, will offer you money or other bribes, to look the other way.

I didn't say anything. I waited for him to continue.

"Bribery is a nasty rotten business. The rottenest damned part of it all is the officer who accepts bribes of money or favors to neglect his sworn duty." He pounded his desk hard and emphatically.

"Can't you arrest them for attempted bribery?"

"I'm glad you asked that question. Discourage it in every way by your own actions. Don't let the gate open the least bit to suggest to others that it might be opened all the way. Some will try it, of course, no matter what. Even there, if your attitude is firm enough it will stop it then.

"Bribery cases are hard to prove and better to avoid if possible. They are suggestive of too many things, which may or may not have actually occurred, and innocent people can be made to look guilty there. If you know of any officer at any time who is guilty of accepting bribes, it becomes your unswerving duty to report it officially. Do not discuss it with anyone other than your supervisor or whoever you may be working with directly."

"If you are working with some man with whom you disagree, do not come running in here. Talk it over with the man. If that fails, see to it that both of you come to see me at the same time."

"Yes sir!"

"I don't like petty tale–bearers, John. When two men work together it might happen sometime that one will save the other's life. He should be ready to do so without even thinking about it. Yet I have seen men come to me with the most trivial revelations about their partners who would not spare their own lives to save theirs. Such behavior is not manly. It is dastardly and cowardly and I will not tolerate it."

I liked that attitude.

"You won't be bothered at all with me on that score."

"One more thing, John."

"Yes, Sir."

"There is a simple solution to the bribery question if it should arise. Never take the first one, no matter how big or how small. Don't take it. It is simple as that. That way you can spit in a man's eye if need be. If you take the first one, though, he can spit in your eye and you will have to take it. He will have you from then on. Every time you hear a knock on the door at an unusual hour, or the telephone ringing, you will think of it and your guts will rattle.

"John, I have been around some rough men at times, and I have been around weak ones too. I watched them sweat out their foul deeds, and some have been killed for them. No good ever comes of any of it. Even the man you take it from will not respect you. He will consider you as a betrayer to yourself, your job, your family and your friends. He will also look at you as a thief who is stealing from him. His indelible thoughts of you will mark you as a weakling and a cheat. Each time he sees you he will let you know. You wili know all these things down inside yourself, too. It is the surest way to make every minute in your life a bad one. It is a way too that you can get other men killed; innocent men, friends, partners, and even the man who pays you for betrayal."

"Your door is always open then, Sir, for questions?"

"Always, John, and my home phone line to you or any of my men."

The assistant chief had told me that the chief didn't like to have to talk to his men that way, about those things mainly, but that he knew that he had to; to be fair to the men who were working for him, at all times.

As time wore on, on snowy days, sometimes we would be at the office for a good part of the day. We would be up on our reports and we would engage in group chit–chat. Some of the old timers would be there and I spoke very little, but listened intently. If somebody suggested coffee I volunteered to go across the street to get it. I didn't want them to stop talking about journeyman revenooering. I wanted to learn all that I could about it.

I asked some of the guys about that big black boat I had seen a long time before as a kid. One guy called the name. I wondered if he had been on that boat down there that day at the battery. All that he said about it was that the whole damned deal was screwed up. He said, "They talked about how fast that boat was. It wasn't anything but a worked over World War I minesweeper. It was noisy. The crew was panicky as hell. It was a third rate operation when we caught that tub.

"Where did you hear about that boat?"

"I saw it tied up at the Battery when I was a kid."

I didn't say any more and someone changed the subject. I was hoping that there had been a lot more adventure involved than apparently had been.

I was thinking about getting my equipment, and I spoke to my boss. He told me to see one of the investigators who was a gun enthusiast.

I answered the phone when he called in that afternoon.

"Hey! I wonder if you can help me find a gun?"

"I'll be glad to. In fact I saw a nice Police Positive 38 for three bucks at a gunshop the other day. Can you go out with us tomorrow?"

"I'll try to go if it's okay with the boss."

I talked with some of the Investigators in the office. They all had their own guns. They didn't want government issued guns.

"You lose the things and you have to pay thirty bucks for a gun that you could get for five in a gun shop."

"You ought to see all the reports you have to write if you lose one of those issued guns."

I bought my first gun for two dollars. It was the Police Positive that I had been told about. It was a nice little revolver, and I kept it for a long time.

There was some delay involved in getting my badge. I had a gun and no badge for a while. I did have a pocket commission though, and I was lucky that no one had asked me to display my badge during that time. The commission was a leather covered folder with my picture on the inside and the certification of my authority as an Investigator. The outside of the commission had the official seal of the United States Treasury embossed in gold.

In public I always stuck close to an investigator with a badge until I received my own. On the subway I carried my revolver in a black leather bag. I also carried in it a flashlight, black jack, and a small sized crowbar, or jimmy. Some of the guys kidded me about it and called me "Doc."

"Hey don't you know that the manual says that you have to wear a gun all the time. It doesn't say anything about a pill bag in the Investigator's dictionary."

"Yeah, I got sores from wearing my gun to bed."

"That's not from carrying a gun. That's from sitting sideways on your ass."

"You ought to see me taking up the collection in choich with that big bulge on my hip."

"What do you do when you take a babe into a hotel?"

They continued, "A cop on the vice squad was telling me about this cop who left his gun in a hotel room one night when he had no business being there. The next day the guy missed his gun and went back to the hotel. He went up to the room to look for it and it was gone. He talked to the manager and showed him his badge. The manager had reported the finding of the gun to the precinct and they came over and got it. He had a hell of a time getting it back. They had to close out the case, and the cop had to sign the receipt for his own gun. What made it worse was that he had five kids and the precinct captain bawled him out. The story made the rounds through the department. They nicknamed the guy after the hotel, and he never did live it down."

"What's the moral of that story, Bill?"

"Keep your gun on you at all times and it never will leave you."

"Would you say that the cop was getting his gun off up there in the hotel?"

"Ha, ha. The cop should have told the captain that his apartment was being painted and that he couldn't stand the smell of fresh paint, and that was why he was at the hotel."

"You don't know Captain Kilhully."

"What kind of goil was he with?"

"She wasn't a goil. She was a lady."

And so it went, and I was introduced to the jargon and joking of the revenooers in the big city. The reporting–in calls came from Harlem and the East Side and once in a while from Westchester.

The office did not own a boat any more. Instead they had available boats of the U.S. Coast Guard which also was a branch of the Treasury Department.

I felt better when I received my badge. I bought a shoulder holster and for a little while I got a kick out of walking around the office in my shirt sleeves and shoulder outfit. I had seen an F.B.I. movie, once, and that's what the investigator did. In a very short time I became used to carrying the gun and didn't even think about it most of the time and didn't even feel the weight of it on my hip anymore.

FIVE

REFLECTIONS IN A TWO WAY MIRROR

Nearly all of us at one time or another, experience the feeling that we would love to walk into our place of business or employment and say, "I quit."

One of the very few times I ever had that feeling at all about any phase of my work as a U.S. Treasury agent came in New York as a result of an assignment. It came at a time when I was tired from long hours, sick with a cold, and when I should have remained in bed. I was pulled off a choice detail which did give me some sort of breathing spell and some glamor to go with it.

In the parlance of law enforcement officers, what I had in mind was to walk up to the boss, and in some bit of final drama, drop my badge on the desk; listen to it tinkle as it fell, and say theatrically, "Have it."

I would then with an about face, click my heels and with bold strides, walk straight for the door and out and away forevermore.

Of course I had no intention of doing such at all, but I thought of it. The personal code I had adopted when I entered the service was an unflinching, "I can do anything for twenty four hours."

I carried that philosophy with me throughout my career, and I saved myself much time and tension by accepting without reservation, whatever detail I might have. Once, years later, I was in the woods at night with a fellow investigator. The lightning had been extremely severe and hammered away close at hand. We had no shelter. The peals of thunder had been sounding off instantly, after each bright flash.

We were soaking wet, and a flash of lightning had peeled the bark from a tree almost at hand. We could even smell that one. Don't let anybody tell you that he won't jump or wiggle when something like that happens.

I had been around storms like that much more than the man who was with me. He became startled and grabbed my arm. You can't say that a guy is afraid when he does that. It is startling but you can't do anything about it. Not in our position.

"When do you think this thing will let up?"

About that time another bolt had struck nearby, and during the peals of thunder that followed, I shouted, "I don't know, but if that bastard doesn't quit within twenty four hours, then I'm going home."

What I was telling the man was that I couldn't stop the storm, and that we had to remain there until our car came and picked us up. We were forty miles from home. In a case like that the best thing to do is to keep things simple. Some guys say, "Nuts," and some say "What the hell," and let it go at that.

That night when the lightning had done a strip–tease with that tree near us I really must have impressed the guy with me. He reminded me of it a couple of different times in later years.

Once a guy told me that when he became involved in a frustrating situation that he thought of girls, all kinds and shapes of girls. He said that it helped him. Later in a stinking swamp on a hot day when he was bitching about the heat, I told him to think about Eskimo girls. He said, "The way I like to think about girls would give an Eskimo girl indecent overexposure."

"Not in this damned place. She'd get her feet dirty maybe."

There are some guys who think that sex is the remedy for all things.

To get back to how I had been disappointed about my unwanted detail, my thwarted feeling and having wanted to toss in my badge; I will tell you of the assignment that I was scheduled to have before it had been changed for the new one.

My original assignment was to go to night clubs on a Saturday night and assist an inspector in taking tests of spirits from the bar. It was easy and interesting too, for the investigator. All that he had been required to do was to keep people from interfering with the tests of the whiskey. It was nice for a change to work at something different and away from our workaday haunts. We had the power of arrest, and the permissive inspectors did not. Some places had nice floor shows and there were also plenty of Saturday night characters about, too.

Most of the time that the inspector had found interference from bar customers it was merely some joker trying to impress his girl friend about his knowledge of whiskies and testing chemicals.

It was a natural affinity for some chemical engineer out on the town for the night to show his girl friend that he knew something about the testing. When they handled the bottles and made boisterous wise cracks, I stepped in as nicely as I could. I never had any trouble.

All in all, the night club detail supplied a change of pace and a change of scenery. Most people were happy that the whiskey which they had been paying high prices for had government supervision. We were really there for the tax interests of the government. Most places kept everything straight in the whiskey line. Some places water would have been added to the whiskey, or there it would have been the practice of the bartender to put cheaper brands of whiskey into empty bottles bearing higher priced brand names.

I saw a guy named Al Reid make an inspection once that was a beaut. He walked down the bar and picked bottles at random. Everyone he picked out for testing turned out to have been watered. Some of those inspectors really knew their jobs.

So I was switched from the inspection detail, and instead of having to travel the night club circuit, I was to stake out a bar and restaurant in downtown Manhattan from four a.m. until twelve noon. I was to start on Sunday morning and continue until I found the man I was to look for.

The boss said, "The man we want is Italian in appearance, doesn't wear a hat, and drives a gray Hudson. It's not much to go on, but from the way things appear we feel that he is hooked up with a huge ring operating in several states."

I was fingering my badge in my pocket. I was sniffling from my cold. It was in the middle of winter, it was cold and there was some snow on the ground. The place I was detailed to observe was near the Hudson River.

"What else does the informant know?"

"Nothing. He is supposed to meet the man in the restaurant that you will be watching. If you see him, follow him and put him to bed."

"Yes sir."

"Good luck. I'll assign someone else in your place on that night club job." I wanted to cuss him out, but I didn't.

A "put him to bed" detail is one where you find the guy, and you follow him day and night, until he goes to bed. Then you slip off somewhere not too far away and grab a snooze. You have to be back there before the guy leaves his house or hotel or wherever he is sleeping. You tail him on foot, by car, and on street cars, buses, subways, els or ferry boats if that is the way he travels. You have to stick like glue, and you have to remain unseen by him.

I started my Sunday morning observation with my cold at its worst. It was bitter cold and windy when I hit the outdoors about two forty–five a.m. I felt better when the car heater warmed up, and I set to thinking about the case I was working on.

I was picturing the immediate vicinity of the restaurant from memory. I was thinking about an observation post indoors, but I didn't think that I would find one. The only mental association I could bring about in connection with the restaurant location was that as a high school kid I had purchased a nut cracker umteen years old for a quarter. The place where I bought the nut cracker was a few doors up from the restaurant. That was no help at all. I would have to check the area and find a definite spot with a good view.

I drove past the restaurant which was open. I went around the street behind it and one block over in front of it. I took in the details of all the buildings nearby. I saw an old building directly in front of the place. That would be the best bet for observation.

It was one of those remaining buildings which had comprised commercial old–Manhattan. It was three stories high and was built of dirty red brick. There was no telling how many and what kind of business establishments it had housed in its time. The chief advantage of such a place would be the low rent. One big disadvantage would be the huge rats which seemed particularly fond of those kinds of places.

I parked the car about a block away. I walked back and tried the glass paneled door leading upstairs from the street. The door was open, and I went inside. On Sunday in that section, very few business places were open.

I sat down on the stairs and was tickled that I had such an excellent view. I knew that there was little chance that I would be noticed or interrupted in my observations. I could hear the rats running around upstairs. We were compatible. They had their chosen places, and I had mine.

I forgot about my thoughts of tossing the "tin" on the boss's desk. I felt good that I had found such a nice place from which to observe. I was sheltered from the wind and could sit on the stairs and look across the street at the suspect's restaurant. Few pedestrians came by on my side of the street.

Monday it would be different, I knew. The occupants of the building would be coming and going. I would have to talk to them and confide remotely in them. I would have to depend on their attitudes as good citizens, to permit me to look out their windows if that was possible.

Nothing happened by noontime. I walked upstairs and saw the name on the door. It did not suggest anything more than a limited, nondescript one–man outfit.

I felt weak and was certain that I had contracted the flu. By the time I reached the car I was having chills and my teeth chattered until I reached 14th Street on my way home. I was hoping that I would again be permitted to use the premises I had used that morning for observation purposes. I felt that it would be some time before I spotted my quarry, if ever. I went home, administered myself the usual home remedies for the flu, and went to bed. I stayed there until one thirty the next morning.

That next morning the weather had become colder, and the wind was stronger. Briefly, as winter goes, the day was a bitch at two thirty a.m. I resumed my surveillance point of Sunday. I saw no activity, but the day was still early. I knew that if I could stay inside during the day, that I would not run any severe chances of my illness getting worse. I felt lousy.

About eight thirty a.m., I walked up the street to a little sandwich joint. I climbed on a stool facing the window. I could look across diagonally at the restaurant and see who was coming and going. It was nice and warm in the sandwich place and there were few customers at hand. I chatted with the owner. He asked me if I worked in the neighborhood. I said, "Yeah, telephone company." I ordered ham and eggs and ate only half. I drank three cups of coffee.

I was stalling for time to let the owner of the business place down the street arrive. I wanted to let him settle down into his Monday morning routine before I asked him if I could observe from his window. I had spent quite a bit of time in the sandwich shop.

I walked up the block and crossed over and checked the make and colors of all cars on the street. There was not a gray Hudson in the lot. I went into the restaurant that I had been observing, and went to the men's room. It was at the back of the place, and I looked around and into the kitchen. When I came out I sat down in a booth and ordered my fourth cup of coffee that morning. It was a little past nine o'clock.

I went to my chosen observation building and went upstairs and talked to the owner of Nondescript and Son, Company.

I hadn't even dreamed that I would be subjected to the kind of abuse I received from the owner. He handed me all kinds of lip and I wanted to kick his tail but good, but I didn't, of course.

"Good morning."

"Good morning. I am a Federal Officer." I started to take my badge out of my pocket and display it to the man.

"What in damdamhell do you want with me? I'm damsick and tired of the government crawling all over me."

"Calm down and relax, Mister. Let me talk to you. I'm not trying to involve you in anything."

"Then what the hell are you doing here? What do you want?"

"Calm down and let me say something, will you?"

I looked the guy over good. I wondered if he was hiding something around there or was up to something wrong. I spotted a reproduction camera at the back of the place. I took another look and was satisfied that no counterfeiting was going on there. He was spouting off all sorts of foul language. I let it in one ear and out the other.

He looked to me to be one of those people who are always sniffing offensive odors. He had developed all the wrinkles for it in the right places in his face. He would be one hell of a guy to have to live with. It wouldn't make any difference if you were his wife or mother, or father. He was that kind of a guy. His appearance was neat and clean, and he had his hair combed back. It was a little too long. Between sniffs he would throw his head back and the hair would reach a vertical position and fall back just like it had been in the first place. I decided that the whole thing was a nervous habit stemming from orneriness.

We both remained standing and after I had satisfied myself by obvious shifting glances about the room I showed him my badge.

He had on rimless glasses with gold ear stems, and when he saw that badge he read it good. He read it with his glasses on and off too. I never saw such a quick anti–tranquilizer react on anyone the way that badge reacted on Mr. Nondescript.

"Government, Democrats, Republicans, and now an I–N–V–E–S–T–I–G–A–T–O–R." He sniffed, he flipped his hair, and he put his hands on his hips and spread his feet like a baseball umpire. He was giving himself a mental fix right down into the honey–bucket of everything he ever knew.

"Let me tell you what those Bastards in the Income Tax did to me. No, I won't tell you. I want to tell you what a no good ding–dong hell of a S.O.B. anyone is who works for the government. You've got U.S. Treasury Investigator written all over you. Stop looking around my place. Stop it. Stop it."

I know that most people have never seen a guy with that attitude but believe me, it takes great restraint just to let such a manner of bastard sound off, and off and off.

I am an easy–going guy at times when other people get shaken up. I had my offical position there and I wanted to observe whatever niceties I could, with everyone like a good civil servant should.

"Mister, I am not from the Income Tax Division. I am not here to argue with you over anything or to question you. You won't let me tell you what the hell I am here for."

"I don't give a damn what you are here for. All I know is that. . .errrr ahhh, is what that badge says. U.S. T–R–E–A–S–U–R–Y, and that is enough for you to go to hell for all I care. Get out before I throw you out."

That kind of talk doesn't get anyone anywhere, anytime. It is not a nice kind of speech at all. I spoke to the guy in a real low tone of voice. I looked him right through the bridge of his nose while I talked. Right straight through and up and down and across that sniffing machine. I stood real tall, and I was a tall guy and big too. With my overcoat I looked even bigger than I was and right there six inches away, was a squirt telling me that he was about to throw me from his premises.

There is a wrong way and a right way to do everything. He was doing nothing right. I told him all about me, who I was, my badge number, and where I lived. I told him to write it all down because if he started throwing me anywhere that those things might be needed later for a lawsuit.

I gave him the reaction that he did not expect. He was baffled, and just then the phone rang. He answered, and his voice was pitched far off–key. He told the caller all about the entire U.S. Government being in the place with him, right then and there and especially Investigator Beezlebub. He had meant Beelzebub the old demon prince, I thought.

I started to leave then, but I didn't. I wanted him to know that he was making me stand outside with the flu in the cold. I wanted him to see how he looked to his fellow man.

I wanted him to know that all people did not feel about their government the way he did. I wanted to ask him where on earth he thought he could find a better Government.

It is odd that in all the odd places I have ever been, that I had to find the most despicable person I have ever met right there in the city, in the form of a business man. The man's attitude in not even letting me carry on a conversation with him was perhaps his most glaring offense toward me.

It would have been perfectly well with me, if he chose not to let me observe from his window. That would rightly be his choice. But to condemn all of the people in the United States and their representatives in government for one wrong, real or fancied, was something else.

Nobody goes around observing people intensely most of their life without knowing what it takes to heat and cool a guy's mind. You can put a guy back on his rocker if he strays from it a little bit. If that fails you can get him off it all the way.

I observed that bird intensely enough, and from the back of my mind I thought of the pencil and notebook routine for response. In the hands of a lawman the mere sight of those two items can get teeth to gnashing or hopes to dashing.

In such a case, a sensitive guy's mind goes awhirring, and his blood pressure goes up. Ask any highway patrolman or city cop.

I pulled out my notebook and pencil. I went through the motions of writing. I looked around and about. I looked straight at the guy as though I was listening to his every word. He had been speaking for some time. I had a good view from where we stood. It looked across at the restaurant. It was warm there and cold outside. I was in no hurry. The guy wasn't either. He wanted to get it all. . .all of it, out of, or into, his system.

He jumped for the bait higher and harder than any rat approaching a trap.

"What are you writing? I demand to see it."

I said nothing and looked him in the eyes. I tried to do it with a smirk a little dirtier than it was silly.

"What did you write down?"

I put the pencil and notebook in my pocket. While I was at it I took a nickel out of my pocket and tossed it onto his desk. "Here's your taxes back and dammit my name is Beelzebub, not Beezelbub."

He ignored the nickel altogether, but his voice changed and he was just a shade more polite. "What did you write down, Beezelbub?" He started across the floor just as I opened the door, and I said, "Read this, you bastard." I took a sheet of my notebook paper and thrust it at him.

I hadn't written a thing. He was disappointed and madder than ever. I had let him down.

I did want to get across to him the real reason I was there. I didn't want to impose on him or interfere with his business. The solid fact was that he had a pip of a spot from where I could see what I was looking for, if it occurred.

When I reached about halfway down the stairs the guy called me, and he said something real nasty. "Don't stand under my window or I'll pour cold water over you, and it might not be water either."

"Anything you got gotta be cold." I turned quickly as though I was going to run back up the stairs, and he ran into his office and closed the door. He never did know exactly what I was doing. I am sure that he would have done everything to upset the case if he had the chance.

I felt discouraged, mad and frustrated. I walked to the little sandwich shop up the street, and drank an urn full of coffee and smoked a pack of cigarettes while I kept my eyes on the restaurant catty–corner from my seat. I wondered how many weeks I was going to keep the whole thing going. I wondered if my nose would stand the constant handkerchiefing. It looked like a ball of fire already, but

I survived the day.

The idea of the four a.m. to noon watch was to cover the whole thing. The suspect had told the informant that he would probably be around there later. When he had said that it was six a.m. and the informer had seen him around there at about that time on other occasions. I arrived earlier and departed later just to be sure.

The description of the suspect as given by the informant, would fit plenty of men. I did not doubt the veracity of the informant; however, I felt that the suspect was a part of the big operation. When you feel like that you keep pushing and keep your nose to the grindstone in law enforcement.

I thought, the "no hat" feature was interesting and could be helpful. The gray Hudson narrows things when looking for one man in seven million. His short stature is helpful. Put all those things together and you have the chance of identity greatly reduced, but when you couple it with the possibility of you and he, two men, being at the same place and at the same time, in the biggest city in the world. Fate remains on the slim side.

I had to find the guy, and I felt that somehow I would. I had a steady mental vision of who I was seeking. I could not go all over New York just looking about. The thing would lose its significance. I kept my eyes open all the time, and I never dreamed that there were so many gray Hudsons in the city.

I couldn't hang around the street near the restaurant. I didn't know where gang headquarters were or who was in the gang. Somebody might recognize me and put two and two together. That would be it. I had to find a spot to observe from, unseen.

I checked the neighborhood in the early morning hours. I found a good observation post. It was in an unoccupied building which had been the scene of a bad fire. It had easy access to the inside. If one did not mind the perpetual smell of charred wood and smoke residue, one could find it a hell of a lot better there than being outside in the freezing winds. It was dirty and dusty too, but the next morning I would be prepared. I would wear an old overcoat and coveralls and a cap.

I spent the next day standing on a wide joist with my feet dangling, where the floor should have been. By that time I was cozy and wouldn't have sat in Nondescript and Son's place to watch fifty thousand nude girls parading on horseback in the street, I don't think. Matter of principle, naught else.

That night the snows came and good. I knew that no moonshiner in his right mind would be out peddling the next day.

I went to the office. I arrived late and caught up on my reports, and the boss found another assignment which was fine for me that day. I began to feel better. The boss and I hashed and rehashed the situation. I told him about Nondescript, and he told me to ignore him altogether and to forget him.

To get into my place of observation, all that I had to do was to remove a couple of boards from a rear ground floor window and replace them when I got inside. That was easy.

The next day I spent on post. The snow had been pushed to the sides of the street by snowplows. Parking would be difficult without becoming stuck or blocking the street. There was not much activity in the downtown area that day. Most people stayed home even though it was a workday.

About twelve–thirty I started home to the Bronx. When the car heater reached a comfortable temperature I could smell the odor of smoke and one hundred years of decay in my clothing. I was warm and the odor was just something I sensed rather than was annoyed by. I went uptown and cut across through Harlem and across the Willis Avenue Bridge over the Harlem River to the Bronx.

Traffic was moving slowly, and here and there I had to wait while trucks made deliveries. They had to be parked in the middle of the street. I had to wait wherever I encountered them.

At one point in the lower Bronx, a sanitation department truck in front of me was taking a long time to move. I could see in the truck's side mirror that the driver was in the cab. I got out of my car to talk to him and to see what was causing the delay.

I saw the cause of the obstruction. It was a gray Hudson. The driver was out of the car. I continued to watch it and chatted with the truck driver about nothing. I wanted to see.

"Whatsamatter with that guy?" I spoke to the sanitation truck driver.

"He was a little Wellyo. He's in that grocery store over there. The damfool was bundled up in an overcoat two sizes too big for him and wasn't even wearing a hat as cold as it is."

Some people say that things like that can't happen, but they do. It happened that day. I had made a mental note of every accessory, and each dent on the Hudson and the fact that it bore a Brooklyn–issued license plate. I had narrowed down the staggering odds to a hundred–to–one. In my mind the hundred–to–one was in my favor, but that was only because of my enthusiasm which had helped me out in a lot of things.

The guy came out. He was short, hatless, Italian appearing, wore an overcoat, and he got into the gray Hudson. I followed him wherever he went for the rest of the day. That was not an easy thing, with the city streets covered with heavy blankets of snow.

Lady luck was with me. I did not lose the guy. At each place from which he emerged, he carried suit boxes which appeared not to be heavy. I could almost swear that what he had inside of them would be empty whiskey bottles. He was picking up empties and taking orders.

Some days on the job for all of us are seemingly longer than others. This one was a short one and a long one. It depended how one looked at it. It was quite a busy one. It was great.

It was about one–thirty when I first saw the man. At nine–thirty I put him to bed. I still had only a place to start on the case, but I was elated.

I watched him go into the house. I drew back and watched his car. I waited until all the lights in the house went out. It was about eleven–thirty when I approached the two–story, two–family dwelling. I walked up a couple of steps and I read the names on the mailboxes by the light from a miniature flashlight which I always carried, day or night.

I went up to the neighborhood plaza area and found a restaurant open. I ordered coffee and went to the public phone booth. I called the license number identification. I wasn't surprised that the gray Hudson was registered fictitiously. In fact, I was happy about it. It told me more than if it had been registered correctly to one of the two names I found on the mailboxes.

Some guys make a living selling real estate. They will know how I felt that day when they sell a hotel or an office building. Some others seek big contracts and when they get one they will know how I felt. One guy I knew called it "That old feeling." I wouldn't go that far. Summarily, it's the appreciation for an hour when a job can be said to have been well done no matter how long it took.

I headed straight for the office. When I went into the building at

641 Washington Street, I kidded with the guard at the door. I matched him for two–bits and won. I told him that it was my lucky day. He said, "You're out chasing someone or something in the snow and cold, when you're down here at this hour. You win two–bits and you say it's a lucky day. Do you know that I haven't talked to anyone in the last two hours?"

"No crap. Well what do you know about that?"

I didn't tell him about the way that the real talker of the day I'd seen that morning had felt. I didn't tell him that I left my house at 2:45 a.m. to begin work at 4:00 a.m., almost twenty–two hours before. I didn't tell him that my supper was two hot–dogs from a freezing pushcart vendor's mobile kitchen on the fly. I didn't have to tell him. He'd seen enough of the comings and goings of the building's ATU Investigators to know what they had to do. After all these years I still remember that the elevator man's name was "Vic," and that he was one hell of a good government employee. He did whatever he had to do on his job and he did it with a smile. He and all the other government employees with whom I'd had contact were honest, hard–working men. That's what made me so mad at that morning's rogue who had figured life all wrong in summarizing S. O. Bitchery in the form of his own government. I wondered if he had ever voted, or tried a little civic work in behalf of his fellow man. He wanted to add rather than subtract. I forgot the rascal entirely when I checked on the gray Hudson. I sure did.

I checked the office records for the names I had taken off the suspect's dwelling. I found the photograph first. There was no doubt that it was my man's picture. I referred to the case report number on the back of the picture. I went to the case report files.

The phrase "Modus Operandi" conveys many things to an experienced commercial crimes investigator. I read the case report twice, and then I read and re–read parts of the case. From all of it I knew that I had a hungry, voracious alky tiger by the tail.

It was a late hour I knew. I also remembered what my boss had said, "My door is always open." I dialed his number and told him of my findings. He was elated. He had it made with me from there in when he said, "John, I knew that you could do it if anyone could. I hated to take you off that detail at the nightclubs, and I knew how you felt, but I admired you keenly when you didn't bitch the least bit at all." The hell of it was that I had–with myself, old Beezelbub.

I thanked the boss profusely. I was sitting at his desk at the office when I called him. I looked at the desk's oak grain patterns shining under the neon light overhead. I didn't see any scratches there which looked as though tossed badges or "tins" had slid there. I felt in my badge pocket and wrapped my fingers around my badge and almost said aloud to it,"Don't ever go sliding across any desk." I recalled the words that the boss had spoken about that same low numbered badge, "A good man carried it before you. Do it justice."

The case turned out to be one of the biggest cases ever. It turned out well indeed. As I have said before, the purpose of my book is not to tell who caught whom, or who did what, it is to relate some personal little human experiences I knew in hearing, feeling, seeing, tasting, and smelling and of all those moments which a law enforcement knows as being tuned to the mind, the heart, the body and the soul. Those things which drift toward us on the winds of time and drift away when the time has spurned us.

In all of this chapter I have been aware, as I have been for years, that sometimes it takes more courage not to do something than it does to do it. I feel that way about walking up to a boss and saying, "Shove it." Things could be worse, no matter how bad you feel they are now.

SIX

PEARL HARBOR DAYS

In my recollection, Sunday, December 7, 1941, was a crisp, sunny day in New York. The New York Giants football team was playing the Washington Redskins at the Polo Grounds in upper Harlem. On my way to Brooklyn from the Bronx, I heard the car radio announcer say that Pearl Harbor had been attacked. The nation was at war, and the long, slow days of World War II had just begun. The blood raced through my system. I had that chilly feeling which expresses itself in the human body at times of shock–provoking surprise.

I said to my wife, Myrtle, "We're in it now."

As I drove across the Brooklyn Bridge I noticed a warship in the river, and I felt for the men on the crew, and wondered where they would be within the month. I pondered as to what fate might have in store for all of us. We were enroute to my partner's house to spend the afternoon. While at the dinner table, a cop knocked on the door with orders for my partner and me to report to 70 Pine Street, Manhattan, to the chief of the U.S. Secret Service.

We kissed the girls goodby and told them that old parting story so familiar to ATU men's wives, "See you when."

On the way over to Manhattan from Brooklyn I kidded my partner about having been Provost Marshal in Paris in World War I. Earlier, in jesting ways, I had heard some of the older investigators kidding him about it. I said, "Jees, I hope I don't get on some whorehouse guard detail because of my association with you."

He laughed, "You could, you know, but anything can happen in a war. I'll probably wind up as a baker or in the mule training section of the Army. He was actually to see the war from a desk in the Coast Guard.

The trip to New York was not long that day. Pine Street was on the lower end of Manhattan and close to Brooklyn.

Seventy, Pine Street, was new to me insofar as Secret Service quarters went. Somebody had truly worked with aforethought in providing new quarters, or maybe that arrangement had been consummated only that afternoon. Despite what some of us say about government red tape and procedure; it can work fast when it is most imperative.

My heart and thoughts were still with Myrtle back at my partner's house. I had left her in a strange place to drive home completely across the world's largest city. It gave me great comfort to know that she was adept with a steering wheel from her days near Raleigh, North Carolina, where as a country high–school girl, she was one of the earliest, if not the earliest of girl schoolbus drivers. She had everything it took to be an ATU wife and still has, or I wouldn't have been able to write this book.

Seventy, Pine Street, was a beehive of activity, with every Treasury Agent for hundreds of miles around arriving by the hour. I met some guys I hadn't seen in a good while, and others kept coming in. New York City policemen and detectives were there too. We were checked in as we arrived, the conversation and fellowship among the men was animated, profuse with hearty greetings and sometimes profane ones given in a jovial spirit. We drifted toward a large room adjacent to the checking–in area, getting out of the way so that things could be done smoothly by the powers that be.

In those days, much more so than now, whenever lawmen gathered in large groups, it was natural for them to play cards to while away the time. Long periods of waiting is something every enforcement officer knows; that time speaks with a drawl.

Cards were produced from nowhere it seemed to me. The games began, and one joker explained to me why he always carried a deck of cards. He said that one of his buddies in World War I owed his life to a deck of cards. A bullet was deflected by the pasteboards in his back pocket. This guy was not taking any chances. I reminded him that I had heard of a cop in New York who owed his life to a prayerbook in his inside jacket in the same fashion, but that guy wasn't spending all his time praying.

I figured that it would be a long, slow night, and entered into a poker game myself. I was dealt one hand which was fair but not good, and I heard my name called over the loud speaker.

I went up to the front desk, and Secret Service Mogul was there. I received my orders and instructions and was introduced to a New York City uniformed patrolman who was to be my assistant for the night chore ahead. This was in the nature of guarding enemy alien property from pilferage or sabotage. The cop, a likable man, was about fifteen years older than me, but without too much apparent joviality about him. He was a good cop. He had had two kosher corned beef sandwiches in his overcoat pockets all the while, and later that night he gave me one and it tasted great. To me, a good cop is always alert to, and prepared for, all situations. This guy was that and more.

When we arrived at the Empire State Building the elevator operators (It was a Sunday night and little building traffic was evident) greeted us like a pair of long lost guardians. The cop's uniform is what did it. No matter what people say about cops, everyone has their moments when the blue and brass looks great. I understood the feelings of the elevator operators. There they were, December 7, 1941, in the up–and–down machines that ticked as a very heart for what was going on in the world's tallest, and target–wise, the most symbolic American structure of the hour.

As I recall, we seemed more like an artillery team. The cop had the usual big belt with the copious cartridge rings that New York Cops wore. I had a chrome plated 32' calibre, 3 inch–barrel revolver. At the bottom of the handgrip, on the metal frame was written, "Detroit Police." It was a honey of a gun, a surplus one at that, but true. It was light and inconspicuous to carry.

I had six bullets on hand, and did not feel at all that I might have to use them; so the size of my ordnance was no personal thing. If I had had the cop's foresight I would have packed a couple of pastrami sandwiches for a pastrami break during the night.

My instructions said to remain at my assigned post until I received further orders. The place was high up in the Empire State building. A safe, sealed by the alien property custodian's office was the chief guardian point, and of course the rest of the place required security measures.

Our stake out point, however lofty it was, punwise, embraced a most generous office area. With all the desks I wondered where the people were who had occupied them, and what their thoughts and feelings were. I felt for them, and since I had hunted men for deeds they had done, I was aware of the sensitivities they knew, and I knew that the office Japanese were either in custody or would be later that night.

I realized that these men did not attack Pearl Harbor, but their people had caused it. They were bound to be lonely and scared, no matter what they might tell anyone otherwise. Now, they were alone, apart from their native land.

As we checked about the office it was completely obvious that preparations were being made by some of the personnel for an extended journey. There were suitcases packed, and on desk tops were assorted items which were to become scarce later in the war.

There were cameras, portable sewing machines, and miscellaneous personal items which had been purchased in the U. S. in view of probable later scarcity elsewhere. We plugged in a small broadcast radio to get the news as it came in. Nobody, anywhere, seemed to know much, and news commentators were speculating. We directed our attentions elsewhere. Beneath some of the desks were little wooden platforms which struck my attention. Recalling the short stature of the Japanese I figured that they were foot rests for whoever was sitting at any particular desk.

The cop went to the far side of the office. He was looking for a restroom. I saw him go outside, beyond an exit door. He was gone for some time, and I looked about to find out what had happened to him. I opened the door and noticed that it had been locked from the inside. It was a fire door designed to keep potential fires from spreading. I had seen and known such before, and I stayed on the inside, with the door opened, when I examined the lock. I wondered why, if locked out, the policeman did not bang on the door. I could have heard him readily. In due time, he was banging on the front door. I asked him where in hell he had been.

"That's a long story. I walked down a thousand and one floors. I should have known better, but I kept going down hoping I would find a door open, but these building bastards are smart, they got things figured out. I didn't get out until I hit the ground."

Jestingly, I said, "Did you find a restroom?"

"Hell, no."

"You mean?"

"No, I don't mean. But I'm going to find one."

"Why don't you try that one over there."

"You federal bastard, why didn't you tell me about it."

"You local yokel, how the hell am I supposed to know your biological needs. You're old enough to be my old man, and I gotta know when you have to go to the toilet."

"Frig you."

"Why in hell didn't you find some more corned beef sandwiches while you were down there with the people?"

"I did more than that."

"What?"

"I got us a corned beef apiece and a pastrami apiece."

"You lovable bastard. What do I owe you?"

"Four bits."

I paid him, and asked him how he had managed to get the sandwiches.

"It's a police department secret. If you wannem, eatem, if not I'll give you your four bits back."

He hung up his overcoat, and I walked over to it at the rack. I patted it obviously.

"What the hell are ya lookin' for."

"I thought you might have had a couple of celery tonics in there."

He said, "Hell no, I keep them in my back pocket," and pulled out a pair of Doctor Brown's celery soda bottles.

Anyone who has lived at all in New York knows that a pastrami on rye calls for a celery tonic, and Dr. Brown's variety used to be sort of a private stock drink in every corned beef or pastrami emporium.

We sat down for a while. We ate and talked the scuttlebutt that men everywhere seemed to be inclined toward. We got sleepy, and stood up and walked around. The lassitude that law enforcement men and soldiers know so well during late but idle hours was beginning to set in. The spoken words between us petered out, and we would look at each other and then respond to the heavy lids that began to spoil the view. We got up again, stretched and resolved to stay alert, come what may.

I went over to the safe, studied the seal, walked around a bit, looked at the industrial catalogues which were on metal shelving and was astounded at the number and variety of subjects. I had to pay secret compliment to the ability of the Japanese to know an easy thing when they saw it and to make use of it. A super spy could have spent years in accumulating what could be had for the asking for a catalogue here and there by mail and by scrutinizing the contents.

The cop was fooling around in a far corner, and I didn't pay much attention to what he was doing until he whistled and said, "Come here." I went over to where he was and saw that he had a little theater all his own, going full blast. I thought that maybe he had found a movie where some guy was playing tennis in front of the Brooklyn Navy Yard, or at least an important bridge in New York.

The picture on the light colored wall was a dilly. So was one of the performers who was more of an acrobat than an actor. He was straight from an oriental kama ritual, but a Caucasian. The girl must have been a stag show regular. She had a cigarette going and was looking all about as though she was watching a fly traveling through the air. She had a vacant look on her face. The gymnastic male kept twisting and turning her about, and I wondered how he could do so without getting burned from her cigarette of which he seemed oblivious. She still wore her stockings and high heeled shoes. Their bedstead was rather inappropriate since it was a narrow, high backed sofa, the only piece of furniture. The background shadows now and then would indicate that there were at least two other persons in the room. Our comments on the situation ran something like this.

"That joker pays attention to his work."

"Probably gettin' time–and–a–half."

"She's probably gettin' paid half–time."

"Yeah, she ain't helpin' the guy a bit."

"I knew this broad who went to a beauty parlor and asked about a certain kind of dye job. The operator got mad and told her off but left a wash pan of dye in a booth for her to do it herself."

"This one got nothing there to dye."

"Yeah, it's disgusting."

"It sure is. Let's run off the next three rolls and see if they are any better."

I tarried at the Empire State Building for that night only. The next morning the employees arrived. Many of them native New Yorkers, were visibly shocked when they saw the signs of intended retreat which must have come during Friday night or Saturday. They asked about their personal effects in their desks, and were dismayed at the turn of events. More than one commented what a nice place it had been to work, and that they had no idea of the treachery that had been about on the part of the Japanese nation toward the United States. By the time they arrived, my orders had come through, and I referred the employees to my relief man. My orders told me that it would be a long, cold winter ahead.

My next assignment was at a dyestuffs establishment of German origin, and because of its product would be allowed to continue operations.

We set up a system of checking employees in and out, and we maintained a close security guard constantly. The hired guards were, from a law enforcement standpoint, a varied lot, but the best that might come our way.

The shining sun in my world there was a little Irish–American named O'Brien, a meter reader with the gas company by day and a security guard with us at night. He was a hired employee. He was plucky, smart, courageous, and had a heart of gold. He received nine dollars a day from the Treasury Department. He told me it helped him greatly because he had a large family and needed more money to maintain them. He was willing to work in any manner of legitimate endeavor. He worked, and was not afraid of work or the details involved in real work.

O'Brien was my man at the dyestuffs firm.

I stayed on the premises for eons. I bought what little personal necessities I needed from a neighborhood drug store, and that first week there was so much to be done that time did not drag.

Little by little, a routine was established and things ran smoothly. The employees were issued identification cards and were generally cooperative. We had a few people under surveillance, and they had to be taken away because of their avowed fervor which was not in the interest of the United States.

The only disturbance occurred late one night at an iron shipping–door at the rear of the building. The guard who was stationed in that area came running up to the front desk, and he was all excited.

"They're breaking the door down."

He had been a bookkeeper, and security enforcement was not at all his forte. He had been stationed at the back door. I went out the front and eased toward the back. I made no noise, and was among the little gathering at the back door before they knew I was about.

"Get up against the wall. I'll be damned! What the hell is this?" There were a couple of old gals there and a bum. The gals stockings were down around their shoes, and they had B.O.

"Just a little party, officer."

"Well, I'll be a sunnofabitch."

"I got everything–wine, women, and song."

"The hell you say."

"Goddamit, Dick, you're a man. Why don't you join us." He offered me a drink from a bottle of sherry. I refused but thanked him.

"I'm working kid. Can't horse around now."

"Yeah, I know. Plenty to go around. How about tomorrow?"

"Sure, any time you say."

"You know something, Dick," one of the women spoke up.

"What's that?"

"I'd marry you if you weren't so damn old."

"O.K. Let's break up the party now. You had your fun, let it go at that. You hear me Buster?"

"I got more than I can handle. How about givin' me a hand."

"Don't worry about that sunnuvabitch, Dick. Me and this beautiful girl friend of mine can take care of you while you gotta steady job. Let's take a drink on it. Gimme a buck, we'll get some more wine."

"Hey look, ladies and gentlemen, I got something to say to you."

"You can say that again."

"It's late now. I've got work to do inside this building tonight, and I'm asking you to go somewhere else."

"Okay. Now we know where we stand. Let's go, girls."

"Damright." "Hey, Dick. You wanna woman, guaranteed? Look us up when the war's over, and we'll love you two at a time."

"Betcha butt on that. So long, Dick."

When I returned to the front of the building I was admitted by the inquisitive bookkeeper type guard.

"Did you catch them?"

"Yeah."

"You tookem down to jail?"

"No."
"Why not?"
"Because they weren't doing anything I could charge them with."
"Who were they?"
"A couple of frauleins and a guy named Herr Schwartzenheim."
"What's the front office going to say?"
"Yours or mine?"
"Both of them, and Secret Service too."
"You wanna arrest them I'll tell you how to find them."
"Two German men and a woman you say?"
"No. Two women and a man."
"What did the women look like?"
"They were real pretty, young, and had nice shapes."
"No crap, I mean no kidding."
"No crap."
"No crap."
"What did you do with them?" The bait was taken .
"I kicked the guy in the ass and sent him home."
"What did you do with the girls?"
"What do you think?"
"You ATU bastard. I know what you did with them. Good Heavens, two of them!"

The chief headache I had there was keeping the men on post. At night, even with their little eight hour shifts as opposed to my own of twenty–four hours a day, they seemed to be away from the scene more than they should be. I decided to investigate. It was the old Adam and Eve thing, except that it was in the form of a spectator sport. From the third floor, the guys were watching a couple of babes in a building nearby. O'Brien was the only one with any original communication on the subject. He said, "Somebody gotta keep a watch on things downstairs."

I told O'Brien that he had better keep an ear and eye open the next night because I was going to raid the bunch in a way that they never would forget. He agreed, and since he carried a gun and was sharp as a tack, he was the only one I was afraid of making things backfire in my plan.

I slipped out of the building and saw the broads in the window across the way. I knew the time was ripe. The girls were hollering enticements at the men at the open window and paid no attention to me. I eased back into the building.

To the truly uninitiated, on a Sunday night after full darkness sets in, there is no place like a huge old industrial building in downtown Manhattan. The street noises are few. The building timbers breathe, the structure quakes, and the heat and cold of things there bring on some odd architectural behavior. An ATU Investigator in New York knows these things but a lot of other people do not. In cold weather it is an especial thing, and unless you know the voices of some things speaking out, it can be scary when you are there all by yourself.

I eased up the back stairs to the third floor and worked my way through an aisle between packing cases. I picked up a board from the top of one of the cases, and got within a few feet of four of the guards. They had a conversational buzz going and their minds were far from their bodies. I slammed the board down hard on a packing case, and if any of those jaybirds had any romantic ideas before that they lost them right then and there. There was a scramble away from the window, and one guy didn't stop until he reached the ground floor. He had thought a gun had been fired. The discipline was much better after that.

The days crawled in their own deliberate way. As in all things, however slow they move, they reach a point where things have changed.

The world of New York had changed. Young girls were going to dances for soldiers. Clerks were going into the army to run earth moving machines, and the kids from the big city finally were getting a chance to shoot a rifle, even if it was in North Carolina or Oklahoma. They were wearing uniforms dyed in the very stuff that I had been protecting. Mothers and grandmothers were going into the churches and temples to pray for the safety of their soldiers, sailors and fliers. The lines for consumer goods becoming scarce were lengthening and gasoline sales were rigidly restricted.

Our people became used to the routine of war in a surprisingly short time. What had been undreamed of just a few short months before, became a way of life. I knew every employee's face in the building, their name and job.

One guy who worked there had a real likable personality and a good sense of humor. He was on a bowling team which bowled on Friday nights. Each Friday morning he would come to work with the bowling ball in a fitted bag which had the contours of the ball itself.

The first time I had seen him with it he was grinning all over. The bag was almost a replica of the standard cartoon bombs displayed to show thugs or yeggs at work. I asked him if the thing had a fuse.

He said, "I thought about rigging it up for fun, with a rope sticking out of the top, but I thought you might not think it was funny."

"You know old so and so, on the desk sometimes?"

"Yeah. I thought of him."

"Well, he really is a nice guy, but he is not at home here. He should be getting his rocks with an eyeshade and a pile of ledgers."

"He looks like it. Do you think we could have some fun with him?"

"Yeah. He'll be on at lunch time today. I'll meet you at the back stairs door. I'll get the rope in the shipping department."

"Great. I can hardly wait."

We rigged up the dummy bomb and put it in a cardboard box which was left untied. Likable guy went out the back door and around to the front. I sauntered to where I could watch the desk. It was routine to inspect packages carried by people entering the building.

"What's in the box?"

"Feathers."

"What on earth are you going to do with feathers?"

"They're chicken feathers. I want to dye them so they look like flamingo feathers. My wife is making a hat."

"They don't dye feathers in this building, bud."

"Well, I'll have to confess. It's something else."

"Like what?"

"Err, aah, don't open it here."

The man on the desk picked up the package and was surprised at it's weight. He opened the box and let out a string of cuss words a mile long. I was truly surprised.

"A bowling ball with a rope on it trying to scare somebody. Well look here, blankety blank wise guy. I'm going to report you to Mr. so–and–so." He called the head–knocker's name.

The guard picked up the phone and said, "Stay right here, wise guy. A goddambowlingball. Jees."

I walked over and the guard was out of character. He said, "This bastard thinks he's a wise guy. We ought to get him fired."

I had to step in, and confess my part.

The guard's reaction was, "You goddam ATU guys don't give a four–letter word for anything." He came back later and said, "Let's try that trick on O'Brien."

SEVEN

SOUTHWARD BOUND

The war came and went. Prices became higher for all things. Apartment houses which had formerly housed stills and piccolo joints, speakeasies, cathouses and gambling joints were being filled with tenants new to New York, and new to New York's ways. The rents were enormous for what was provided. The housing laws in effect were ignored in those places, and families were doubling up and felt lucky to be able to sleep in shifts or crowded rooms which were better than they had ever known before.

Copper prices had soared and it's availability was limited. Sugar and space could be bought only at outrageous premium prices. More jobs meant that more people were patronizing legitimate bars and drinking legal whiskey. After a joint was raided and padlocked a family or families would seize upon it for living quarters. Some janitors dressed in new suits and smoked better cigars. The wise guy absentee owners from other places switched to the next bigger car for more pleasure, because of the hulk of brick, mortar and broken plaster they had purchased for a bargain was truly that, and a prime moneymaker.

Our dialogues with informants were shorter. The moonshiners were openly complaining, and what few there were, were getting caught because people who needed space would tell us things. Even those sources of information faded out and the job became a patrol routine rather than an investigative one.

My partner and I carried out an ambitious plan. We made a systematic check of every building in violation areas. We climbed stairs and descended them all day long. We felt every hallway door. We sniffed at each door. We checked each chimney flue.

We came up with four of what we called "piss–pot" outfits, and as motley a bunch of defendants as one might find. Some were using syrup to make mash instead of sugar. At the door before we banged the place, we could hear the operators walking around sounding like they were in a swamp. The syrupy goo would fall on the linoleum and the moonshiner would step in it. With each step he made a sucking sound and had to make an extra effort to pick up his feet and put them down.

We hung around the sugar stores, and what little sugar the owners could buy and sell, found us tailing it. We tried to make informers out of the sugar dealers, but what we could learn from them was nearly nil.

We would check in at the Police Division offices. Heretofore they always had numerous moonshine complaints they couldn't handle, and gave them to us. We found that what isolated few they had were family grudge complaints.

The sugar stores with "Azucar Cubana" and nothing else printed on the painted windows closed one by one, and some of them became occupied by gypsy families. They became points for palmistry and phrenology, and if there was any prediction in them it was that the moonshine business in New York was shot to hell. To be sure, the gypsies would have preferred the tenements or the open road, but I guess they were doing the best they could in an overcrowded place. It took a hell of a lot of gas to run their big old Chryslers and Cadillacs, so they had to stay put.

More and more we cruised the city streets. The days dragged by slowly, and we racked our brains for clues. We checked carefully every scrap of information no matter how unpromising. The monthly reports contained less and less, while the reports from the Southern States showed that their men were working their tails off. The pioneer spirit of the olden day's distillers was showing itself in their descendants. The hollows and swamps were busy places in some areas.

The word got through to New York and there were discussions and predictions that the whole Yankee ATU shebang would be roaming the hills and lowlands of the South. As the youngest member and having plenty of service behind me, I was often kidded about being transferred. I talked it over with the boss and he said that there were some who might go, but that as active and experienced as I was, he would have to think twice on such a thing.

Inactivity was doing me no good and I was afraid to get in a rut that way, so I thought of moving on. At the end of '47, and beginning of '48, I was with my wife, on vacation at her home in North Carolina, near Raleigh.

One night I cooked a steak out in the yard at the farm where her folks lived. I was in my shirtsleeves, and the radio news broadcasts described the wild and heavy snowstorms in New York. The silvery moon, the one that seems to be North Carolina's very own, was in its full glory that night, and the gentle whispers in the pines across the road were talking and I was listening.

Myrtle's father, Mal Weathers, was a great kindly man, and as honest in all things as the day is long. He and his wife had eight children. His wife, Minnie, had passed away when only two of the girls had reached maturity. With the help of the kids, and through his own fortitude and determination, he carried on.

The household illumination was provided by kerosene lamp, and refrigeration, what there was, was effected by an ice–box, or storage in a food safe in a cold room, and some things like eggs and butter could be put in a bucket and lowered into the well, and spoilage retarded.

That was at the beginning of 1948, and rural areas all over the country were not served by the power lines that many people today take for granted. Pap had a nice farm, a fine milk cow, an abundance of hogs, and plenty of beef available at hand in the pasture. My city lips would smack while I downing chocolate milk–shakes made with pure cream. Whatever livestock would be slaughtered, even chickens or turkeys, had been fattened up on corn for a good while so that the meat was in top condition.

The kids, all but Bob, who was a senior in high school had left home. Pap was not feeling too well. It was hell leaving him when we headed back to New York. The papers had carried stories of moonshine raids. The balmy weather, the moon, the pines and all the songs of the nearby woods were working on me and I was a sitting duck.

When I told Myrt she said that I was off my rocker, and said that I would get over it when we got back to New York. I didn't.

Myrt, never one to stand in my way in an undertaking, consented to go South if I was transferred, on the one condition that we would not live out in the country. She said that she had enough of feather quilts, outside toilets and wood fires.

At New York I talked to Mr. Carroll, the Investigator in Charge for the Southern New York district. I told him the full story. He was most understanding and kind.

"If that's what you want, John, I won't stand in your way."

He picked up the phone and called Mr. Dunnagan, the enforcement chief at 253 Broadway. The next morning I went to see Mr. Dunnagan. He, too, was most gracious and emphasized that I should not go if I was thinking that perhaps I would be transferred South anyway. Later I felt that he thought I was pushing to get to North Carolina before I was sent involuntarily to a state further South. When I explained my full feelings to him, he consented, and said, "Hell, they'll want to get a man like you." He picked up the phone. The next Monday morning I was at the office of the chief of enforcement, ATU, at Baltimore, headquarters for the upper Southern states.

In about three days I walked into the Post Office building at Raleigh. I took the elevator to the third floor. I spoke to John Whiteside, the ATU group head. After courteous and welcoming amenties, he said, "Are you ready to go on a raid?" I looked at his khaki's, high–top shoes, and wide gun belt with the big 4–inch barrel '38. I looked at my own carefully pressed suit and my shined oxfords. He grinned, and said, "Drop us off from the car. You won't get your feet wet."

I didn't have the faintest idea where we were going other than we were headed for a place called "Broadslab," and that we were going to raid a submarine distillery whatever the hell that was. I watched every inch of the route we took, and in about an hour we joined a constable, and set out for the locality of the distillery.

I made mental shorthand notes all the way, and such notations spanned my mind something like this.

1. Left at the funny colored house.
2. Right at the place where the sign says "Fresh Fish Daily."
3. Cross the bridge on the other side of that funny looking barn.
4. Go by Mingo Swamp Church.
5. Turn left where that triangular slanted thing that looks like a

two–legged sawhorse, sits at the edge of a field. (It was a cotton weighing device.)

And so it went until we came to a rural church. We drove in back of it, and the others got out. Someone said, "See you in an hour. Keep away from Four Corners."

I drove the offenhauser–headed Ford Tudor to the nearest town. I watched my speed all the way in, and checked my watch between points, and was making more notes about turning and topography and country architecture. I went into a drug store and had a soft drink, looked at the magazines on the rack and came out. I still had about twenty minutes to kill. Three or four guys were standing near the car. They were friendly, and were dressed neatly in clean overalls.

"You're a new ATU man aren't you?"

"No."

"I'm Ed Barfit, this is ol' soanso, and this is soanso."

"Glad to meetcha."

"You're from up North. Saw you come up in Whiteside's car."

"Yeah. I guess you guys live around here?"

"Yeah, we're farming folks. Too wet to plow today."

I didn't know whether or not it was, but I said, "It sure is," and they agreed. I noticed that one of them had hands too soft and too white to have been on a plow handle for a long time. He saw me looking at them and grinned. They waited for me to drive away, and they tailed me until I headed back toward Raleigh. They turned back. Their outfits must have been in the other direction.

I found my way back to the church where I had dropped the others. "It's not ready to run," they told me. They got in the car and directed me out of the area by another route than we had taken going in. We went to another place in the same fashion. I went into another town, and when I returned they had a moonshiner in custody, and I got my first look at a submarine still. It was nothing but a big wooden box with a galvanized bottom and sides, and had a hole cut in the top for the cap, which gave it a submarine periscope appearance.

That afternoon I went to a department store on Fayetteville Street in Raleigh. I bought a couple of sets of khakis, six inch high top shoes, and a cowboy belt. That night I dressed up in my room, looked in the mirror and thought, if the New York guys could see me now. The phone rang. It was for me to go to work and I was ready.

EIGHT

VANITY UNFAIR

"I'll kill you. . .you son of a bitch."

"Balls."

That was our dialogue at dawn in the swamps of North Carolina, and the bucket of mash in the moonshiner's hand came crashing down on my head. The bottom rim struck on the top center of my skull. He was daring me to arrest him. I sure as Hell wasn't going to let him get away. I moved in.

It was all over in a hurry. My speed accounted for that.

"Federal Officer, you're under arrest."

I straddled the man face to face. My head was wet and sticky. We had gone down hard, with me on top. His face hit the muddy ground. I turned him over and he began to cry.

The blur in front of me as I shifted, was a forest of red feathers patterned against a gray sky out there somewhere.

I tasted that liquified salt which, even unfelt or unseen tells you it's blood. I looked into the face of the man beneath me. Was it a face or was it something I was dreaming about? I wiped my eyes with my shirtsleeve and looked again. What I saw made me think that the man had struck a tree root or stump when I knocked him to the ground.

I could smell the stink of swamp mud mingled with fermented mash, and right then it didn't seem to me that there was one good thing anywhere in the world. My head was hurting, and my arms didn't have the strength they should have. I rested heavily on my antagonist.

I noted the hardened overalls fabric where muck of one kind or other had adhered in spots. I knew it was mud, spilled mash, soot from the firebox and sweat from the day before and the week before too. It could have blood drawn by the mosquitoes down there and smeared by scratching with grime coated fingernails. I almost felt sorry for the poor joker.

"Whose gonna kill who, feller?"

"You can bet your ass on that."

"What are your eyes so red for. . .cryin' like a baby I guess."

I could feel his muscles pulsing under me and pushing the sobs all the way up his body to where they came out in that sea of blood. It was one hell of a noise I had to listen to there with the thump keg whompin' and the birds practicing up their songs for the rich people all the while.

It's funny but I can still remember that a mockingbird and a cardinal redbird were singing louder than the rest. A bluejay out there was raising a ruckus and telling me that my partners were working their way toward me through the swamp.

"Get off me, you mother."

"Balls. Don't push me too far. I'm on top."

"Get off."

"Glug."

"One more try like that. . . . ."

"Glug."

"Gees."

The strength was back in my arms and I got up and stared through the red feathers at the guy. I talked softly.

"Federal Officer. Damn if you ain't ol' Geather Jarratte. I see you now, Geather. Why'd you want to clobber me? Bad business clobberin' Federal Officers. Lemme wipe the blood off your face."

"Whaddya mean it's my blood, Geets, Huh?"

"You listenin' Geets? Stop crying, dammit."

"Sorry, Geets, they're coming in now. They won't like it at all."

"Hear that bluejay out there, Geets?"

"He's tellin' us they're here coming for you, Geets."

"You still there, Geets?"

"Ought to be ashamed of yourself callin' ol' Race a sunnuvabitch, and talkin' about killin' folks when you don't mean any of it."

I didn't remember my partners arriving on the scene.

"You were really out on your feet when we got here, Race."

"What hospital is this?"

"Yeah, I should have known. The closest one."

"How do you feel now?"

"Lousy, got a headache that won't quit."

"I remember now. I rode with it as best I could when I was jumping over that pipe right at him."

"You know something?"

"What."

"It's funny, but I can see that bucket coming at me yet. I can still see the printing on it, "Grandma's Molasses."

"We've got it in the car trunk. Might need it for evidence."

"I got all the evidence I need. Right up here."

"That's usin' your head, Race."

"Yeah, I'll save the bucket to show my grandchildren."

"Yeah, tell 'em what a great impression grandma made on grandpa."

"Hey can't you guys get serious about anything?"

"Yeah, Nurse, ya wanna see where the mule bit me?"

"I've got a clean mind. I don't want to see it."

"So have I. He bit me on the hand."

"I used to think that revenooers were crazy, but now I know it."

"I'd love to catch you at a whiskey still."

"What would you do with me if you did?"

"Put you on Bearcat County probation."

"What on earth is that?"

"Come on over here Dollbaby, and I'll show you."

"Race, I think I'm going to tell this guy's wife on him."

"Barney's?"

"Certainly."

"You can't do that, Honeychild."

"Why not?"

"Because he's not married."

If she thought Barney was crazy after that she sure didn't act like it.

I still had the sense of levity that helps revenooers to keep going sometimes under adverse circumstances, but I had a strange feeling about being out on my feet there in the swamp with a prisoner in custody. It seemed that something from the past was sustaining me, like having the right kind of training for a job when training counted most. I thought of what Mike had said about when he and Barney came up.

"You were covered with blood on your head, neck, face and shirt, and you were holding a cloth sugar bag at your head talking to him as though you were the head chaplain in the moonshine brigade."

"Hell, he was the one with the blood all over him. I saw it."

"Yeah, that's true, but it was your blood. He didn't have a scratch on him."

"I had been wondering what you guys would think when you got there. I knew you weren't too far off the way those bluejays were screaming, and I got up off him."

"It was eerie, I'll admit, coming up on you like that. That swamp was full of holes over our heads, and the briars and brush was tough to get through. That guy was glad to see us more than you were."

"Yeah. He was scared. I guess that I startled the hell out of him."

"You know what he said?"

"What?"

"I'm afraid of blood."

"He ought not to be now. I gave him a four–barrel transfusion."

When Mike mentioned the cloth sugar bag on my head, I recalled a conversation years before with a revenooer from further down South who had told me of a shootout he and his partner took part in. His partner was killed and so was one moonshiner. He was shot three times in his midsection, and was bleeding bad when he wounded the moonshiner and captured him.

"I didn't think we were going to get out of there. I was bleeding badly and I had my gun cocked on this guy telling him to pray that we would get out of there, because if it looked as if we might not to me, then I was going to snap that trigger."

"What we had down there," he continued, "was a nightmare, and as serious as it was, a lot of things were running through my mind, all the nice things about my partner, his plans to retire in three months, and how in hell am I going to stop this blood flowing out of me. I saw some empty sugar sacks lying on the ground. I picked up a few and stuffed them inside my jacket and zipped it up and said, "March, you bastard." I followed him out of the swamp with my gun at the back of his head, thinking about who would tell my partner's widow the bad news and what his five kids would think about it."

I guess that I stole the deep–south revenooers act for myself by some form of retention. I used determination and an empty sugar bag to come out of it better than I might otherwise have. . .that morning in Cottonmouth Swamp.

It was a demonstration of how acute observation and training can be in a field where both are really needed.

I took a real good look in the mirror and was reminded of the biggest thing that had been prodding me that morning. My three day old new style crew–cut would probably be messed up for life. I recalled looking at the hearty mop of hair and the heavy beard on my oppressor at what times I could see him clearly, and how I had thought, you're gonna go through life with that nice fat hair. Poor me is gonna have an embroidered scar right in the middle of that thin silky hair that never would stay in place until I had it crew–cut three days ago. Now they call the same kind of haircut a flat top and charge two–bits extra to cut it.

I remembered things I had read, good and bad, things philosophers called vanity, but that didn't help at all. What I really wanted was to be able to continue getting crew–cuts without having to worry about having an ugly scar there.

I thought of old Heidelberg, the scars of honor, the movies of World War I, when all the German Aces had scars on their faces from dueling over the honor of beautiful women.

I thought of the time that I put my leg clean through a plywood door panel in an alky raid in N. Y. C. The only problem that went with it was merely the possibility of losing a leg that I had had for years.

This was different, that nice new easy to care for crew–cut that permitted me to go bareheaded in a windstorm without my hair looking like a rat's nest. Gees, I had it that way only for three days. I wanted to cry when I looked in the mirror.

I thought about the night the New York detective accidently turned a still faucet while I was bent over, shutting off the gas fire. My belt had acted like a funnel and the boiling mash poured down on my backside, thank goodness, instead of on my front side. I got over that okay.

But how in hell are you going to get over a 32–stitch scar tissue job in the middle of your beloved, bee–utiful, bejabbered pate?

A funny thing which happened the day before was still fresh in my mind. While I was waiting, under observation, I thought of it. It too had to do with my crew–cut.

I was slipping up on a still in operation. I got real close to the two men there. When they began to move around quite actively, I ducked behind a stump which was rather small considering my size. The two moonshiners were talking about girls and I could hear what they were saying. They were lying like hell to each other.

"Me and her did it twelve times wass night."

"I worked too hard yesterday, deliverin', so I only got it fourteen times. That's why I feel so good today."

"Me and her sister did it eight times wass night before I met her."

"Yeah, that's why you're so tired today."

"Yeah. Eighteen times a day is enough for anyone got to go to work."

"I wonder if 'dem wevenooers wike it da way we do."

"The way they hang around all the time in the woods it don't look like they have time for it."

"I don't know about dat. I was up in da men's wess woom at Federal Court wass term, an dat one dey call Barney, he was tandin' up at da unerall nect to me, and I wook down to tee what one of dem wevenooers wook wike."

"Well what did you see?"

"You tee dat young tapling up da path?"

"Sure."

"Well he was just wike. . . .doddamit, dere's a wabbit up behind dat tump."

"Let's shoot him."

"Hell, no. We make too much noise. It wook wike a wittoo wabbit. I tneak up on him and gwab him and we have barbecue wabbit for wunch tomorrow."

The crew–cut was just visible as I sought to conceal myself.

A time like that is a serious thing for a revenooer. He has three choices of what he is going to do next. They are, 1. Wet himself laughing. 2. Make a noise laughing and give himself away. 3. Hold his tongue and his kidneys as far back as he can.

"Here, Bunny, Bunny, nice widoo bunny, tum to Charwey."

"Bet your ass I will Charwey."

"MA!"

"Ha, ha, ha. You're under arrest. Ha, ha, ha. This is almost as bad as the night Aunt Tilly got caught in the wringer."

"One going your way, Barney, down the creek. Watch that sapling." I hollered as loud as I could. Charley had a sheepish grin on his face. If I knew Barney, I knew he would be in there close enough to hear the conversation the two moonshiners were having.

Barney and his man came out of the swamp in animated conversation and joined us. I turned to Charley and said, "Don't let it get you down feller, it's all in the game, some good days, some bad, and you never know from one day to the next. There's a million guys in this country right now who have ten times as much trouble as you have."

"Deeder Trite, I tot you was a dodam wabbit."

His buddy spoke up and said, "Take it easy on me fellers, how would you feel if one of you didn't know a daddam wevenooer from a doddam wabbit?"

"You're the Torter twins, aren't you?"

"Yeah, I'm Buck and he's Charley. You're Race Bayley, aren't you?"

"No, Race Kearins. This is Barney over here."

"I know, I been hearing big things about him."

"He hears it all the time."

"Doddam, dem two guys are a tircus awright. Barney and Baywey they call demselves. Ha, ha, dat's a good one."

"Race why don't you put something in that book you're always talking about writing. . .about today. We had enough for a chapter listening to these guys."

"Yeah, I'll call it 'The Torters and the Hair.' "

Barney wasn't to be outpunned that day. He said, "Hell no. Title it, 'The Farmers Torter.' "

Charley, as it turned out was quite a joker despite his being caught that day. The still wasn't a very big one and we destroyed it with axes. While we were working we were carrying on a running conversation with the Torter boys. Charley said, "Dat pun about da Torters and da hair nearwy had me tumped. . .Det it?"

Barney said, "I don't reckon you're going to get your full twenty two today, Charley."

"Oh, we jut hortin' awoun'. Deeder Trite, don't tell dat to da judge, he wock me up and trow away da key. I never will det any more."

Buck Torter had been quiet. No doubt he was thinking about his predicament for which I couldn't blame him. Charley was a ball of fire and told us how he'd been a cook in the Army over in the Pacific.

"I'd alwayed det me plenty of sugar, and waisins, and yeat, and I made a nifty widoo outfit to wun off a batch when I tould. It wadn't bad, but when I went down to my hidey spot I pwetended I wad helpin' wit' da ditwattin and da waundry, and da wootenant tought dat I wad da tmart't duy in da tumpany. I didn't dwink mytelf, but I wolled up tum dood pwoffits, until a tongue tied targeant from anudder tumpany tame awong and poiled it all for me."

"What did he do, Charley?"

"It wadn't what he did dat boddered me. It wad what he taid to me. He asked me a whole wot of twettions and I wouldn't antwer him. He wad a tough duy too."

"Why wouldn't you answer him?"

"I twied dat one time before wit a tongue tied'twanger in Wattington, D.T. and he whomp da hell outen me."

"You don't seem to get sore about it, Charley."

"Hell, no. Dere's a wot of tings inna world I tant change, and I wet well enough alone. I ture would wike to doe and tee my dal tonight, but I weckon I spend da night in jayoo."

"I dunno. Why don't you boys promise us you'll be at the Commissioner's in the morning about ten o'clock?"

Buck brightened up at that and said, "We'll be right there at nine thirty on the courthouse steps. You can bet."

Charley had to get in another word before they walked up to their house not far away. He said, "Do you weckon you would have taught me if I hadn't went up dere wookin' for a wabbit?"

"I reckon so, Charley. Not only do I look like a rabbit sometimes but I can run like one too, and so can Barney."

"Dat ture make me feel better. I tink I doe tee my dirl now."

We watched them walking across the field, laughing, and joking, taking the bad with the good, the world by the minute instead of the hour, day, month or year. We watched them separate at the middle of the field and walk off until they were out of sight. We knew that Charley was on his way to see his girl. We knew too, that Buck would soon be making arrangements to get another outfit so he could supply his customers.

The nurse startled me as I lay on the table watching the ceiling mostly, and dreaming.

"You were grinning like you'd just caught another moonshiner."

"I was thinking about something funny that happened yesterday."

"Your friends went out to eat lunch and buy you a shirt to go home in. We'll let you go in about a week."

"Barney and Mike are okay. Good workers, and have a good sense of humor."

"Mr. Kearins, I'd like to say something to you."

"Call me Race, Dollbaby."

"Stop your clowning for a minute. I want to say something serious to you." She had what I call a fast southern accent.

"You want me to get you a date with old Barney?"

"Look, you had a close call. It was a lot closer than you probably think. You'll have to take some time off from work. You lost a lot of blood and that bone on the top of your skull isn't exactly like it was yesterday."

"My head is full of bones."

"You're not kidding."

Barney and Mike strolled in with a new shirt. Barney was already calling the nurse by her first name. They stood talking while Mike pulled a red shirt out of a paper bag which said, "The College Shop." The shirt was long, and in big white letters was printed on the front: "N.C. State Playmate." It was a girls "shortie" night gown, for college students' wives and sweethearts. They also had bought me an undershirt. I put it on, and then the playmate shirt. In no time I had an audience of nurses, a couple of doctors, and an old lady who went around the hospital with a four–wheel cart full of heart diagnosis equipment. She said out loud to everybody. "He must be the one who escaped from the roadgang last night."

I looked in the trash can at my blood–stained shirt and undershirt. I turned to Barney.

"Did you get my notebook out of my shirt pocket?"

"Yeah. It's in the glove compartment of the car. I don't know whether you'll be able to read it or not. It's messed up with mud and blood."

Five days later we left the hospital and began the one hour drive back to our post of duty. I was in the back seat of the car and I was thinking "Grandma's Molasses."

How in hell are you going to tell someone that you were conked on the head with a Grandma's Molasses bucket. It doesn't ring true in ordinary conversation at all.

"In Cottonmouth Swamp at daybreak too."

I knew that I wouldn't be able to dodge the issue entirely. I recalled how a friend of mine used to explain away his miscellaneous black eyes and bruises about the face and neck.

"A garter belt snapped on me."

That was all he said, and nobody persisted in questioning him any further.

Later on I was to attempt telling what really happened, and I found any true explanation to be quite complex. Instead, I merely said, "Well, sir! There was this rich, good–looking babe. . .and she was wearing a diamond studded garter belt that was tight as hell. We were shacking up, see, and going through the preliminaries. Well, sir! You know how a feller gets curious about things like that. Well, the dern thing snapped and caught me on the noggin. Ha, ha, ha."

"Damn, Race, I'm glad it happened to you instead of me. Gosh, I'd never be able to tell the truth about it the way you did. What were you doing with your head down there, anyway?"

The ride back seemed longer than usual to me. I shifted restlessly in the back seat. As we hit the outskirts of home I saw Barney eyeing me in the rear view mirror. He was grinning and shook his head.

"You sure are a pretty sight back there, Race. Only your mother could love you like that."

"You bastards will get yours yet, and plenty of it, by the time you've been in this business as long as I have."

NINE

SOONER OR LATER

It happened on a Thursday night, when most toddy wagons rolled. Barney and I had spent the better part of the afternoon tuning our official cars and checking our radio equipment. We were going to work moonshine transportation on the Scallywag Swamp Road from ten p.m. until daybreak. The town of Scallywag was situated on the far side of Bigsnake Swamp from Teddybear Inlet.

The road had some sharp curves on each end, but the center stretch was long and straight. It was made for the big engines and medium size cars, used by moonshiners and revenooers alike.

The weather man predicted severe thunderstorms for the area that night.

After we had put in a set of points on Barney's Ford, checked the timing, and cleaned and gapped the plugs it sounded a little better.

The car had been cutting out on Barney at high speeds, and he nearly had a wreck because of it the night before.

We tried the car out before supper, and at one hundred it would cut out. I swapped cars with Barney and drove it on Sandy Plain Road.

I was on the Cat Tail Bridge and gunned it full range on the far side near Preacher's Bend. The fuel supply choked, and I was glad that I wasn't meeting anyone on that curve. I figured that the fuel pump wasn't right, and that at best it was clogged. When we got back to town we blew out the fuel line and it helped some.

We ate supper at Honk's Drive–In. As hot as the day was, we ate a bowl of chili each and topped it off with fried chicken and all the trimmings. We went home and hit the hay to get ready for the night's work ahead.

The telephone woke me up about eight thirty p.m.

"Race?"

"Yeah."

"This is Det Cleve."

"Hi, Det. What's new?"

"Bunk Barnabee and Hilton Moses are tripping down to Scallywag tonight for fifteen pieces." (Fifteen cases, ninety gallons of moonshine in half gallon Mason jars.)

"What'll they be riding?"

"His gal says the '54 light gray tudor. The one that's really red–hot."

"Good. We'll snag it for government use."

"Mr Race, I want to warn you about something."

"Thanks. Go ahead."

"Be careful. Bunk's been sportin' round the juke joints all day with that gal of Big Daddy's."

"Ruby Lee?"

"Yeah, and Big Daddy don't like it. Bunk's been into the juice getting up his courage. He's scared to death of Big Daddy. Bunk might give you trouble. He's bad when he's had a few."

"Thanks Det. I'll see you later."

"Okay."

"Yeah, so long."

I made a pot of coffee and while it was brewing I sat down in the kitchen and thought about how we would work Det's information. I thought of Big Daddy having the same model and color car as Barney's, and how a few days before Bunk had scalded his car off at the sight of Barney's car approaching him on the Hildersett highway.

We'd have to change plans now. I knew we couldn't leave anything to chance in a running tilt with Bunk Barnabee while he was under the influence. I'd take the running road–block.

We couldn't have Bunk thinking that Big Daddy might be coming up on him. I'd put my car ahead of him where he could see that it was a black coupe instead of a gray tudor.

Barney laughed when I told him about it.

"They got plenty to fight over." Barney gestured with his hands and posture.

"Yeah, plenty to go around all right."

"I told you what she said to me the night I surprised her with Hootinowl Hibbs over on Vinegar Hill."

"Stop bragging, Barney. She just likes guys with cars the same as yours and Big Daddy's."

We knocked off the banter and became serious and made our plans; our last official plans together.

At ten minutes before ten I pulled from the Bigsnake Swamp Road on to the logging path at the far edge from Scallywag. The broadcast radio was crackling and I knew that there were storms brewing in the vicinity. I hoped they would be quickies and hurry up and come along so the road wouldn't be too slick later.

The wind grew stronger, and the trees outhummed the grunts of the frogs. I figured that Bunk would come by about two a.m. after the highway patrol cars thinned out some.

Barney was going to station himself at the Scallywag end. Before we parted Barney pulled up alongside.

"All you gotta do is lay behind him, and flush him my way."

"Okay, Grandpa. Anything else?"

"Yeah. Watch that number three curve this way. It's a bitch."

Barney laughed into the night and said, "Yeah. So is Ruby Lee."

He gunned it and took off like a striped ape for the second last time of his life.

I sat parked on the log path and listened to the night sounds and watched the lightning flash through the trees from a distance. At times like that I lapse into a third consciousness that's just there and doesn't interfere with what I am doing.

I just think things, any old kind of things, and I get ready for the night at the same time. I sit there and eat stuff out of a can, and drink warm soft drinks or buttermilk. I get out of the car and walk around when the fluids say to. Hot chocolate is the worst liquid to keep you hopping.

That night, on one such occasion, I anointed myself with insect repellent to discourage the mosquitoes, and walked to the edge of the road. Getting down into the ditch full length, I waited for the next car to come along.

I wanted to be sure that I could get a good look at anything passing by. A pickup came by and I read the license number with ease. It was a petty moonshiner's rig bound for a case or two of Scallywag moonshine. I made a mental note of it the way a guy would note a pigeon when he is hunting for partridges.

I went back to the car and turned the radio dial to an all–night station. It was a hell of a long way off, but it came in loud and clear. That happens in car radios at night.

I could hear animals gnawing away at supper, further back in the swamp. I felt very sorry for their main courses which had been other animals in a place they called home.

I heard a fox cough, and I knew that my short wave radio hum was bothering her kits. I didn't hear any traffic, so I threw my flashlight beams into her face, tossed a piece of tree bark toward her and she took off.

There wasn't a sign of a star overhead. I remembered how close and vivid the stars had looked on my first night visit to the Bigsnake twelve years before. I still had the echo of city streets and tenement house routines in my night hearing then. I was impressed because the mosquitoes were not nearly so pesty as those I had known on many summer dawns on Manhattan's lower east side.

Night life in the swamp had truly intrigued me. It didn't seem half as numerous as the wharf rat population of the big city, or as close at hand. Some of the guys in the crew on my first swamp night those years ago, had expected some kind of maidenhead reaction from me. They dropped me off to observe a pesky little pot outfit for thirty–six hours. I had thought that it would be real spooky quiet down there, like a big city cellar deep in the ground, but it wasn't. I went in at eight p.m. Tuesday, and they were to come for me at eight a.m. Thursday.

What I remember most was that my rubber boots were too hot, how cool my bare feet had felt in the muck, how the sun looked so orange through the thick treetops, how busy the animals and birds were, how they worked, how they breakfasted, how they sang, and how they chastised each other. Of course I remember how no human being had approached until noon on Wednesday when Case Swaney came into the swamp.

I didn't hear any car stop on the road, and the first sign I had of Case being there was when I looked about a hundred yards away and saw him approaching. I hid behind a bush and watched him checking for strange tracks, stopping to listen, and putting his feet one at a time into tracks that he had made going in the time before.

It took him so long to come by me that I was concerned that my feet might go to sleep in my squatting down position. I wasn't in any hurry. I wanted to see him do something. He did have a Mason jar case under his right arm, but I wanted more than that to connect him with the still, and I had twenty–four hours to let him do it.

Case sat down on a stump a few yards from me. He took off his shoes and reached down beside the stump and came up with a jar of clear liquid. I supposed it was moonshine but it could have been water. He took a nice long pull, smacked his lips out loud and said, "Hot Damn." I knew then that it was whiskey.

He got up, leaving the jar case. Cradling the jar of whiskey in his left arm, carrying his shoes in his right hand, he walked down to the still and went to work.

I let him get the fire started good with lightwood knots, (turpentine saturated chips from old pine stumps).

"What have you got there, old timer?"

Case had a foolish grin on his face, and turned and ran. I didn't want him to fall and hurt himself so I caught up with him in a hurry and tagged him on the shoulder. That means "You're IT". . .if you ever played tag. That's the usual routine, and when the moonshiner feels revenooer on him like that he stops. Case was no different than the others.

"Tough luck, old feller, but it's all in the game as you know."

"That's for sure. I'm Case Swaney. Don't believe I've seen you before. Thought I knew all the revenooers. You from Raleigh?"

"Yeah. Johnny Kearins. They call me Race."

"Had a feelin' I oughtn't to come in this mornin'. My sixty second birthday. No way to celebrate a birthday, is it?"

"Let's see what we can do about it, Case. I've got some potted meat, sardines, crackers and some colas." I had three bottles of the stuff I'd stached in a stumphole.

"I gotta little bit of stuff left in a jyar I kep for emergency. We kin use that. I got some cake, ham and biscuits, in a fruit jar box up yonder a mite."

"You got an axe hid around here anywhere?"

"Yeah. Got it hid. Once in a while them logmen come by and help themselves to one, and then you fellers are apt to come by so I keep 'em hid so they won't be stole or confisticated."

Case swilled the remaining whiskey he had before I could stop him. We sat down and ate most of what we had except some of my canned goods. I destroyed the distillery, and we walked out to the road and hitched a ride from a moonshiner bound for Scallywag. He said that he was going to visit a sick cousin there, but that the cousin could wait because he wasn't that sick. For a while I thought that the guy who picked us up was some of Case's kinfolk, but he wasn't. He was one of his customers.

That day, twelve years ago, had been kind of festive, and it was nice to remember as I sat in the same swamp with Barney being on the other end and waiting for Bunk Barnabee.

I had a few brief communications with Barney and went back to an individual world of thoughts and fancies that people in lonely places know so well.

I could smell the ozone before the thunderstorm. The overhead was a dirty and windy gray, that even the lightning didn't suggest as transparent. I thought of other nights.

I thought of Bridgie, a girl of my teens. How certain man made stars overhead in Loew's Paradise Theater had cast their spell on Bridgie and me one snowy night during the big depression.

The radio announcer interrupted my thoughts with a commercial. They were two hours behind our time out there. I checked my watch and called Barney. I could hear his broadcast radio playing "Good Night Irene" in the background. He put the microphone close to the broadcast radio and "Good Night Irene" came in too loud. The announcer said that it was twelve minutes past one. The rains were slow in coming. We had seen the same things pass on the road and our conversation was routine until Barney said, "I'll see you in my dreams, Irene."

"Yeah, I'll see you in my dreams. Drive carefully."

When I did see him it was not in any dream. It was in a nightmare, and a hundred more since.

At one–thirty I heard the car coming when it was still a mile away. The driver wasn't wasting any time getting around the curves. At one point I thought the guy had lost it.

Something must have scared him because by the time he passed me he had slowed down enough for me to read his license number. There were two people in the car. It was Bunk Barnabee's. . .the one registered to a cathouse in a phony, but legendary name.

The name was that of a man who was alleged to have died from complications of a broken leg which he suffered as a result of jumping naked from a third floor of the local hotel. A woman's husband had caught the pair in bed and chased the poor guy until he jumped from an open window. They said that his last words were, "You'd think the scoundrel would have more consideration for a fellow ninety–eight years old." At least that was the legend, and every drummer or traveler who had visited Scallywag, carried the story with him. Bunk Barnabee went a little further and registered his hottest car in the man's name.

Bunk had one hell of a sense of humor when he wasn't drinking, and there were all kinds of stories told about him. One thing he never joked about was Big Daddy, because he took both him and his girl, Ruby Lee, in all kinds of seriousness.

I could tell by Bunk's driving on the curves that he had more than a few, so I called Barney.

"The Eagle's flying high."

"Okay. Keep contact, Race."

"Ten four."

"I hear him coming. Gees, that motor sounds pretty. I'm gonna whip my plug hard and stay with him."

"Watch number three curve this way. It's a bastard."

"Ten four."

At six minutes past two Barney said, "Coming your way, Race."

I went out to the road driving in the same direction as Bunk. I rolled along about thirty–five until I saw the reflection of Bunk Barnabee's lights. I stepped it up to sixty until he came up behind me, then I slammed the accelerator to the floor board. He would try to come around me, and I would try to put a stop to the foolishness. The race was on.

I tried Bunk out for size. He was a tight fit. He didn't slow down at all when I tapped my brakes lightly for the effect when the brake lights came on. It didn't work and I had to jockey to keep him from hitting my left rear.

In all of it I was conscious of not hearing siren sounds or seeing a red light back there somewhere. I was hoping that Barney's car hadn't conked out. I had my hands full with the steering wheel and had to time to grope for the microphone or talk into it either.

The bad curves were in front of me. As I came to them I measured the outer and inner edges of the road and took them outside–in with Bunk right on my tail. I had it figured just where I would tap and twist.

I felt the bump. It was real light, but enough to send me into a slide, which I straightened out the split second that Bunk came up on my rear sideways. We bumped that way, and I went into the ditch which was low at that point. I ran with my left wheels in the ditch and gunning the car for all it had. I hit a low point and turned ever so easily toward the road.

Back on the road I braked hard and stopped along the right side of the road. My own car was making so much noise in the ditch that I didn't hear much of what was going on behind me. I knew something bad had happened when Bunk's lights were not behind me. I slammed the car in reverse until I came to the wreck.

Bunk had hit the ditch and lost control. The car was lying on its side, and somewhere in it were two guys, a zillion pieces of broken glass and enough moonshine to get the whole town drunk for a month of Sundays.

You don't really know how heavy a car door is until you try to open it while it is lying on its side and you have to open it straight up. I pulled hard by bending down and straightening up my legs as I stood over the door. The two men were conscious, and I yelled at them to turn off the ignition. Gas and moonshine, together as they were, could make one hell of a little hades.

The gas fumes were strong. Bunk said, "That's the quickest I ever got sobered up." I was conscious of Bunk touching my arm. It was too light a touch for a man his size, I thought; and my thoughts went back to Barney.

"You all right, Hilton, and you, Bunk?"

"Yeah. We're okay, but that guy back there, your buddy I guess, I'm afraid for him."

I started to handcuff the pair to a tree and rush back to Barney. Instead I said, "Dammit, let's go back."

We climbed into my coupe and I turned around and took off. I breathed much easier when I saw lights approaching. Bunk said, "That ain't him."

He was right. It was just another load of shine, we calculated mutually, and the driver kept going. Bunk began to cry. I thought it was shock from his accident until he put his hand unsteadily on my leg and sobbed, "I should have stopped when I saw them flames behind me in the mirror."

"Barney."

"Was it Barney, Mr. Race?"

Right then what I wanted to do was to knock the hell out of both of those guys. At the same time I felt sorry for them and I straightened out every curve but good. Hilton joined in for a good cry and I wasn't far behind. It seemed as if they were more afraid of what they would see than I was.

I knew that Barney never strapped on his seat belt. I had asked him about it and he replied, "I don't fasten my sleeping bag zipper either because a snake might get in. When I want out of a place I want out no matter where it is."

I thought, and said aloud, "Maybe he was tossed out."

I didn't believe that he had been, but I didn't want to give up to negative thinking. Bunk and Hilton had gotten out okay from their wreck. There might still be a chance for Barney. Three in a row was asking a lot, I knew, but I asked it anyway.

I recognized the human companionship of Bunk and Hilton, and I said in fatherly fashion to them, "We all gotta keep our heads in this. You hear?"

"Yes sir. Thank you, Mr. Race."

I didn't hear the rest of what he said.

"Oh my God."

I looked at the flames reaching upward from the car. In the firelight we could see it lying on its top fifty years out in the swamp. The three of us ran over close to it. The trunk lid had fallen open and I saw some familiar objects being charred. I saw a couple of axe silhouettes, the spare tire, and Barney's Goody box for his raincoat, hat and canned goods. It hit me hard when I thought of Barney's face when I had caught him stashing a box of rubbers in back of the spare tire.

"What the hell are you doing, Barney?" I had asked him.

"Squirrelin'."

"Squirrelin' what?"

"Aincha seen a box of rubbers before?" He had held the box out for me to see.

"Goin' on vacation?"

"Not with a government car, you jerk."

"Not on official time either, I hope."

Barney had ducked his head into the trunk and reached up behind the spare wheel and dropped the box. He had slammed down the lid of the trunk and grinned a silly grin. "You'll never know."

I was thinking those things while I was running around the car. The heat was terrific, but I kept looking for what I didn't want to find. I made one final stab at it.

I practically stuck my head into the flames, eyes broiling and wide open.

I'll never forget the feeling I had when I saw that Barney wasn't in there. I jumped back and dived into the mud to cool off. The rain was coming down hard by then and the lightning and thunder peals were sharp and close together.

"He ain't in there." I said as soon as I was wet down good, and I saw that a car had stopped on the road. The driver was talking to Hilton and Bunk. I looked at him and recognized him as a moonshiner I had arrested a year or so before.

"Anything I can do, Mr. Kearins?"

"Nothing, but thanks just the same. I appreciate it, Roscoe."

Bunk said, "Roscoe, if I was you I wouldn't tarry here. We got enough help for what we can do and there's no use you getting in trouble."

Roscoe took off, waving his flashlight. His car was parked a bit up the road, and he took a beeline for it through the mire. He never did admit that he had moonshine until a couple of years after that. He said, "Hell, a bit of moonshinin' ain't nothin' to seein' somebody get burned up over or hurt either."

Moonshiners generally have more compassion for their fellow man than most people think they have.

I thought that an alligator had a hold on Roscoe when he screamed. We rushed over to him and he was waving and shouting, "There's a dead man over there." I didn't even see him leave.

I fell down in the muck beside Barney and wanted to pray, pray hard a million prayers in that split instant my hand rested on Barney's stomach and my ear pressed his heart region. I felt the stomach move before I heard the heartbeat.

Barney! Barney, you great big, beautiful, alive–livin' bastard. I love you. I love you. Instinctively I took his gun from its holster and stuck it in my belt the way I was supposed to do.

I had calmed down some in body and mind, even though I had vague sensations of burnt tissue on several parts of my body.

"Take good care of him, and don't touch him."

"You bet, Mr. Race."

I rushed to my car with Hilton, and gave him my raincoat.

"Cover him with that, but don't move him."

"Sure will."

Hilton ran back into the swamp with the coat, and I picked up the microphone speaker. I could hear the cracking of sound from the electrical storm. I was afraid that I wouldn't get through.

"Officer in trouble. Officer in trouble."

"Come in, officer in trouble."

"How do you read?"

"Loud and clear."

My voice took on a new pitch. The guy must be outside the storm area. I continued,

"Scallywag Swamp Road, casualty, possible fatality. Hurry, hurry, hurry. Need ambulance. Five miles north of Scallywag."

Luckily, the guy who received the message knew the area and knew what I was saying.He was able to get the message through to Daisy Hildersett Hospital.

I heard the distant wail of the highway patrol siren as it roared toward us clearing the way for the ambulance following it. My mind flashed back to the distant reception I had earlier on the broadcast radio. I was almost negative in my thinking about the message getting through.

My eyes were hurting and felt caked with some sort of emulsion. My pantslegs had burnt places in them and so did my shirt. My legs and body were stinging at those places, too.

I rode back in the ambulance with Barney. I had given the government car keys to the patrolman, but he had a rush radio call, so I had to let Bunk drive the government car back to town.

"Don't try anything funny, Bunk."

"What on earth do you think I am?"

Hilton spoke up and said, "Let's catch old Big Daddy with it, Bunk." I thought Bunk popped Hilton a bit too hard, and then I remembered how he never joked about Big Daddy, not one ounce of Big Daddy's four hundred pound frame, anywhere, anytime.

"What about regulations?"

"Screw 'em for now."

I climbed into the ambulance, and we raced off to town at what I thought was a neat pace considering the guy at the wheel had a high floorboard in his rig.

We went to the hospital where I'd been treated a couple of weeks before. The same nurse who had treated me came into my room the next morning. When she saw me she rushed over and said "Dollbaby," and I wondered, what the hell is this? My eyes were bandaged and I couldn't see, but I sure could feel the squeeze she gave me. Only the little quiver she had in her voice kept me from giving her a pat on the fanny or someplace else. Then I had the awfullest thought, Barney is dead.

"Where is he?"

"Room 218, down the hall. He's doing good."

"Conscious?"

"He was. He's asleep now. He was asking about you, and that he hoped you'd caught some guy named "Bunky" or something like that."

"That's me." I heard Bunk speak from the back of the room.

"Goddam' Bunk. I appreciate your staying here, but you can go home, you know."

Hilton spoke up. "We know. We're waiting for Ruby Lee. That's Big Daddy's girl, coming to pick us up."

I waited for the sound of a slap but it didn't come. Bunk spoke this time. He was really worried.

"I'm mighty concerned about Mr. Barney and you. I feel like it wouldn't have happened if I hadn't tripped down to Scallywag."

"Forget it. All that's part of our job. I appreciate your thoughts though, and don't forget to be at your hearing a week from Wednesday at ten o'clock in the morning."

"I got it written down. We won't go nowheres. You can bet on that. We'll be there for sure."

"Good. Hey Bunk, is 'ol Ruby Lee a ball of fire like they say she is?"

"Man, you think I'd be messing around with anything at all of Big Daddy's unless it was a ball of fire? She's pure, pure, what I'm afraid to say in front of this here nurse."

"What time is it?"

"Twelve–thirty."

"Dern. I been asleep."

"You sure have."

Ruby Lee came in and the nurse went out.

"Ruby Lee?"

"Mr. Race wants to know if you're a ball of fire."

I thought of the guy who jumped out the hotel window.

Ruby Lee came over to my bed and hugged me around the shoulder. She was one hell of a big woman, big up, big down, and big all around. She purred some and said, "You hurt all over?"

"No."

I wanted to know what the hell she had in mind when she said that. From what I had heard of her I was afraid that she was going to climb in bed with me. I wished that I could see her face. She leaned over and smothered me, and left a big imprint of her lipstick on my cheek and said, "Thanks for not getting rough with Bunk."

Bunk and Hilton roared, and I felt around the sheets with my feet to make sure that I wasn't showing someplace I shouldn't be showing. You know how those hospital gown creations are.

I didn't know about the lipstick smear until three days later. It didn't hurt me any and it gave a few people around there who needed a kick, a kick.

I wondered about the dollbaby routine from the nurse, and I found out what it was all about the next morning at washing up time before breakfast. I was glad that I hadn't even tried a teensy–weensy touch of familiarity. She was one of Barney's girlfriends.

Barney hadn't told me about her because he didn't want me to call him to go to work while he was at her place. We both cried when she told me that Barney would never walk the woods again or even drive a car. I left the hospital after five days.

I was hoping that somehow, some way, Barney would be able to get away from the wheelchair after a while. I drove him home when he got out of the hospital. He was sitting in the back seat with pillows propped around him and with his nurse girlfriend by his side.

As we rode along I looked back at him in the mirror. Once our eyes met, and Barney grinned and said, "Don't laugh, you bastard, you'll get yours sooner or later if you stay in this business."

I talked to the judge about Bunk and Hilton, in and out of court; and he saw it my way. He tempered justice with mercy and didn't send them off but gave them a fine that they could afford, and a probation routine for a couple of years.

I asked Barney if the car had cut out on him and he said, "No. I was hauling ass into that number three curve. The road and shoulder blended in together in my vision and I took the turf some, and as far as I know that was it."

TEN

BLUE STARS IN PARADISE

I laid there in the hospital bed that five days, and I did a lot of thinking. I had a dialogue going with Barney's girl, and she kept me posted on his progress when I didn't get around to see him. I had bathroom privileges, and my main problem was that the fire had done some damage to my eyes so I was quite confined. I was trying like hell to keep my chin up, and I did, except when I'd think of the little things Barney and I had known together in our work, like him buying me a college girl's nightshirt when I was hurt a few weeks before, and like me catching him hiding condoms in his car trunk, and the way he punned with me all the time. It hurt to think that it would be different from now on without Barney. I'd had other partners, and things happened and broke us up and I thought of those too. For the pleasant part of my thinking in that bed I thought about Bridgie, a gal in New York I ran around with in my late teens.

I had a job on the side while I was going to school, and I always had more cash to play with than my school chums. I flashed a roll at movie box offices, candy and soda places, and whenever there were girls around.

My roll consisted of twenty–five dollars in bills. There was a fiver at each end and fifteen singles in between. I kept it rolled and intact with a rubber band and in my left trousers pocket. It was a neat little pile in those depression days, all things being considered, and it gave me confidence enough to ask any gal in college for a date no matter what kind of a steady job her old man had. When I had that roll I walked with my toes pointed out the way I'd seen a rich guy do in a movie, and I kept my shoes shined to high heaven so that everyone had to notice me.

One of my buddies who saw me walking with my toes pointed out asked me if I had to go to the bathroom. He was serious, and I started walking like an Indian again.

I was making about twenty bucks a week with my "enterprises" as I called them. I didn't have too much time to spend with girls, but I spent all my time thinking about them, even when I was painting signs for neighborhood stores, and working two newspaper routes over on the West Side, going to school, studying, tinkering with cars and working on weekends at a swimming pool in summer. All the girls I thought about were bad, that is except for Bridgie, who was a nice, happy, good–looking kid. I didn't pay much attention to her until I had a disappointing experience with a rich broad whose dad had a steady job with the telephone company. Bridgie was a real poor kid with a wonderful mother and sisters and brothers and an old man who wasn't worth the powder it would take to blow him to hell.

That rich broad really got me shook up on that one date we had. Her name was Marcella, and her mother called her father, Horace Dear, and he shook my hand like he was poking a wet fish at me. Mama was still a good looking tomato and I liked her except when she called the stoop a piazza. She asked me if I was from Niew England, like view, because she was "in school there you know." I had been there too, in Saint Mary's, at Lawrence, and Lawrence High School, but I didn't tell her that because we didn't have any millionaires there. I did say that Mother went to Wellesley and that Father dabbled in textile mills and textiles which went over swell with her old man.

"Republican, son?"

"Democrat, sir."

"Democrat?"

He said that one as though I was getting ready to rape his wife and daughter, and him too, maybe. It was one hell of an uncomfortable piazza then and there for me. It wasn't much better for Marcella either. He was Bridgie's old man in reverse, but only financially, and he still had eons to go before he could become a telephone company branch manager. It was himself, and not the company with the fancies against the poor people.

"Al Smith is an upstart whippersnapper, and Herbert Hoover is the people's salvation."

"Balls, sir."

"What did you say?"

"I said, "Is that all, sir?"

Mama came to the rescue. She simply said, "Horace Dear, you have an ugly mind sometimes." She had good ears, good hearing, and a nice build, and I liked her for it. Since I was some kind of a scion to her notion, I had it made with her. Marcella changed the subject momentarily. She said, "Johnny got a hundred on the high school regents exam this year." Papa spoke up and said, "On what subject?"

"English."

Mama helped out to break the political spell that had been rearing its ugly head.

"New England upbringing, you know. The Wellesley influence."

"Father went to Harvard," I lied matter of factly.

"Be home by ten o'clock and no later. What's the name of the movie?"

"It Happened One Night."

"With that Gable fellow, I suppose."

"Yes sir, and Claudette Colbert."

"Do you work with the Consolidated Edison Company, Mr. Sir?"

"I told you I worked with the telephone company."

We were saved by the bell on that one. He had only inferred that he worked with the company, and I had known what he meant by that. The phone rang and he went inside the house to answer it. I was getting even with him for calling me a Republican.

As we left after chatting with Mama awhile, with great rapport I saw Papa drive out from the rear of the house in a telephone repair truck. I hollered "Goodby, Mr. Sir," and took Marcella by the arm. She said, "You're a vulgar bastard saying 'Balls' to my old man, and we walked toward the movie house.

On the ten block walk I thought of the lousy dialogue we all had at Marcella's house. I recalled each word, each moment.

I had always considered myself to be one of "Big Jim" Farley's boys, so I had to tell her papa that Al Smith had done a great job as Governor and that he took the blue color out of the poor peoples' milk, and that he had helped the widows' cause.

"Ruzervelt is the one I'm afraid of." He said the name like it had an extra "I" in it. Mama and daughter came out on to the porch. Mama said, "What a lovely rose you brought my daughter." Since it was my first date with the girl I had stopped off at a florist's and bought a single rose. It was supposed to mean something.

I had to get the girl home in a hurry too, because her old man had placed the time she had to be home at such an hour that we had only about ten minutes to ourselves outside of the movie. We didn't even have time to discuss current events or the high school student–president campaign that I was managing for a buddy.

I gave that gal the full treatment at the ticket window. It was at the RKO Royal, or Westchester Avenue, and the marquis had a zillion lights overhead. It was real bright. I looked around to see if any potential pickpockets were about. She took it all in and I could have socked her when she said, "You ought to buy a wallet."

I went back to dating the poor kids, and I remembered a real honey. Her name was Bridgie. That was short for Bridget. She had a good sense of humor, was a real nice kid, and her old man was practically unemployed. Sometimes during the summer, he would get a job umpiring semi–pro baseball games over in "Joisey."

I liked the guy a lot to begin with. I listened to his tales and those of his upstairs buddy who lived in the same place. They swilled home–brew and talked of "French Dolls" that they claimed they had dated when they had regular jobs before the Wall Street crash. That kind of talk was supposed to make their wives jealous.

I liked the way the kids in Bridgie's family were shaping up. There were five of them, and they were all clean and nice. The oldest three were girls and the others were boys. The boys were pretty good ball players for their age. The oldest girl had started work and had a job in a bank. She and her mother were working hard to keep the brood on the right track.

The girls got their get–up–and–go from the mother. She was quite good looking, neat, and hard working. She looked tired all the time though. Her old man was strictly a liability. He wouldn't even help her lift the trash cans to the street.

The family lived in an old tenement house on the ground floor; and the mother was the janitress for the building.

They never asked me who I was, what my family was like, or what they did. The only thing that they really knew about me was that I went to the same school as two of the girls and that I was able to take my date to the best shows and things like that. They didn't even know that I was a signpainter.

Ruzervelt won. The nation's theme song was "Happy Days."

Bridgie and I ran around together quite a bit, even after prohibition was abolished and Bridgie's old man had switched to 3.2 beer(3.2% alcohol content). He became a fixture in the new bar which had started up on the corner down from his house.

When I bought my first car the old man really had a fit when he saw it. You would think that I was his son–in–law the way he showed off me and my car to the neighbors.

I couldn't have commanded more respect from him if I were president of both major baseball leagues. I wasn't Johnny anymore in public, while he was around. I was Bridgie's beau and everybody on the block had better damn well know it.

He personally saw to it that the young kids on the block didn't climb all over my car and mess up my wax job.

His favorite moments were when I drove him up to the corner bar and waited while he bought a growler of beer.

More than a few times I slipped him half–a–dollar, or even a dollar, as we pulled up outside the bar. I said something like "for a little night cap maybe," and I was parroting the hell out of some movie actor I had seen in a similar beneficent moment on the screen.

Before he would get out of the car to go into the bar he'd say, "Honk the horn good and loud when you're ready." I would, and he would come out with some guy and introduce me to him as "Bridgie's beau." He never failed to add "Dat guy's old man really has the mazuma." My father had been dead for a long time.

I will have to admit that I was eating it all up like a cat in a bowl of fish. The way those guys from the bar looked at me you would think that I was president of the biggest bank in the country. A couple even called me "sir." I guess that Bridgie's old man laid it on thick about me and my car when he was lapping up a brew while his growler was being serviced.

A growler of beer cost two bits. The growler was a combination milk pail, too. It held about two quarts. All the poor people in those days bought their milk "loose." They carried the milk pail, or growler, to the store and had the grocer fill it with the milk.

Real beer drinkers had separate beer and milk pails. They said that the milk ruined the pail for good. An old German once said, "Biss in it, yah. Milk in it, Nein."

Milk bought that way was cheaper than by the quart bottle. Those were the days before homogenized dairy products. On the top of the milk in the bottles there would be two or three inches of cream. The cream was thicker and darker than the milk. You could tell good milk by the amount of cream layered at the top of the bottle.

The loose milk was for the poor people. With all of it you got what you paid for.

In the grocery stores or dairy stores all over the city, there was a big milk can sitting someplace around. Usually it was in a corner or off to the side. It was a shiny metal affair of at least ten gallons capacity. There would be a metal scoop hanging on the can. This had a curved handle. It could reach to the bottom of the can. It looked like a big empty tin can at the bottom and it held a quart or pint in measure.

Grocers always seemed to me to engage in measuring out their milk in sloppy fashion. Food should have better care.

Between the flies and short measure, the blue milk that came from water being added, a cat around to lick up the spilt milk, was a hell of a way to buy groceries.

The beer trips with the same can met more sanitary exposure. At least everything at the bar was new, and the shinier the better, seemed to be the motto of a lot of bartenders.

They were always mopping up with dish towels, or polishing the glasses, or the bar, or the mirror at back. About the only thing in a bar in those days that a cat did was to catch a mouse once in a while. Sometimes he would sneak up to the free lunch counter for a snack of ham or baloney if the bartender wasn't looking, which was not often. Cats didn't lick beer spouts either.

The bartenders of those times were not at all lazy men. Most of them had finally found a job with a steady income that way, and they took care of it. They didn't let the beer slip all over the growler the way the milk fillers did. They took pains with giving the beer a nice head of foam but not too much.

I had to tell you something about the way the growler was in those days of milk and beer, and no honey.

Bridgie and I dated quite a bit for a long time. We had a lot of fun. I remember one winter night with Bridgie that was a beaut. It was a real snowy night and there was at least a foot of snow on the ground when we started out while it was still snowing. I wanted to test my new car in rough going. I did. We drove up to Loew's Paradise in the West Bronx and I drove most of the way in some dual–wheel bus tracks that helped a great deal.

The Paradise had blue stars revolving around the dark ceiling. After road–testing my car to my satisfaction, I was happy and was dreaming of being out in the woods in the great outdoors. There would only be me and the night and a bunch of moonshiners out there and they were catching it from me. I would be known as some kind of an ace or something like that. I wanted to be a Revenooer more than anything else in the world.

Bridgie and I had a ball in the movie house that night. There were only a few other hardy souls there because of the snowstorm. The picture was a good one starring Joan Crawford. Bridgie said to me, "Johnny, I'm snug as a bug in a rug" and she leaned her face against mine, and we both knew that such nice moments were rare in everybody's life. They were much rarer for Bridgie than me the way things turned out.

She was a pretty brunette and looked real Irish but she was of German extraction a long time removed from Germany. She had those blue eyes which are blue–blue and almost shiny in the white part which sent off a glint from inside that came only from a nice friendly disposition.

My longings inside the theater for the great outdoors became a reality when we came out of the movie. The snow was coming down hard and heavy and the big flakes were sticking to our clothes.

I looked at the snow piled high against my car where the snow-plows had shoved it. I borrowed a shovel from a Sanitation Department worker, and between the two of us we managed to get the car out.

The ride to Bridgie's house and then back uptown to mine was a nightmare. Bridgie got home about two a.m. and her father bawled her out. I got home about three–thirty. My mother was so glad to see me in out of the storm that she forgot to chastise me until two days later.

I guess I scared the daylights out of Ma since she had told us many times as kids about how severe the snowstorms were in Maine, and how the people there had to have tunnels from the house to the barns so that they could feed the cattle in winter.

It didn't help either that Uncle James died when he was thirteen years old. He died in a snowstorm, and was on his way home from school. That was in the month of October, and they didn't find him until the following April. He expired about one hundred and fifty yards from home they said.

I didn't think of those things at all out there in the snow. I thought of me and Bridgie being out there like that, but mostly I was thinking about the amount of alcohol in my radiator and whether or not my motor block would split from the cold.

Ma didn't care about me having a car and tried to discourage me against buying it. Pa was killed in one.

I eased Bridgie's problem over getting home late that night from the movie. I took her pa down to the growler house and explained it on the way down. He said, "I'm not sore at you, Johnny." I thought he was a pretty good egg and I slipped him a buck and said "one for the road," and I winked and waited for him to come out.

The next night he slapped the hell out of Bridgie and used his feet on her. He found some pictures of nude women in her pocketbook. She never was the same after that, at home, with me, or anywhere. What hurt was the real truth about it in the first place. She took the blame for her kid brother. She had found the pictures under his pillow when she made his bed that afternoon. She was going to throw them down a sewer when it got dark.

I didn't know about it until a long time later when I met Bridgie's sister at a Legion dance. It wasn't a nice thing for the family, and it tore them up to think that the old man would put the boots to Bridgie the way he did.

Another dirty part of it was that the old man was looking in Bridgie's pocketbook for money when he found the pictures. He took forty five cents, which was all that Bridgie had.

I talked to Bridgie after that and she was not the same kid anymore. She was nice and all that, but she didn't have that animation around the eyes and in her smile the way she had it before.

She said that she hated her old man and that her mother did too. She told her mother everything, and her mother understood. The whole family left the old man when mama found out that papa was showing the nude pictures to all the guys in the building.

I thought about Bridgie for a long time, but like all things in those days, there was so much to everything; so much to see, and feel, and hear. I had to go on fast to other things. Things I didn't even know about then. I wasn't mean at all, but to keep up with things, I had to get meaner and bolder. That time is a time when a lot of kids get lost on what they want to be and do.

I don't really know if I did get bolder really, but one thing was for sure. I got a hell of a lot older in a hurry.

I got a little ahead of myself when I told you about the dates I had with Bridgie and my new car. I wanted to tell you the whole story of Bridgie so that you wouldn't get the idea that she was some kind of a chippie or something. She was a nice kid with a nice ma and family except for her shiftless old man.

I saw a kid coming out of church in Savannah one Sunday morning a couple of years ago, and she looked just like Bridgie. She had silky, well–groomed, black hair, cut in bangs, and her real blue blue eyes were set in a colleen smile. Her complexion was just like Bridgie's too. It was that healthy pink.

I stared at the kid, and my mind was back up in the South Bronx. She was Bridgie all over again except that her old man was a nice looking, well dressed guy who paid more attention to his family than Bridgie's old man had.

The girl had on a neat plaid dress and a Buster–Brown collar that wasn't too high or too wide. It was just right. She had a cute figure. She was Bridgie for sure. I didn't want to talk to her either like you might think I would. I was afraid that her teeth wouldn't be as white and straight as Bridgie's, and that would spoil my whole mirage. I wanted that re–run to be the same in detail as the last time I had seen Bridgie before her old man killed her in spirit.

The last time I ever saw Bridgie was in a bank in New York. She was working there as a teller. She looked harder, very neat, and was almost too business–like, and a little too direct.

I've seen other women with the same kind of approach. It was the approach that a woman has when she has been hurt badly by a man. They seem to be perpetually resolved that they will never give any guy, any kind of a guy anyplace, a chance to hurt them again. That time with her old man was a long–lived nightmare.

Bridgie asked me what I was doing those days and I told her that I was chasing moonshiners. She said, "I'm happy for you, Johnny. I'm glad that somebody I know is doing exactly what they have always wanted to do."

I'd seen a lot of things on the job that were difficult to behold, and I wasn't easily disturbed about things I couldn't control. I had a lump in my throat when I left that bank. The thing started deep inside me and reached up higher while I watched that gorgeous hunk of woman counting out my money. I watched her fingers and saw no wedding ring there. I didn't ask about it on account of that man–father thing that had to be still bothering her.

I wanted to say something like, "Remember the time we got snowed–in up near the Paradise, or that Sunday afternoon near Budd Lake when the train came out of nowhere almost on top of us on that dirt road." I didn't though. I asked her where she was living, and she said, "Over on Broadway with Ma and the kids."

I let it go at that, when she started to prop on her elbows on the counter and say something. She leaned forward a little bit, checked herself halfway, and put out the light that was just beginning to shine in her eyes a little, from away back inside where the little girl was.

"How's your mother, Bridgie?"

"Real good."

"That's swell."

A guy came up in back of me and mercifully ended it for us both. I moved to the side and made room for the guy and said, "Bye now, Bridgie."

I walked away wishing that I had been like some of those Southern guys I had seen in Washington so much. If I had, I would have leaned over the counter, right then and there, business or no business, to give her a little hug for so many nice yesterdays.

I just didn't have it that way, that's all. It was the least I could have done in view of the ugliness she knew from another guy who just happened to be her father.

Bridgie would have known and appreciated it if I had acted like I wanted to. She'd know that it didn't mean we were in love, or that I was showing off with a good looking gal. She'd know what it really was. It was an acknowledgement, that both of us once had good things going together, that I wanted to give her. I guess we did pretty good, but it could have been better on my part.

I looked back when I reached the revolving door to the outside and she looked at me. . . that last time. I waved, and she waved back.

The next time I visited the bank I looked for her but she wasn't there. The girl who was working her cage told me that Bridgie had been transferred downtown to the main office. She said, "Bridgie got a swell promotion and she deserved it." I thought to myself that Bridgie deserved anything that was anything but bad. She was that kind of a girl and that kind of a woman too.

I have thought many times since that it was remarkable how I recognized Bridgie after so many years. I did have to look down at the nameplate on her counter to be positive though.

A couple of years ago I was in New York and bumped into a guy who'd been in school with Bridgie and me. He had just retired as a New York City detective, and I had seen him from time to time in my work as the years wore on.

The guy said, "You remember that good looking gal you had a crush on, Bridgie Whatshername??? Her old man was a swell guy."

"Yeah I remember her, you bet. I remember too that her old man was a son–of–a–bitch. What about Bridgie?"

"Well, anyhow, she had a tough break. Had a good job. Kept her whole family. Good looking as hell and wouldn't give anyone a tumble. Real uppity and never got married."

I was half impatient, half angry. I snapped, almost savagely, "What in hell happened to her?"

"Lemme tell ya, will ya? Ya act like ya still gotta crush on her."

"You said it. I didn't."

"Well anyhow, she studied and worked like hell. Got a job in a bank and went to banking and accounting schools at night. She made real good, but I guess all of it was too much for her."

"What happened to her?"

"She got T.B. She went to a sanitarium, but she didn't last long."

I remembered sort of a cough that Bridgie gave the last time I saw her but I figured it was from smoking, or nothing at all.

"She went off real quick. No suffering, I heard. Things were too far gone. The bank and her insurance took care of the family pretty good."

"She'd have to do it that way."

"Got two good looking sisters. One of 'em married a fire captain."

I hardly heard the last part. I said, "So long, feller."

I walked north on the concourse toward the subway. I looked across the street over toward the Paradise, but I didn't read the sign on the marquis. Instead I looked up the street. At the exact spot where I'd been stuck in the snow a hundred years before I heard a young girl laugh in the way that only a tickled young girl can laugh in her happiest years. It was that laugh that Bridgie had when I got my car out of the snow one night so long before. It was like an echo from beyond.

I turned around and saw a couple of young girls of high school age. They were having the silly giggles by then.

One of them said, "Edgar Allen Poe lived right down there. The one who wrote all those weirdies. Right down there?"

"Sure."

"Gives me tickles down my spine. It's weird."

They went back into the silly giggles just about the time I was wondering if they still had those blue revolving stars in the Paradise and whether or not anyone went to movies on bad snowy nights anymore.

I felt something wet and hot on my cheeks. I looked back for one long, final look at a place called yesterday. I looked again for Bridgie and a guy named Edgar Allen Poe too.

"Nevermore."

I hurried on to the subway.

ELEVEN

THE MANUFACTURERS

One night I went down to the country to see a man who had called me about "some strange goings on" on a road near his farm.

I knew the area to be a likely place for a huge distillery, and I was elated, and went to see the man. He was well acquainted with what consisted of normal traffic. I met him down the road from his house on a wooded lane, and as is usual we put forth the usual amenities toward each other like, "Howdy," "Cool weather," "Maybe get some rain soon," and the little preliminaries of greeting one finds more of in the country nowadays, than in the city.

He had walked from his house to our meeting place, so I suggested that we ride about some after learning that he had noticed for "the past few nights," a rumbling of heavy trucks along a secondary road removed from his own.

"Now that sort of thing just isn't right at this time of year hereabouts," he said and I agreed. No tobacco was headed for market. It was not the season. Nor was it the season of any activity of heavy transportation in the area. "A feller lives in the country all his life, mostly in the same place, and he can almost see what's moving on the road away off without getting within looking distance," he reminded me in quite folksy fashion.

At this stage of the game comes one of the greatest of challenges to an investigator, and while I was talking to the man, who had said about all he could in the way of transmitting worthwhile intelligence about the matter at hand; I was speculating in my mind.

I speculated about the area, the gangs who had operated there, the likely places for a still, for miles away even, from there. I recollected the things I had heard and seen about the operations of the various gangs, but I centered on one. It had to be them. Their plant had been cut down a short time before in another place, and now they would be setting up again. With the man, I sat in vigil just in case what traffic he had heard on the roads might be repeated that night.

When we had reached a point on a side road, he said, "I know they came along through here, but they kept on going until I couldn't hear them anymore. I didn't hear them slow down or stop at all, so they must have gone on ahead." I knew that the distillery could be located a long distance away, but I did not think it was. Right then, all that I had to go on was an old man's word that he had heard some trucks late at night on a country road, and that he thought they didn't belong there. I thought so too.

I would be content this night to sit with the old man and listen, without trying to follow the trucks. One thing was for sure—if it was the gang which I thought it was, then they would be up and down that road plenty during the next few weeks, if they lasted that long.

From what the old man had said, I was certain that it was a "setting–up" operation. We heard one truck, and a pickup or a car, and they were running not too far from each other. It happened just about the same time of night the old man said it had happened before. He said to me, simply enough, "That truck ain't got no business down there at this time of night." I thought the truck had much business at hand down there, but not legitimate of course.

I took the old man home after that, and told him not to speak to the neighbors about the matter, or about having seen me at all, and not to be too impatient if he didn't hear anything from me "for even a couple of weeks if necessary."

I was the only one then, on duty at the office; the others being away or on vacation. The next day I went over to the county ABC enforcement office and sought some help. To my surprise, they had been working on the situation themselves, and had seen the trucks and equipment in the area, but they did not know where the still was but only some possibilities of where it might be.

We decided to work the investigation that night with men on the ground and a radio car concealed in the area. It rained like cats–and–dogs that night, and we neither saw nor heard anything of trucks of any kind. From where one of the ABC men and I were concealed on foot we saw a car come by. We were almost certain that it was that of our chief suspect who had a penchant for riding the roads while things were happening in his outfit.

The next night we obtained more help. Seeing the big guy's car in the area was a booster for our enthusiasm. He was a long way from home, and while we could not declare, to the point of absolute certainty, that it was he. . .we decided to plan as if it were him.

We discussed the whole situation many times and speculated as to who would let them operate on their property and where a suitable place might be. We tried to recall all past information. I checked the sugar sales record for the area. No boost there. It had to be an outside gang.

One of the men, the most familiar with the area, had settled on a few possible or likely places. To one of these points I went afoot with an ABC officer, and we planted ourselves in an open field by the side of the road, to wait. We were prepared to wait the whole night if necessary.

To be at such a place with such a purpose takes much preparation for an officer on observation post. First, we decided for all enforcement personnel to remain out of the area during daylight hours. The next chore was to obtain the necessary personnel, cars and radio equipment to follow our plan. We placed personnel quietly and inconspicuously on post.

Each man of course knew the nature of his duties. Those on ground observation took warm clothes, something to stretch out on, such as a sleeping bag, and enough food to last for a day or two just in case.

I had bread, milk, canned meat, and some cookies in a canvas waterproof bag I had for the purpose. This from the very beginning of its use had contained a can opener, (twist type), a fruit juice can opener, an extra pocket knife, a couple of spoons, a fork, and a quart thermos bottle with three cups which screwed to the top. The bag was not difficult to carry and could be used for a pillow or a seat. In one of the bag pockets I had a can of insect repellent spray. The portable radios we carried; raincoats and other required gear could sometimes even make an extra can of peaches in the kit seem heavy.

The idea then, was to have what we needed and no more. The fact was that we never knew what we would need in sum total. Usually, we carried more than we felt we would need.

On this night, we were dropped off in good order. My partner and I sat alongside the road in the field, and we talked of this and that. With our gear not far away in a dry drainage ditch we commenced our vigil.

My buddy began to take hard–boiled eggs from a paper bag in which he must have had a dozen. He nibbled on them and put the broken shells back inside the bag so that he would not leave any sign of our observation post should something cause the violators to become alert later.

To the violators it doesn't take much, if they are alert, to consider every possibility in all things. A cigarette butt, even though extinguished, can reveal previous human presence at a spot. They can be tossed curves too.

In regard to that I heard another officer say, "you couldn't pay me any kind of money to carry those things in my wallet." Not for any still. I'd hide the car ten miles away and walk back before I'd take a chance on my old lady finding those things in my pocketbook; me with six kids the way it is."

"How the hell ya gonna explain it?"

One officer I know well, carried prophylactics to discard on wood's paths where he had driven his vehicle on investigations. It worked remarkably well for him on one occasion and fooled the operators who had noticed his car tracks entering the woods where he had concealed the car while checking their distillery. One of the moonshiners said later, "We figured that some of the neighborhood sparks had been lovin' up."

Out there on post whether it is in dark fields or deep woods, doesn't make any difference. Discretion is vital, and sometimes the best discretions can backfire. The investigator had to be one step ahead in the game, and that is more fact than philosophy.

With all these things grasped well in mind, my partner and I found ourselves that night about nine p.m. getting into position to see and hear all that happened nearby. By joint agreement on all scores we felt that we were in a likely place to witness something close at hand. We mutually agreed that a path leading from the other side of the road looked A–1 as a probably location.

Off in the distance in the woods, though it was dark, we could hear a power saw being used, and we wondered if it wasn't being used to clear a vehicle path.

It was a cold, windy night about the first part of the year, and although it had rained in the section the night before the day's wind and sun had done a good job of drying up the fields.

We had a good post, and sat down in the field, not far from the road. We were in one of the high spots in the whole area. We could see lights in the night at a good distance, and could hear the tone of rolling rubber on roads a long distance away.

We checked our radio communication with the radio car driver who was out of the area. We contacted the other walkie talkie post to ascertain if we had a good communication facility, or bad. Things were fair, and we were in business for whatever transactions might be at hand.

We slipped most of our gear into a good place of concealment that we had located. This was a rock overhang, a couple of feet down, in a drainage ditch.

It is at such times that we hear all the sounds of the night in every form. We seek the moving lights far off, scan the dark sky overhead and "J. B." and I are in a little secret world of the nonce. Nobody except us know exactly where we are, and a guy out there riding the roads in a big car, would dearly love to know.

It's too early yet at this time for any real action, so we sit there——the two of us. Each one is thinking about what's out there in front of us, and all the while we're alert but good.

Our minds wander to different things, and in those we think of the places all over the country where other Revenue Officers are right then in vigil at other kind of places; like mountain tops, valleys, swamps, on plains, and in cities.

We think to ourselves, gad, all the tall tales those bastards are exchanging. I wish I could be a little bird for a while around some of those guys. Hell, they are thinking the same thing about us. We think of all of them as members of the brotherhood. We think all in all that they are a great bunch of guys, and that we'd go anytime, anywhere, with any of them. I think, ol' JB's a pretty good boy.

It is at such times, as sitting in a field, or on a mountain, or in a swamp, or in a cellar, or on a roof, we anticipate action and lengthy periods of waiting at the same time. We appreciate some sort of tranquility about wherever we are, and we can glance about in any of those places and see what we are looking for. . .if our attitude is right.

We wonder why guys take other kinds of jobs for a living, we think of our own appointments, and our amazement at the opportunity to play cops and robbers and get paid for it. We see it, and feel it, all out there before us, and say to ourselves, "Some day I'm going to write a book about this. I'm going to put it all down." The other guy says the same thing to himself. But nobody will write the book. Nobody will write a book just like it all happens. Nobody has the time.

You hear your Buddy say, "Race, what'cha thinking about so hard?" He asks you if you want a hard boiled egg. You do not. He has a whole settin' of eggs in a brown paper bag. He's on his third egg already and you haven't really noticed but you did because you saw him carefully putting the shells back into the paper bag as he peeled the eggs.

You saw that, and you heard two cars on another road, and watched the white mist of their lights going up and down hills far away and around curves all the while you were thinking. You heard dogs barking, and you were scanning the sky for those satellites up there those nights.

I say, "I' been thinking," and J.B. says, "I thought I smelled wood burning."

"Yea, you thought you did, but it's all that stinking sulphur in those rotten eggs you are eating."

"I like hard boiled eggs. Make a man out of you."

"Yea, I hope the hell you sleep in a single bed."

Hey, no crap, J.B., you know what ol' whosis said about you and your hard boiled eggs?

"No, that bastard's liable to say anything."

"He said that you like hard boiled eggs better than he loves good old country poontang."

"That sunnuvabitch. How about an egg, Race?"

"No thanks, I gotta thermos jugga coffee in my sack, I think I'll get me a cup. Want some?"

"Psst. . .Hey Race,. . .Shhh. . .I see him, J.B., he's checking tracks, ease on over here, keep down."

"Can't tell if he's white or not."

"Gees, we got the right place, for sure."

"It's twelve fifteen a.m., something's gonna happen."

"Shhh, something coming thru Buckles Crossroad."
"Lights coming this way."
"It's a truck, ya bet."
"Yea. Still got his lights on."
"Comin' up Jason's hill."
"Just around the curve now."
"There goes his lights out."
"Yea, that guy on foot up the road, he's turned his flashlight on."
"Hot Dam, there's two trucks."
"Let's ease right up to the edge of the road."
"Watch that guy on foot."
"He's on the other side of the road."
"Yeah, we can't screw up now."
"They're goin' down that path sure enough."
"How do you like that?"
"They're slowing down for that guy with a flashlight."
"Gonna be hard to see much except silhouettes as dark as it is."
"Gotta get close as we can."
"Here he comes."

We know one of those guys on the big truck is smoking a cigar, know it's a stake body truck, and we have picked off the silhouette, the both of us, and we agree on the make and model. We know whose truck it is, but can't see the license number, or the real color of the truck, and mostly we know it distinctly by the funny shaped white background square with lettering on the cab door.

We can almost figure who is driving the truck. We haven't see it, but we know there's a hell of a big still out there. We watch the truck turn into the path we thought it would, and we wait until the pickup truck follows him. We wait until the guy with the flashlight has fulfilled his vigil and has gone a good distance down the path.

We slap each other on the back, call the radio car and the other walkie talkie post and say, "We hit, we just put 'em to bed." We say just enough to communicate your direct concern. After all, somewhere an officer on the same frequency might be somewhere in or out of his car, and the wrong people could be nearby and listening.

And so we waited. . .for just about an hour. We heard the trucks coming out, and they weren't straining. That meant no whiskey coming out. That meant that no whiskey had been run. The bulky material that was in the back of the big truck, going in could have been a boiler, or could be a still on it's side. Sure. They were just getting ready for the big first run tomorrow.

"Tomorrow night we're gonna have your asses good, misters."

"Duck, Damit."

The trucks came up and the first one switched his lights on at the road. He turned left; the pickup followed, and he turned left.

"Nah he didn't see us."

"What the hell is this?"

"Run like hell, he's on top of us."

We run like hell. My cap gets snagged on a briar clump close to the ground.

"Slam, bang."

"Gees, he missed the road without lights."

"Goddamit! my cap, I lost it. I hope they don't find it, or we're screwed up."

"That bastard was right on top of us, wonder if he turned over in the ditch."

"Didn't quite sound like it, no glass busted."

"He's racing his motor. Let's move while he's making noise."

"Yeah, gotta get my cap."

"Steady now, they're not far off."

"We gotta get that cap."

"Goddam briars."

I find the cap and put it on my head.

"What's this?"

"A hard boiled egg."

I pick up the egg and put it in my pocket, and think, Gees, J.B. had a whole bloomin' bag full.

We're still not far from the moonshiners. There's a car over there almost at hand, and we move away ever so agonizingly slow when the driver races the motor.

There's two guys out there. One's name is "Stupid Sunnuvabitch," and the other's "Blindass Mike," and they're excited as hell.

We hear them talk about what will happen if the boss comes by and sees them in that predicament.

"It's gonna be your ass, "Blindass Mike," if he does come by, or if that truck turns around when we don't show up. Old rat'll tell the boss sure enough."

"Goddamit lets get out of here, lemme drive, and you push."

"There ain't no way out like that."

A guy is walking around with a flashlight.

"Lemme get a pole," one says.

I squat down behind some skinny briars right next to a pine tree, and the man's light comes to just within a few feet of me.

"Hey, Ellsworth, let's cut down this tree."

"Stupidsunnavabitch, we got no axe, how you gonna cut down a tree with no axe?"

"Yeah, dat's right."

The light is all but directly in my face, I'm glad I had retrieved the cap.

"Hey Ellsworth, I found something."

"What is it now?"

"A aig."

"Goddam stop foolin' around wit' hen nesses."

"Yeah, a fresh aig," he mutters to himself, and walks off toward the car.

"Come on Andrew, Goddamit less get dis so and so out of here."

"Yeah Ellsworth, I'm gonna look in that ditch over there, maybe find a pole."

I think our radio and gear is in that ditch.

One thing I know for sure, he won't walk away with that radio.

"Andrew, you stupidsonnavabitch, come here."

Andrew goes to help Ellsworth. I realize that we have arrested the same pair just a month or so ago. So does J.B., so we back off some more while they are trying to get the car out. We reach safe concealment.

We check the time. It's been forty–five minutes since they holed us up. I can feel the stings of briar cuts all over my hands and face, and I relax. I touch my cap to make sure it's still there.

We both say "whew," and we mean it. It's tough to be so near to everything and yet be close to nothing.

I said, "J.B.? You know what?"

"What, Race?"

"You reckon that bastard'll try to make a milk shake with that hard boiled egg?"

"You sunnavabitch."

"It ought to make a man of him. Huh."

We jump up and down and slap each other on the back. We can't wait to get to the radio, and we can hear the car grinding to no avail. Lights are coming up the road, and moving fast. The pickup has returned. They call each other by their names while they push the car out of the ditch with the pickup.

The pickup driver pulls alongside the car, and says, "Don't you dumbastards say a thing about this to anyone, because if you do and the thing gets screwed up, there'll be hell to pay and you both better head for California fast."

"Naw suh, we're not going to say nothing to nobody, nobody atall."

Right then I knew the guy wouldn't say a word about the hard boiled egg to anybody, because if he did someone might want to check the place where he had found it, and want to know what the hell he was doing there in the first place.

We went over to the radio, and I talked into the mike and said, "Pick us up."

That night we went back with several radio cars and more men, including a stand–by crew.

At about the same time the very next morning, I was laying about a mile down the still path with a walkie talkie. I had been there some time and was freezing marse off.

I could have reached out and touched the big truck as it came by, loaded with sugar. The driver had his parking lights on and I eased out into the path and got his license number, just in case. I ducked back beside the path when I saw the parking lights of another vehicle coming. I watched it go on down the path. It was a pickup truck.

We had men around the still, and about that time they called, and I received them well. A voice said, "We caught four down here."

I said, "Take care, two trucks are on their way down now."

I called the cars but could receive no reply. Either they were too far off or my radio was not working.

I saw the trucks go down and they had turned around before they reached the still, and was coming out. I radioed the men near the still.

No reply from the radio cars. The damn radio wasn't working just when we needed it. I kept trying. I ran up the path in back of the big truck. The driver had a long way to the road, but he was moving slow.

Something was wrong. I banged the walkie talkie with my fist and I heard a sputter. I called into the radio and heard the beautiful words, "Go ahead."

"Mayday, come in, close in, block the road."

I had contacted one of the radio cars.

I jogged along behind the big truck. I had been running for over a half mile after frantically talking into an inoperative radio. I figured by now that I was going to get one of those guys when he bailed out of the truck.

I saw the lights coming up on the cars, one from each side. There was a grove blocking the truck driver's view, and I saw the lights on the truck go on full beam. The truck headed into a field. I saw the bailout made and the running figures, and I found my second breath. I headed one of the jokers off and he sprinted for the grove, and I saw someone come out of the grove and tackle him about the time I had him. It was J.B. When I saw who he had caught, I said, "Well, I'll be dammed, Andrew, what in hell are you doing here?"

I couldn't stand it. "You gotta gun, Andrew?"

"No, Mr. Race."

"Let me search you." I reached into his jacket pocket and felt what I was looking for.

I asked Andrew where he had gotten it. He said, "I found it last night in a hen nest in a field."

"I believe you, I really do."

Andrew said, "Yas suh, that's the truth."

"J.B. you know old Andrew here has been robbing hen nests," and I tossed him the hard boiled egg.

"All right Race, you sunnavabitch," and I ducked the egg when it went sailing by.

Our score was impressive, a hundred percent success. When I told my informant about it, he merely said, "I figured them trucks had no business on that road at night."

TWELVE

THE WHOLESALERS

Once, in the role of a corroborator, I accompanied another investigator on a trip to the North Carolina mountains. We had a load of apples on a pickup truck. My partner was a native Southerner, and his accent was right for the area. My mode of speech was real Yankee, way out of place in our setting, to buy moonshine from area dispensers. We whipped that by my playing deaf. Literally and figuratively, I was to keep my ears open and my mouth shut in conversations with the moonshiners.

We had acquired the load of apples we were to peddle, for appearances. The place was apple country itself, and anyone who wanted apples could get them almost for free. We were wholly aware of the situation and figured that we could get down to business more easily without having to actually merchandise apples.

It did give us a reasonable presence in the area, to have the apples, and we let it go at that.

Mainly we were after two individuals, and our aims were to make moonshine buys, and a successful prosecution. The pair was notorious, and the sheriff had requested federal assistance in getting a conviction against them and removing them from the community.

We "hit" in both instances and in another one, too. That one involves an obliging old man who lived on a crag which our truck could barely ascend, even with a load of apples holding down the rear. The truck would slide on stones in the roadway and go sideways toward a steep drop–off. This was on my side and I was the passenger.

I was there chiefly to move fast, and unexpectedly so, in case of trouble or violence. I looked down, and wasn't particularly worried about our immediate safety. We had a few feet of terra firma on our side yet.

I was wondering how we were going to get the rig turned around. I couldn't say anything of course, but the old guy, Charley, came out of the house, whiskey jar in hand, and practically shouted out his wares.

An old Model B Ford was parked at the side of the house. It had been at one time, a pickup truck, but the rear had rusted away. The tires were up, and apparently it had been running regularly, judging from the tracks leading to and from it's parking place.

My buddy asked him if he didn't have trouble getting in and out of the place.

"Nawsuh, never, except oncet when I was sober. Ya see down thar by that tree yonder; well that's what I was drivin', that 1928 Willys–Knight down thar all by itself. I just let it sit thar, just as a reminder like."

I figured that he had to do that anyway, as it was a long way down there, and a long way up, too. I just grinned at him like I didn't know a thing he was saying. It was hard for me to keep it up, because he was telling about his old–timey way of "makin' likker" and I was interested.

He said, "Got the best place over thar for makin' it. In all copper too."

I grinned stupidly and watched all the while he carried on a petty moonshine transaction with my partner. He told Charley I was deaf from falling into a gasoline tank.

"Was he sober when he done it?" We bought the moonshine he offered and backed downhill a mile before we could turn around.

I felt sorry for the old guy. He was sticking his neck into the noose. He had been recommended as a source of good likker by our first target, when he told us that he, himself, was "out of the stuff." This was a way of giving himself time to check on us. We had a good story set–up, and had studied a plausible background for it, and we embellished that in our plan.

My partner carried out all the details, and I merely had to look, listen, and grin. I had to try real hard to stop laughing when he described me as being "That feller who fell into the gasoline vat over at Statesville a few years ago and it deefed him. And it would have blinded him too if he hadn't hit his head in the fall and had his eyes closed on account of being unconscious when he hit the gasoline." The first man had said that he had heard about it but didn't recollect knowin' the feller, but that he knew gasoline was bad when it got inside the ears.

He looked at me with some wonder and compassion at the same time and said, "My uncle used it one time to purify a venial disease, and it dam near ruint him for life." He had then told us to go over to the ridge and see "Ol' Charley," and he told us where Charley lived, and that's how we had gotten up with Charley.

We finally made our first contacts with the two we had really sought in separate instances. In one case we had a man on our hands who severely resisted arrest. I came at him with complete surprise. I guess that was because he thought I didn't know anything about what was going on. It took some mental and physical gymnastics to place him under arrest. A relative of his family was watching it all with a 30–30 rifle pointed at us.

We stood up after the scuffle. We had handcuffs on the man, and we were all surprised to see his fourteen year old sister holding the rifle and drawing a bead. At such a time an officer has one of several ghoulish choices of action. None are any good. You can't shoot a handcuffed man in the back. You can't shoot a fourteen year old girl. You are commanded in the authority of your warrant to "hereby arrest" and the man is named and is in your custody.

Bluffing was the first choice, soft talking to the girl was the second choice, and the third choice was that she might unnerve and present a chance to get the gun away from her. This was a hope. The real communication would be with the man, and to have him make the decision for the girl. I took out my gun and let him feel the steel of it on his neck, and then I spoke. When I did, he said, "You sunnavabitch, you tricked me," and he struggled some until I rammed the barrel deeper into his neck, and he was impressed more solidly.

"Tell her to drop that gun or I will drop you at the count of five."

He told her to and she didn't. At the count of three I cocked the trigger alongside his ear, and that did it. He was in front of us all the while and facing her gun. He told her to drop the gun, and she did it without hesitation. Others started to come out of the house some seventy–five feet away, and I slipped the cuffs off before they reached us. Mountaineers have a mania about being seen by friends in handcuffs. It is the ultimate in ridicule. Sometimes it is a fatal mistake on the part of the officer who does it. It does not always stop there.

We took him to the U.S. Commissioner, after explaining to his family that we were Federal officers, and told them where we were taking him. They knew all about the bail procedure and who the commissioner was. When he was released on bail, he shook his head and said, "You the first man I seen who can tell a lie without even openin' his mouth." He added, "I was glad when you took them handcuffs offen me, though." There are many connotations in some things when there doesn't seem to be any room for anything else. I attended his trial and he pleaded guilty and was sent to prison.

The number two man on our expedition proved to be somewhat disappointing to us, and we wondered how in hell he ever got to be a moonshiner of reputation. We said little to communicate. He said less. He sold. We bought. He carried out the cases of whiskey from a dense growth of honeysuckle near his house, strewn with footpaths from past ventures. He loaded us and we left. When we came back to make the knockoff buy and paid him with the badge he said, "I guess you got me," and we took him off. He pled guilty too.

In all instances we had stand–by crews not far away. When we made the knockoff buys, we radioed them. They came over and knocked off two stills, and found some more liquor which they destroyed.

When it came time for sentencing, old Charley received more time than the others. We tried to talk to the judge but when he displayed Charley's record to us, we couldn't say any more. It seemed like Charley was always sticking his neck out, for something like thirty years or more, and he never learned. It didn't help my feelings when Charley never asked me about my deefness which wasn't.

It didn't help me when we got ready to back down the hill from his house, the three of us, my partner, Charley and me. Charley said, "Roll down the glass, please." I did and to his wife, a white haired woman bent over a washtub on the porch, he said, "I'm goin' over to Mr. Walter's, don't know when I'll be back."

"I reckon so, Pa," and she never turned around. She just kept washing clothes in the wooden tub. Mr. Walter was the United States

Commissioner over in town.

As we backed down the hill, I looked for a while at the house in front of us. It looked like a fairy book drawing of a house in which lived elves and leprechauns together, on a high hill. It had been there many a year, and Charley, a pleasant little guy, must have felt what I was thinking. He said, "I raised a passel o'younguns on that place and I didn't do it with the crops I raised on that hill."

One of the crew who went back on the follow–up seizure said that Charley's still was a nice little copper outfit way down below the house, next to a spring.

"I don't know how Charley carried the sugar down and the moonshine up."

Charley did though. He'd been doing it a long time. I asked Charley how he turned his truck around. He said, "I go around the house. I couldn't do it with this thing though," meaning our truck which was wider and longer than his.

I asked Charley if he made deliveries and he said, "No, I don't go out much anymore. The last time I made a delivery the Feds were waiting when I got there, and I lost a Hudson Six right then, and all my whiskey too."

The wholesaler is right up next to the big league manufacturers. He takes a lot more chances, and sometimes his timing must be uncanny to have things click for him the way they do. He's mobile. He delivers and gets around the challenges of taking a cargo of moonshine to its destination.

He is stationary when all his assets are stored in one building. He takes chances when strangers come up to his place and want to buy a large quantity of whiskey. He has to haggle with them, to size them up, to watch their faces, their mannerisms, and their hands. Are they rough, are they those of a man who sells whiskey, or are they those of the undercover man who pops in, makes a buy, and is gone, only to come back with a badge and a warrant, and his fellow officers? He has to be sure, even if it means turning down some good sales now and then, although he can't do this too often.

He must judge whether the guy is all right to sell to. He must look at his clothes, look at his car, look for all the signs. Is the guy too educated to have just eased into the trade? Does the purchaser know the language spoken among wholesalers? Does he know the right ones in the trade? Does he really know them? What is his story? Why did he come to me? Who got caught a while back who might be passing out information? What guys have I doublecrossed? What women have I scorned? Have I cussed my brother? My sister? My father? My mother? Have I done what they wanted me to? Ma hates this business. Maybe she wants to get me out of it the sure way——through my pocketbook. What have I seen up or down any road I've traveled the last month? What did not seem right? What about my friends? What about my neighbors? Have I paid all my bills? Have I seen this guy before? Have I seen him in somebody's house? Have I seen this guy at a cockfight? At Miami? Baltimore? Boxwood? Charlotte? Winston–Salem? Wilkes? Danville? Benson or some other city, or county, or place, or testifying in Federal Court? Does he taste the moonshine? Does he know how to proof it? Does he bicker about the price? Does he really have the dough to buy what he asks? Who sent him? How well does that man know him? Go over his approach, his manners, his clothes, and everything you have seen and know about him. . .and get his damtag number and tell him to come back Monday on account I've run out. By Monday, I gotta know all those things or else, and I'd better not forget one of them, not one. If I do, I'm hurt bad.

His further thoughts are that if he is fooled by an undercover man: My whiskey will be gone, and my business too. Perhaps my car will be gone too, and the expensive road lies ahead; the road of lawyers, and courts, and trials, and judges, and juries await me; and if I'm lucky I'll be given a stiff fine. If I'm not, I have three or four years probation, and possibly the same amount of time in jail. If I don't get caught for a while, I've got it made.

You just try putting yourself in his place.

It's tough as hell for a man in a fast acting business to turn down new sources of money when your motto is "make it fast while I can." What makes it worse is that even the guys you buy from sometimes wonder about you when things go wrong, and when you really have all you can do, to mind your own business without sticking your nose in theirs. You have to worry about your old customers, too. If they get knocked off or get pushed too hard they might talk for a buck, or the informers fee, so they can get back on their feet.

You have to worry about constables, policeman, deputy sheriffs, sheriffs, county ABC men, state ABC men, Federal men and for that matter any busy body along your whole work route at all times of your work day.

You have to worry about getting a staching place. You have to worry about getting cars and license plates which are not traceable. You worry about getting good personnel who won't panic or kill somebody in a chase. You watch the daily papers to see what's what. You listen to the radio, watch the TV news, and see what gives in the news that might interest you. You watch the ground and the road all around the staching place.

You look for signs. You slip into the courts once in a while and listen to the moonshine cases to see what's new in men and equipment on the side of the law. You look for new faces on the witness stand. You stop and you chat with the law when you're clean, and you size them up so you will know them in a passing car at night——and you can bet your tail they're doing the same thing with you. You don't depend too much on the crows you've got spread out watching the place where your main stache is. They are human too, and are not always alert.

Only the damn law is always alert it seems. Sometimes you buy from guys who want only sugar in payment because the Feds are clamping down on sugar sales in the area. It ain't enough you have to go through all the routine to get the likker to sell it, you gotta be a nursemaid to the guy who makes it on account he don't know everything about his own business.

It all takes time, and having to make the new contacts gets you sweaty outside and sticky inside, and you cuss the hell out of yourself for not going to college. Now you gotta have the moonshine though, or no mazoola, so you set out for the country store circuit. They look at you like you are crazy when you ask for one hundred pounds. "Twenty, maybe," they say, and you take it and pay top price. You gotta have six hundred pounds of sugar.

You try twenty places and you come up with three hundred pounds in all. You look in the rear view mirror, and the Feds are laying back on your tail. You take off and say to hell with it and you shake them off. It's only for then though. They have taken notice of your activities. They figure you are going into the manufacturing end in a big way. For them you bear watching.

Gees, now is the time to take that trip to Florida, but you know you won't. You sweat it out, and every strange car has six Feds on the inside and one in the boot. They are figuring what it will take to get your kind of meat in the right place. One of them is liable to be an income tax man wondering about the new house you have, the new cars you bought, or all them country hams hangin' in the smoke-house.

A week later when one of your cars gets knocked off with fifteen cases and your driver is caught, you can feel the ulcer seeds sowing themselves all the way from the roof of your mouth to your stomach. You talk with your driver. He's a good kid.

He didn't panic. He pulled over and ran like hell when they bumped him, driving sunsabitches. He put up a good ride and a good run, but he was outrun. He didn't say a thing. But it's bad enough. Then the lightning strikes the outhouse.

He tells you without thinking anything of it that they told him he had fifteen cases on before they even looked in the boot. They even said fifteen cases and spelled out the word fifteen one letter at a time. They told him fifteen cases, "E–I–G–H–T–Y damn gallons, boy."

That's what he had, too. They know plenty without the kid even opening his mouth. They either saw it loaded from the main stache––in that case it's all gone––or. ol' soandso the consignee, helped them with a pure, sweet, soul–satisfying set up. The kid did right. He gave them the car key. He didn't make 'em mad. They would have towed the rig into town anyhow, and you think, and the ulcer seeds start sliding down and getting bigger all the while.

You can't get at your stache. They're watching it sure as hell. You gotta check around and see who got caught, and who didn't get caught. Among those who got caught can be a traitor sure enough. Among those not caught can be a guy who is getting bigger, spreading out, and got his fingers in your cookie jar. You gotta take care of the whole thing. You alone. Nobody else. Most of all, right now, you gotta figure the next move, and figure it for sure, for perfect, for everything.

You think; I'll find a young kid and give him a dime to walk around the barn where the whiskey is and tell me what he sees. That won't work. Those Feds, if they are there, will give him a quarter and send him back so confused he'll think he's playing a game.

That Florida trip sounds good. No, wait a minute. The McKloyes know the liquor is in the barn, and it'll be gone when I get back. You gotta tell somebody, dammit, and you can't tell anybody.

Why innahell didn't they ask the kid more questions? They know enuf already, and you know it too but won't admit it. Why don't you just lay off a while. You can't, the damn sweat outside and stickiness inside won't stand it, that's why. You'd ask the big boy in manufacturing what he would do, only he will say, "If you chicken that easy, you got no business bein' in the business anyhow."

He might see to it that you got out of the business as a liability to the profession. Worse than that, you know what he would do in your shoes. Nothing. Nothing at all until he got ready. He could afford it. He's big and I'm little, and now you know why he got big. He did the right thing at the right time just by knowing it, and not having to figure it. That is he did it after he learned it the hard way. He'd been up and down, home and away from home, on account of his business a number of times. Now he was one in ten thousand with things on his side the way they are.

Somebody else takes the rap for him. The kid'll take yours, but only this time. He's useless now. You gotta stand by him till it's over and then it's goodby for him and you. You'll treat him right so he won't even tell his own mother about the outfit. Those things are another kind of moonshine.

One Sunday afternoon or just about the hottest day of the year, I received a phone call from the supervisor to come down to the office. It was about two o'clock, and for some reason it was deemed advisable to terminate a large undercover whiskey–purchase investigation that night. It remained however, that completing would be accomplished by final knock–off buys. The investigation covered a wide area of about a fifty mile stretch.

When I arrived at the office there were a few investigators on hand, and a couple of officials, and we had a discussion about procedure for the wind–up.

One large scale violator was situated a good distance away from the major portion of the others. It was decided that a final buy be made from him first, so that the word would not get around, before we could strike in full force. It was suggested that a young investigator hide himself in the trunk compartment of a car which would be driven from Raleigh to the violator's premises by an undercover investigator.

Other buys had already been made from the violator and this was sort of a coup de grace, or a "knock–off buy," which in enforcement parlance is considered as "paying with the badge." In this fashion the moonshine whiskey is seized on the spot, and the violator receives no money for it.

In this instance the thing would have to be done quickly, and the pressure for haste was on all around. More investigators were appearing at the office, and the assignments were being made.

The idea of having a man concealed in the trunk is to enable him to offer assistance to the undercover investigator, if needed. He could help too, in ascertaining the source or moonshine stache of the violator. Frequently, it is the practice of a violator to drive the purchaser's car off to the stache, or to his source, and while the purchaser waits at the violator's premises, the moonshine is obtained and the car loaded by the violator. The reason for this is to thwart seizure of the stache, and confiscation of additional whiskey, by keeping the location of the stache known to an absolute minimum number of people.

When the Investigator in Charge suggested the young investigator to ride in the "boot" of the car, the fellow was gone for the idea.

I suggested that we check out the car to be used, and was told that time did not permit such. I had been through a bad experience a long time before whence the car had a faulty trunk lid, and a faulty exhaust manifold.

In that fashion I had occasion to go on a tour of dusty, bumpy dirt roads in the back of a Ford Coupe unbeknownst to the driver who was a well known moonshine wholesaler. Unfortunately, he could not obtain any whiskey at several places, as we had been active in the area with a saturation drive not long before. The trunk lid was rusted, and squeaked so that if I did try to emerge at any time, I would be telegraphing my movements to all within one hundred yards.

When I came out of that trunk a couple of hours later, I had been eating dust and dirt, and soaking up gasoline fumes on the entire trip, and I was a sad sight indeed.

I had forgotten that occurrence even though it had happened a long time before. I had resolved to inspect any spot where I might have to lay concealed in a small space in the boot of a car driven by only the Lord might know what kind of driver.

I suggested that I would go instead of the younger man. He truly wanted the experience, and since I felt that he might be in for more than he could reasonably handle, I suggested that I accompany him when I found out the make and model of the car to be used. It had a huge trunk, and so with the undercover investigator at the wheel, we set out for the knock—off buy.. We were in the passenger section.

While in the proximity of the moonshiners house, the young investigator and I climbed into the trunk and our driver closed the lid. I tested it to see if it could be opened from the inside. It could not. The lock mechanism was faulty. With an oh well, what the hell attitude, we had to accept things like that. An investigator recognizes them at such a time when all things must move. I did tell the driver of such, just in case.

It was not long before raw gasoline fumes were making themselves felt to both of us. The stench from the exhaust was mixed in with the smell of raw gasoline, and the heat inside the trunk at four o'clock soon made us soaking wet. We hoped that the job would be a quickie, and we stretched out the best we could. Our driver called out when we were approaching the moonshiner's house. I felt the car bear to the left and the familiar bouncing up and down to be found in riding over private vehicle paths in the country.

When the car stopped, I could hear sounds of what might be a family at leisure on a Sunday afternoon. I heard kids playing and shouting, and voices in the distance. I heard the voice of the moonshiner in greeting.

I thought to myself, that joker must be having a family reunion, no sale here today.

Not far from where the car was I could hear a horse running up and down, and much laughter.

The moonshiner entered the car and allowed "how it was hotter'n a June bride in a feather bed," and he explained to the U. C. investigator that "That thar horse my young un is ridin' was a plumb hard thing to find." He was in no hurry, and went into detail that he had been looking for some time for the right kind of animal for his seven year old daughter.

I knew from memory the place where we had stopped and I was visualizing people gathered on the front porch, and about the yard, and I knew of a big barn at the side of the house. I was hoping that the guy had the whiskey in there.

It was more comfortable now that the fumes were no longer strong, but the gasoline odor persisted enough so that I realized that the tank had a leak in it.

The preliminary conversation over with the moonshiner still had some doubts about the U. C. investigator, and he thrust and parried.

"How long you been knowin' old so and so?"

"And where'd you say your home was?"

The kids were causing some distraction with the horse, and the moonshiner must have felt good about it all and he changed his topic.

I had been afraid that things had somewhere taken a turn for the worse, which is an easy thing. A little thing could have, another event there, someone said this, and someone saw that, and bingo, it's so easy for such a deal to bog down.

We already had this guy, and this was to be sort of a corroborative buy, but I was glad that I'd come along with the new Investigator. It wasn't exactly the place right then to be desired for a new man, with the mechanical conditions of the car involved, and with the guy asking questions of the undercover man.

Alone, or with somebody else, there isn't much you can do in such a situation but wait it out; but with a bit of company at hand it makes the waiting a little more bearable. Thusly we waited.

After about thirty minutes, the whiskey man proved that he had a hell of a sense of humor. We heard his conversation and his jokes (both up front were in great rapport now) and we forgot about fumes and were having a hell of a time to keep from laughing spontaneously.

The one that topped all things off for us in their conversation came from the moonshiner. He said, "Do you know how many bottles of shoe polish it takes to dye a white horse black?" Of all the screwy things I could think of being on anybody's mind there, the very last, at least, would be the quantity of dyestuffs necessary to change the complexion of a horse. With that one, we both just about had to hang on to each other to keep things quiet. The U. C. man was doing a whale of a job and had by then knocked out all suspicion on the part of the moonshiner.

The moonshiner said, "What time is it?" U. C. replied, "Four forty–five p.m."

"We might as well get comfortable, I ain't got none at hand, and I tried to get some off this other joker, but he ain't home and won't be until eight o'clock."

At such a time the investigator thinks all kinds of things like, that means three and a quarter hours more in this sweatbox, and I can't move, cough, or breathe heavy. If that sonnavagun keeps up his jokes, they're gonna think that gas tank is leaking sure enough out there. He then thinks how he refused that soft drink on the way down for obvious reasons ahead. He did the right thing.

An investigator once told me that he suffered the tortures of the damned night when he was with a guy in a trunk in similar circumstances. He called the man what he thought was the "coarsest sunnuvabitch I'd ever seen."

The car had been parked behind a rural church by a driver who had left in another car to go down the road for a road block if necessary. The moonshiner was to approach it and load it. He had already been paid, and accepted the chore, so it was more than a good bet that the deal was coming off without a hitch.

The two guys were in the trunk though, and could raise the lid if they wanted to if no one was around. The grieved investigator told of the incident thusly, "Here I am with this bastard in a tight trunk, and I halfway have claustrophobia anyhow. This guy is having a hell of a ball at my expense. He kept whispering about running water, and about drinking a lot of water which he said he had before he left, and how his stomach got full of gas sometimes after eating chili like he had done that night."

"I didn't know him too well, and when I moved or whispered anything he would say, 'Shhh! I heard something.' I was so stuffy inside, I would squirm and almost get sick. I became more conscious of my bladder for the nonce, and I occupied my thoughts with that for a while."

"The moonshiner came up and when he got out of his car, he left the motor running, and came to the trunk and my friend was on him, and over to the car and cut the motor off before I could get started good."

Later the guy told me that he'd said what he did to get my mind off that small enclosed place. He told me that he felt that there never was any use in worrying about a damned thing if it was something you couldn't do something about. His idea was that something could always be worse, and he sure did suggest it to me.

In our case, years later, our troubles had nothing to do with claustrophobia. We just were sort of impatient to get going with the thing, and on to some of the action at other places. We realized that the guy might not be home at eight o'clock. It was a good bet that we would be the last ones to come in with our quarry that night.

We stood fast, and the U. C. man was trying to make things as lively and easy for us. He suggested to the moonshiner that he would leave and come back later and the moonshiner did not want that. He was hepped up for a sale and afraid he might miss out on it that way.

He compromised. He said that he would give it a whirl about seven o'clock and that if the guy wasn't there that he would try another place or two.

We finally started on our merry–go–ride, but not in a merry way.

The car was an older model, and after the U. C. man got out of the car, the moonshiner attempted to back up and turn around.

The automatic transmission became hung, and after backing up some the car would not go forward. This occasioned about a fifteen minute delay, and the U. C. man said, "Hell, I'll drive it and go along." The moonshiner said, "No, I know these old things, I'll make it. If I take you, the guy won't sell to me even."

We were off.

I knew the area quite well, or at least I thought I did until after I had slid around in the back of that trunk so much, bounced over rutted roads, and listened to that motor roaring at wide open speed. We braced ourself against the top, and the bottom and sides of the trunk the best we could, and the fumes and dust were unmerciful. We arrived at number one place. Not home yet. Our driver left a message for him. We went to number two place, and number three place, and no sale. He left word that he would be back later.

We were to get twelve cases of moonshine (72 gallons). One guy had a few cases. That was no sale. We heard the conversations and finally we headed back to number one. He was home, but said he didn't have it on hand.

"Had it stached. Come back in an hour."

The moonshiner went home and advised the U. C. man, who must have been worried as all hell about us, as we had been gone so long––faulty transmission and all, and by then "God only knows where."

The moonshiner had wanted to open the trunk "to see if it will hold twelve cases." The U. C. man had said that the back seat would hold it, and that he had hauled twenty cases that way. (He had retained the trunk key himself though." The moonshiner was satisfied, and away we sped with a driver who was in one hell of a hurry. The U.C. man had also told him that he was tired messing with him, and that if he knew a hell of a lot about moonshining, he'd had the whiskey a long time ago, and that his (the U. C. man) time was valuable.

We arrived back at number one place, and the man said, "I only had ten boxes on hand, but I borrowed two."

Now the real fun began. The seller was not at all as gullible as the man buying from him. He wanted to see inside the trunk. "Man, just slide it in back here, in the car, dammit. I been keepin' the man waitin' about six hours now." He'd taken up the plaintive manner of the U.C. man.

"I don't give a damn he been waitin' ten hours."

"Lemme see them keys, I'll open that trunk." (We would have been glad to oblige, but we couldn't get out unless the right key was manipulated in the slot in proper fasion).

"Gimme a match."

We could hear the lock being toyed with, and through a little crack we could see matchlights. Simultaneously, we could smell the raw gas fumes getting stronger under the car. Our moonshine man smelled it too, and said to the other man,

"Damit, you sellin' whiskey, you supposed to act like it. Damit I been keepin' the man waitin' six hours now, and you gonna set his goddamn car on fire. He's a big man. He liable to do anything, you burn his damn car up."

"I gotta see in that trunk."

"I'm payin' you the money, and you got no more whiskey here, you got nothin' to fear. I'm the one takin' the chance, but I'm in the damn whiskey business so I gotta act like it, not like I'm a detective."

Such words at such times are music to the ears, and my partner and I nudged each other. The action was at hand.

Our man must have felt good about it all right then. The two men walked away, and we heard a door chain rattle, and we heard a door squeak.

They loaded the back seat compartment of the car with twelve cases, and our pal of the twelve cases had backed the old car to get it turned around. The transmission was stuck in reverse, and there was some pushing by hand, and some knocking around with a truck or another car, and the mechanism shook loose.

By this time my nose was running, and so was my buddy's. On some of the bumpier roads, we could now be a little more free in our movements without detection as the whiskey in the back no doubt would be considered to be shifting if we moved some.

I wondered if we would be able to get out and do the job we were supposed to do. We were scheduled to scramble out when the trunk was raised and take our man. We were cramped to a severe degree.

When we rode into the moonshiner's yard with the cargo and stopped, the U.C. man played it real smart. He had told the guy he didn't have the trunk key and hoped that it didn't cause any inconvenience after he had left. He said that the key didn't work most of the time anyhow. The moonshiner didn't seem to care.

The moonshiner went into a long spiel about how the guy was so stubborn with "puttin' the moonshine in the trunk, and how he had to finally tell him that if he was worried about being in the moonshine business, he had no business bein' in it."

U.C. must have been diddling around the trunk a while. The moonshiner went on rambling about "fellers ought to tend to business, and that a feller has to take a chance once't in a while."

We heard the trunk lock click. We eased out of the trunk in fairly good fashion, and since the guy was on my side, I put my hand on his shoulder and said.

"Federal Officers, you're under arrest." My knees were shaky and buckling, almost, they were that stiff. I leaned all my weight on him so he couldn't break away. All three of us just sort of blocked him. I told him, "It's tough luck, that's the way the ball bounces." That chit–chat tends to soothe in such a rather unexpected situation.

Later, when he found out we had been in the trunk, he said, "Man, oh man, I wish I'd known that, you'd be sitting down peaceably in a creek over your head, or lightin' up the sky a long time ago."

I said, "You didn't do it though, and you oughta be goddam glad you didn't because what trouble you're in now is nothing compared to doing things like that and to hear you talk like that wants to make me kick you in the butt.

A short time later we were talking, and he said, "I didn't mean no harm a while back, but sure enough I'd have left that car by the road if I'd known you were in there. Mister, you couldn't pay me enough money to have your job."

I said, "I guess that makes us even then, you couldn't pay me enough money to have your job either."

The same sort of deal was worked in another area that night, but it went off in a jiffy, and the guys in the trunk had a rope tied around the inside of the trunk lock lever, just in case. They had more time to get ready in the first place than we did.

About a month later the "hidey in the trunk" maneuver was tried again not too far away and the moonshiner who had a friend with him, just laughed. He said, out loud, "Well, now, in there, Mr. so and so, and Mr. so and so, won't you come out of that boot and come into the house for breakfast. You know we quit the moonshine business two years ago."

The U.C. man driving the car, and who was from a very distant area, drove off, of course, and to a point where I was waiting with a receiver car, (to remove the whiskey from the buyer's car so that he could hit a few more places).

They told me about the no–go deal, and the funny part of it was that the moonshiners had named correctly one of the guys in the trunk.

The moonshiners never did know for certain that anyone was in the trunk though. They just weren't taking any chances, that's all. The undercover investigator said, "You've got the politest dern moonshiners I've ever seen." That may be so, but in all of it there was something surer than politeness, to be ready for such. They talk, and they listen, and they look, and they figure maybe you'll be back later and if you do, you can bet one thing, that they'll remember you from talking to you and looking at you and listening to you and they'd know that car again if they saw it anywhere even piled up behind a wire fence in a junkyard along the road, two years later. They don't miss a trick and most tricks miss them, but not all.

THIRTEEN

TRANSPORTERS

It is not always easy for the moonshiner to get his finished product from the stills to the distributor and consumer.

It can be a very tricky business. A great deal of planning, cunning and effort is devoted to this phase of moonshining by liquor law violators.

I have known them to use hearses, tank trucks, wagons, baby carriages, wheelbarrows, pushcarts and homemade creations on wheels.

The carrier's can was a favorite device in Harlem years ago. That consisted of a custom made copper container with a pouring spout. It fitted snugly into a suitcase which had been previously purchased for that purpose. To an observer looking into a transporter's car, equipped thusly, it would appear that the owner was merely transporting clothing or personal belongings. It served to deceive someone noticing the driver walking across the sidewalk with a suitcase.

In using the carrier's can on arrival at the speakeasy, or distributor's, the transporter would empty the contents into a five gallon tin can which the speakeasy owner kept on his premises.

He would leave after being paid, and walk out with the suitcase. Not always though. A known moonshiner taking a suitcase from a suspected car was a sitting duck for an alert officer.

I had a real break one time on the lower east side of Manhattan. I saw this guy pull up beside the curb a short distance in front of where I was parked. I was on a surveillance detail for something else.

It was about seven–thirty in the morning and activity on the block was just beginning to stir at a good clip. My hopes were on the wane for any activity by my suspected operator, so I watched this bird get out of the big brown Chrysler.

He walked around to the trunk of the car and opened it. When he lifted up the trunk lid I saw stacks of cardboard boxes. Now cardboard boxes wouldn't be suspicious in themselves, but what got me was the size of the things. The driver took one out and walked across the sidewalk and entered a building. It was obviously heavy judging from the way he carried it. I became curious about what was inside the carton. I approached the man.

As I got closer I saw that the carton bore the brand name of a popular cigarette manufacturer. I knew that the intended use of the carton was for cigarettes.

"Hey Bud."

"Yeah."

"Federal Officer. What do you have in that package?"

"Alcohol."

I almost keeled over. It is not customary for a moonshiner to answer so positively and abruptly when he is caught in the act. He made no attempt to run. I remained on the sidewalk.

"Where are you taking alcohol to in that building?"

"Second floor. Photographer's. He uses it in his business."

"Is that taxpaid alcohol or denatured alcohol you have there?"

I wasn't in any hurry. The guy knew I meant business too. I wanted to do the thing right, to have the correct answers when I got up on the witness stand.

Believe you me, that's the easiest way for any officer, but things don't happen like that every day either. Not things like a guy coming out and telling you point–blank. He wasn't the first guy I'd ever caught and after you've been up there on the stand with some sharp lawyers with a year's time to prepare; to ask you why the hell you did something in a split second, what you said and saw, you pay attention on the scene. It sure is one whale of a way to stimulate your memory, believe me.

"The taxes been paid on that alcohol?" I asked.

"You kiddin', you know better than that."

"Yeah, but I want to hear it from you."

"Hell, no. You got me right here red–handed. You're gonna cause a lot of curiosity."

"How?"

"The people see me standing here talking to you."

"Nuts. Did you know who I was when I walked up until I told you?"

"No."

"Then how in hell do they know who I am? I'm curious about you."

"I'm curious about you too. I always thought if I got arrested the cops would be all over me, all excited about a pinch."

"I don't get paid for the number of pinches I make. I get paid by the year. I like to learn all about this business, and I take it that you don't really object to what I say."

"No, because when I really tell you what I've been doing and how long I've been doing it, you probably won't believe me."

"I'm wondering about you now. Do you have a job, a legit one I mean?"

"Yeah, and I'm on my way to work now. I hope you won't tell my employers about it."

"They have any part in it?"

"No, legitimate one hundred percent people. I gotta kid who needs a lot of expensive medical attention."

I bent over and picked up the carton. I put it in the trunk with the others. I noted the number of containers. I opened the carton that had been on the sidewalk. The five–gallon tin can was the big–city universal container for moonshine and alky. I smelled of the contents. I put my finger inside and wet it. I waited for it to dry. By those little signs I was positive that it was alky, about 180 proof.

I watched the guy's feet alongside me, while I was bent over. He moved them slightly, nervously I thought.

I told him that he was under arrest. We both got into his car. He handed over the keys and I drove him across town to the Federal building for processing as a prisoner.

"How long have you been at this business?"

"Eight years."

"What?" I could hardly believe my ears.

"This car yours? Registered right and all that?"

"Yeah, I kissed it goodby when you told me you were a Fed."

"Now look, buddy, you said you were curious about me and the way I approached you. I'm curious as hell about you."

"Ask me anything, I've already convicted myself. I want to get it off my chest. I really do. I'd like to tell you about it."

"Okay, go ahead."

"Well I found out about this racket and it paid good. I didn't think it would last. I had my own philosophy about it. I would continue at it until I was caught. I would just do it and pay the consequences and quit when I was caught. In the meantime, I figured that if I wasn't caught, I would keep at it. The money was great. I'm not sorry or anything like that."

"How about the time you tripped the first time out. Were you nervous?"

"Nervous and scared, but I made it okay. Then after about the third trip I figured it out. I wouldn't associate much with known alky or moonshine guys, and I would have a legitimate job, and maybe drive like I had a load of eggs or something like that. I guess that the first time a guy drives across a bunch of railroad tracks or on a bumpy road with a load of eggs he is pretty nervous. But you know he's gotta get used to it if he is going to deliver any eggs."

"Right."

"So I pretended that I had a load of eggs back there. I quit looking in the rear view mirror, and from side to side. I just drove soft and smooth. I've been stopped at license check stations, and just figured that I had a load of eggs. It worked too."

"Did you always use cigarette cartons to carry the cans in?"

"Not always, but for a pretty good while."

"Gees, buddy, what gets me is that you're matter of fact as hell."

"What do you think the judge will do with me?"

"I can't even give an opinion on that. My job is to find and apprehend violators and to report the facts. I wouldn't even begin to say what a judge would do. I couldn't. I don't even know what judge will try you. I can say that you have been frank and truthful about what you've done, and that never hurts."

"Tell me something. Who told on me?"

"Now you are being illogical. It doesn't make any difference, does it? Maybe nobody told on you. I can't tell you anyway."

"But after eight years, it's hard to believe."

"I know, it's hard for me to believe it too, but I believe it."

"I'm caught. Will you tell me quite frankly what your best advice to me would be, man to man, being real honest about it."

"If you want to be real honest about it, tell the truth."

"That's the way I figured. That's why I said what I did."

"I'm not telling you how to plead one way or the other. That's up to you. Get a lawyer if you wish. He might think differently about it."

The guy did get a lawyer. He told the judge about his own guilt. He wouldn't implicate others. The judge took into consideration the value of the seized transport car. It was the guy's first time up in court. The judge was pretty nice about it all, I thought.

I'll have to admit that the seizure did make me feel my oats. In split seconds I was able to take in a lot of things I never would have thought I could. I remembered the picture on the Civil Service exam. They showed to us, and later asked what was depicted there, where it was, on what side of the room, and what the guy in the picture was wearing in detail. Time and time again I knew what they were trying to find out about me.

I had to write here about that guy because what he had done was really something. He kept whatever he was doing to himself, and thought things out so that he didn't arouse people's suspicions.

I sensed that he was relieved when he was caught, that something he started so long ago, so timidly, had ended even if it was a long time after it had served its purpose. I never heard of the guy again.

What he did was to carry out the general idea which so many moonshiners were concentrating on. The many factors this guy had going for him are rarely embraced in one operation. What they're really seeking is the big hit, the kind the race track gambler always pursues but never makes.

If you've read the action and adventure magazines, or went to movies about devil–may–care sort of guys, you probably are aware of the "ridge runners" who transport moonshine from the hills of the South into the cities. Those guys are real characters.

You can't really call them true moonshiners, because almost always they never own the stuff that they are hauling. They take it from one place to another on sort of a contract basis, and take their toddy wagons and their driving seriously.

A number of veteran stock car racers obtained their start through making moonshine runs or hauls. They would carry a load for good distances in rapid time. It wasn't that they were in a hurry but they figured "having a good head of steam up is the best way to avoid capture."

Pursuing revenooers were never so naive as to park beside the road, and wait for the moonshiner. The time it would take to get their cars started would permit the fast traveling moonshine runner to gain enough distance on them to evade even close pursuit.

The best way to intercept a moonshine runner in action was to cruise the winding roads about sixty miles an hour. If the runner was on a regular run known to the Feds, it was likely that he would come upon them and try to go around them. Then the fun began and it was anybody's race from there on. It was car vs. car and driver vs. driver.

In other days the runners would resort to smoke screens, tossing jars of moonshine or oil in the path of the pursuing revenooers. Strict penalties for such has virtually eliminated those practices.

Familiarity with the routes they were running was a must for both the moonshine runner and the revenooer. Reinforced front ends, milled heads, Offenhauser heads on Ford motors, dual exhausts, extra–leaf springs, hot plugs, overinflated tires, and other tricks of the trade were the rule for the fast drivers, be it moonshine man or revenooer man.

The '36 Ford coupe and '40 Ford Tudor were great favorites of both law and outlaw in the prolific years of moonshine races.

Motors were kept perpetually tuned. Practice runs, and sometimes what amounted to automobile acrobatics in sparsely populated sections, were all of the essence in being a mountain moonshine transporter or a pursuer.

Both the chased and the chaser would often enter into a jargon at some gas station or country store and discuss area moonshine cars as though they were personalities. They would talk of the merits and demerits built into those vehicles, and of new trends in racing, and about the legendary figures of the mountain speedways.

Some guys would put a padlock on the hood to keep service station attendants from messing with service which they personally wanted to give their cars. It kept competitive eyes from knowing what kind of motor the vehicle had, and those little extra special features the drivers cherished as their own.

We had a mountain transporter specialist who was working in our area in such official secret fashion that we were unaware that he was in the area. He had a padlock on his hood. He stored the car in a local garage one night.

The next morning the garage attendant called me at the office. He said, "We got a car down here that got something curious about the hood."

"Yeah, what is it?"

"Got a padlock hooked onto the front hood latch. Looks suspicious as hell."

"What kind of car is it?"

"A '40 Ford."

"Damn, I'll be down and take a look. Thanks."

I went to the garage and looked the car over. I looked at the license number and I looked at the inside of the car. I had to smile. I knew the car and had no doubts as to who was driving the car. The guy stopped by the office a little later and told us that he had come into the area the night before to make some undercover contacts.

Years later I was talking to a moonshiner and he told me about being approached by a guy with a padlock on his motor hood. He said, "He might just as well have come into my place with his badge on his coat, that padlock was so noticeable."

The chase of the moonshine runner didn't always end when his car was out of action from fatigue, or crash, or even tumbling end over end on a steep mountainside. The pursuing driver would have to take up the chase on foot in many instances to catch his man at the scene. I once heard an old moonshiner runner say of a revenooer, "He was a flying fool, a maniac at the wheel, and fast as a deer on foot."

In those early times the government cars were mostly seized ones, and here and there one was seized intact with a high powered motor and later used by the agents. The government economy procedures did not permit the expenditures to put or keep a pursuit vehicle in the same condition that the moonshiners kept theirs.

The ridge runners had the edge just about all the way on the narrow, curvy, steep roads they knew so well. They were born and reared in those hills and foothills, and got their hands greasy at an early age handing shade–tree mechanics their wrenches.

The small cow–pasture type of racing just had to come along in that environment and it did. The local speedsters would assemble and compete in dirt racing arenas in the rural sections on Saturday and Sunday afternoons. They would have contests for small stakes or participate in wagers compatible with their limited means.

Some developed reputations from this. The sport became more popular and lent itself to spectator admissions for a fee. Purses were provided, and the whole thing became organized and went from there to big business. It moved to town. The asphalt tracks with more and more accommodations and features for driver and spectator sprang up throughout the South and in the North too.

The best drivers deserted the ridges in favor of the "long green" currency of the asphalt pastures in the populated towns and cities. Stock car racing was a real going concern. Moonshine running was left to the poor people, but moonshine running had helped a lot of drivers get their start in the world of racing to go on to being some of the best drivers in the world.

I have heard colorful legends of these men in their early ridge running days and of some of their almost unbelievable feats.

Some would run road–blocks to go on to escape. Some spun their rear wheels with such force in maneuvering with their powerful car that a rear axle sheared and left the driver stranded.

Others would run away from awesome smashed hulks of burning steel and glass amid the sound of glass jars breaking, and the shouts of men's voices pursuing them.

Others' last view on earth was of only space in the night sky, and then the dark hulks of trees below as they hurtled toward them.

The bane of the moonshine runner was to be caught redhanded by revenooers on foot who had been waiting for him at a supply stache or moonshine terminal.

I have heard moonshiners say that it was not fair to catch them on foot when they had gone to all the expense and trouble of buying and maintaining the fastest car they could get.

The conditions of disposal for forfeited seized vehicles was either that they be sold by public auction to the highest bidder, or be turned over to the seizing agency for official use.

When the government was finished with their cars they were sold on sealed bids, or given as surplus to other federal or state agencies for official use.

If a finance company had an interest in the seized car and their equity was recognized judicially, then sale would be made by the U.S. Marshal's office for the district, and the finance company would obtain the amount of their investment balance on the vehicle less interest and charges.

Advanced procedures for insurance requirements and more allotments and provisions for additional personnel have placed state motor vehicle agencies in the position of eliminating some of the old time motor vehicle registration tactics.

Not too many years ago the registered owner of a car was sometimes listed from a tombstone. The address given was a vacant lot or c/o general delivery and in just about any fashion any wag would dream up for the occasion.

In the cities the moonshiners learned a long time ago that high speed chases were taboo. Once in a while some guy would come up from the rural south backwoods to try his hand at moonshine transporting up North. He would ignore the rules of the city. The results were pitiful. He was up against born and bred city drivers who knew all the one way streets and short cuts, too. He was a sitting duck.

Once such a guy sent word to me in N. Y. that he would suck my Plymouth up his exhaust pipe. Not long afterward I got behind him. He took the left side of a street car headed west on 125th st. There were people at the corner of Lenox waiting to board the street car.

It was ticklish but not too much so. He bounced through the red light at Lenox. It was green when I got there and I went right through. I gained on him and at 7th Street he made a right. I had the red and green car lights lit, and the siren wailing as we went up 7th.

A couple of police cars got into the act and were at my rear. I watched the traffic pedestrians and cars, and my partner watched the car just in case of a bailout.

I tailgated that rascal and pumped the spotlight handle up and down smack on the back of his head and onto the mirror. He was losing speed and his courage. I gave him a light calling card on his rear bumper telling him that I was dropping in.

I saw his brake lights go on and he started around the corner to the right. A cop on the corner saw it. When the guy pulled over to the curb he didn't get out. He stayed in the car and was shaking all over. The cop got in the car with him and called him a crazy son–of–a–bitch, and when the guy saw the three police cars right there, he said, "Is everybody in New York the law?"

The tops for oddity in transporting moonshine in my career was carried out by a blind man up in Harlem. For his vehicle he used a baby carriage chassis with a wooden box mounted on top after the baby compartment had been removed. The box had a hinged lid on top. It had a padlock too.

The blind man said that he didn't want kids or folks "pilfering with my mess when I'm not around, or when I can't see 'em." His "Mess" carried four five gallon tin cans of moonshine nicely enough. His only ally in his work was the darkness of night when he could listen to more than other people could see. He had squeaky hinges on the box cover to help him.

We had been waiting for the moonshine to arrive after an informant had telephoned an order for delivery of four cans. The informant made the mistake of telling the moonshiner to "be sure and bring it in your new Buick," so that we could make an impressive seizure. When he told us that we doubted that the moonshine would be delivered at all.

The moonshiner's canniness came up in reply to his suspicions in the form of dispatching the blind man and his squeaking baby buggy. A seizure like that was a headache in more ways than one. An investigator couldn't give the guy a license to transport, and he had to be humane too. The solution was more in the heart than the head.

The guy's predicament appealed to the compassion of the powers that were, and the quality of mercy was not strained. The blind man did not go to jail, but his activities were placed under close supervision and his talents directed toward other channels.

The Buick guy did a hell of an ugly thing when he sent a blind man out to deliver his moonshine. When a guy did things like that he called attention to himself in the eyes of the law. He called for increased vigilance of his affairs. He wound up in the pokey for all of it.

It wasn't long after the blind man thing that we had Mr. Buick before the eyes of a judge. The judge felt the same way we did about it and sentenced him accordingly.

During Prohibition, in the cities, a moonshine vendor was to be found near any place where people were congregated. Some of these equipped their persons with assorted contraptions to contain their merchandise. Some would use a hot water bottle in an ample inner pocket. They would have rubber hose attachments and siphon a drink with their withdrawn breath into a container at so much per drink.

Others used rubber automobile tubes strapped about their bodies.

Only the moonshine–man's ingenuity limited whatever means or device he used to purvey his concealed spirits.

Boats and airplanes have been used. The small outboard motor boat is still being used in the tidewaters of Virginia and North Carolina and other Southern states.

The most used form of transportation for moonshine today is the old rundown car, with little financial value. False registration, or sometimes none at all is used. It can be abandoned by the operator who takes rapid flight on foot when he knows he is being pursued. The car can be stored in woods or out–of–the–way places when not in use, and thusly is not much in sight of officers for the purpose of recognition.

The speed potential of today's cars has surpassed the capability of highways to accommodate them at full acceleration. It is no longer advisable for personal safety, and the safety of others, to challenge these cars at open throttle on difficult roads, moonshine or no moonshine. It means suicide and death to do so.

The government has given serious consideration to the matter. Wisely it has appropriated more money for undercover operations, more personnel, and newer and better equipment and techniques for its law enforcement officers.

I am not saying that a few unthinking individuals are not continuing the practice of moonshine running in new high–powered cars. The answer to this could be personal comfort's sake.

To employ such with the idea of a speedy getaway can be disastrous, and an invitation to any would–be pursuers to tighten up their opinions of the runaway. He is inviting the avowed attentions of some shrewd and able people who are acting in behalf of the public, and who can be when aroused, highly detrimental to his operations and well being.

I have seen moonshiners using brand new trucks, but these are usually the big guys. One night we were tailing one loaded with about 1500 gallons of moonshine. We were at his rear. We were without car lights hoping to take him to the main stache of the whole gang.

He missed a dirt road in the fog, and went by it. He started to back up, the way one of those dump truck drivers you've seen do. He held the door open and leaned way out so he could see around the cargo section of the truck. If he'd been driving a horse he would have whipped it to death at what he saw.

He saw us back there or at least the reflection of our bumper from his tail light glow.

He slammed the door and poured the gas to the truck. We turned our lights on and took out after him.

We pulled alongside. I was in the front passenger seat. Another revenooer was driving, and one was in the back seat. The guy in the back recognized the driver and called his name. I took a good look at him in flashlight illumination.

I saw him twist the wheel hard. I saw the big truck coming over. It looked monstrous. I heard the grinding of metal and the breaking of glass and I felt our car as it started over on its side. I felt the rocking as it settled back on four wheels. I jumped back into the front seat when the car leveled off. The driver raced the motor and I felt the car pulling out of the ditch where we had been pushed. We hit the open road and caught up with the truck.

It went through a man's yard, down a dirt road, through a cemetery, around trees, under trees, against tree limbs, and what have you. We were right at its rear. Somewhere it would have to stop. We had a full tank of gas. We could hold out.

After several miles the truck began to sway lightly. It swayed more and more until it came to a lumbering slow speed. The rear tire went flat. I got ready to begin the chase of the men on foot.

I tried to open my door. It was jammed tight by the impact of the crash. I went out through the open window when the truck came to a stop. The man on our back seat went out the door on the other side. We took after the two men who fled from the truck. It was an easy chase. We caught both.

Hell, with the memory of that leaning smashing truck still fresh in our minds, we could have run clear to Atlanta to catch them.

It is not always easy for the moonshiner to get his finished product from the stills to the distributor and consumer.

It is not always easy for the revenooer to catch the moonshiner as he takes his finished products from the stills to the distributor and consumer.

But the moonshiners, one way or another will transport, and the revenooers will pursue them—–one way or another too—–but I doubt if it will be in crazy, high speed chases on busy roads. It just doesn't figure any more.

FOURTEEN

RETAILERS SOUTH

Most of the time with moonshiners, the retailing end of their crimes are things which continue day after day and night after night. The retailer does well to keep his business as quiet and inconspicuous as he does and at the same time advertise widely that he has a product to sell.

The retailers are direct and discreet. They say to their neighbors, "If it's against the law to have it and you don't want it, don't buy it; but don't tell on me."

I have heard it said many times that if moonshiners at any level would divert their energy, ingenuity, and ability to retain good will, that they would be a tremendous success in legitimate enterprise.

As such applies to most this is pig tracks in the mash, especially if one would go back to their beginnings. Summed up for all nearly; it resolves toward the fact that they never had a chance at anything in their lives, other than in merchandising and manufacturing moonshine.

The difference for a lot of them in the beginning was in tilling rocky lands and eating on restricted diets. They lived in old houses with open windows and leaky roofs. They commoded in the elements. Their clothes were washed in iron pots over a backyard fire. They washed their bodies in tin tubs in the kitchen. They wore somebody else's clothes, ate Ford and Chevvy dust on a dirt road and watched kids and women folk in the house get thinner. They all got sloppier, and didn't seem to care any more. They tried to get warm while asleep under a one hundred year old quilt thrown on top of feathers in a canvas.

They stuffed newspapers and cardboard in the walls and a piece of tin beneath the floor. They shivered in winter, sweated in summer, and swatted at a million flies that plagued the table.

They had a million mosquitoes at hand to torment them with their sounds and their bites while taking the nourishment gained at supper away. The mosquitoes left night welts to be attended to with tobacco juice in the morning. The stink of chickens, pigs, wet babies, dogs, cats, wood smoke and kerosene was all about them.

Unwanted odors of burned–out oil and damp upholstery came from the three–wheeled, broken–windowed, motionless, dilapidated wreck of a rusty car in the front yard, driven three years ago for about fifteen miles altogether, after fifty good dollars was paid for it.

There came sounds of kids crying, pigs squealing, roosters crowing, dogs barking, the house creaking, the wind whistling, and the rain dripping down inside.

The landlord cussed louder all the time, and the only thing to take it all away was the news that came in the paper and over the radio so they could see how other folks live––exception, "maybe, just maybe, if a fellow could go to sellin' moonshine."

These were the facts many old moonshiners had to face, and were the ones that helped them decide to separate the reflected moonbeams from the honeysuckle scents in their own front yard. Some made the transition, and prospered. Most did not. For some, prosperity did not have much evaluation by total degree.

To them it meant little things one at a time, things like screens on open windows, a glass window in the outhouse, a house where the chickens would go to roost instead of in the trees in winter time. Sometimes the chickens froze in the trees with their feet remaining on the branches while the rest of the chicken was on the ground. The family would have chicken for supper.

It meant little things in a way, but their possessions, their wants, their hopes, their needs, and their very worlds were big little things. These men then would be the sellers beginning, vending by the drink or by the jar. Their house was a place where drunks gathered. It was where the transporter pulled up in the back yard twice a week, at night, without lights. He talked to Pa or Ma in a low tone, opened the car boot, took out a Mason Jar case, half a hundred pounds heavy, slammed it down on the porch, got paid, and took off up the road without lights.

The kids don't know for sure but they think it's Chet from over Red Bull Swamp way. They only see him in the daytime when he comes to take the order for that night. Sometimes Chet doesn't come and Ma and Pa are waiting. Later the drunks get impatient and sometimes nasty because the whiskey supply has run out.

Pa tells Ma that Chet's still got hit probably. He's right, Chet's outfit got hit and his hands were caught at the still that day, but Chet will be here. He's got contacts and can get an advance from another supplier––unless the beer buzzard was flying the area today. Then everybody was hit.

That beer buzzard pilot didn't miss a thing, ever. There are stories told about him. Once they said he spotted a fifty cent piece on the ground in a meadow from the air at eighty miles an hour on Saturday and came back on Sunday in his car and retrieved it. Of another alleged time the petty sellers said that he could smell mash and booze so keenly that "he once smelled them pouring them old cockballs on a passing airliner."

The best any could do though would be to spot a case of moonshine in a honeysuckle bed, or spot the "keyhole" in an overturned submarine still. This would be the result of axework on the top of the submarine still to spoil the circular hole where the cap had fit while the still was in operation. The keyhole told the pilot that the still had been destroyed and to pass on to a productive one.

A good pilot in an L–5 or L–19 observation plane didn't miss many stills, and if Chet's was gone through it was a good bet that every other one for several miles around was too, unless they were in buildings. There weren't many of those though. The still hands felt like they were trapped while working inside.

One moonshiner told me that he would rather sleep in one of them old sleeping bags than work inside tending a still. He elaborated on his feeling that he didn't want to sleep in an old sleeping bag and have some highland moccasin or rattlesnake crawl inside some night. (Sleeping bags were part of our night surveillance equipment.)

Once I visited a pair of dillies in the retailing by–the–drink line. It came about on a real balmy spring afternoon after a well dressed smooth talking man stopped by the office where I was working on reports. He told me, after suggesting that I close the door, that he had information relating to a huge distilling syndicate in another county. He said that with a bit of luck I could meet the chief of the syndicate by ruse.

As I said it was a balmy day, and the open road and outdoors I had become to know and love, beckoned quite strongly. I set aside my reports and contacted another Investigator who would drive the informer and me to the syndicate headquarters area and drop us from the car.

Enroute, my hopes were dimmed when the informant said, "I saw the still. It took up an acre of ground and a tractor trailer was unloading ice at the still right then."

"What were they doing with all that ice?"

He replied, "For the cooler."

Had we been closer to Raleigh at the time, I would have turned around, but I figured that maybe the guy was stretching things a bit to make it look good and that maybe he had seen some kind of a still. I wanted to meet the "kingbee" too, and see what kind of sting or honey he had.

With all the water available in creeks, branches, and rivers, no self–respecting moonshiner would have resorted to ice as a coolant unless——that during a run on an inside plant his water supply gave out and ice was fairly available.

The informant and I dropped off on a dirt road in a section which might be referred to as "way–way out" in the country. We proceeded to the alleged still site at the head of a pond. He said that he had walked across the dam and at the other end took a path which went to the distillery.

Immediately I noted the terrain, the width and condition of the dam itself, the swampy area in front of the dam and little things which did not denote in any way the proximity of any still of even modest size. At the end of the dam I saw a footpath such as used by bait diggers, trappers, or some other people on occasional walks. Was this the path at the end of which my informer had said he had seen a tractor–trailer being unloaded of ice?

The man was dressed quite well, and I told him to wait and that I would go through the swamp and make a complete circle to see whether any traffic had cut through the circumference. That was one way I could be wholly certain of my companion's credibility or veracity.

I checked all around the edge of the swamp and found a footpath which had not been used of late but had been well worn. I followed it and it led to an overturned submarine still of unimpressive size. I felt sure that my informant had adopted some tale that he had heard of this outfit and for some particular reason get me in the area——or perhaps even more so himself. I went back and told him what I had found and admonished him for fabricating. He said that he had not really seen it but that he had heard of it. We walked back to the road.

I asked him where the Kingbee had his headquarters. He pointed to a house on a hill and beyond a plowed field. We would go to the house, and we would be tobacco workers from Durham, muddy boots and all, out for a ride and right then thirsty for a drink of moonshine. As we walked across the field a man came out of the woods and my informant told me that the man was the Kingbee of the Sinnerkit.

I was annoyed with the turn of events but not at the informant altogether. I had met screwballs before and learned to take them in stride. I was thinking that if this guy hadn't showed up I could be winding up the case report I had started that morning.

The man approached us with a friendly smile. I sized him up for any latent kingbee qualities but I saw none. He was a big man. He had fair features, light blue eyes, and long blond wavy hair which dropped beside his cheeks. We greeted him and he said, "Hi Fellers," and we commented about the weather and crops.

The only thing my informant added to the conversation was, "It sure makes the sap rise inside a feller, especially us tobacco workers from Durham." Our acquaintance said, "You tobacco workers from Durham are O. K. in my book, hard as you all work and all that."

I don't know what it says in the "Tobacco workers from Durham field manual," but mine didn't provide for a situation like this. I just kept quiet and I glommed the Kingbee's haberdashery. The guy didn't have anything on but a pair of overalls and they were split along the backside. This was a real cool cat in more ways than one. I guess he didn't know that syndicate chieftains are supposed to wear silk underwear, nylon overalls and a shoulder holster.

The gang–guy was about thirty–nine or forty, and my informant was about forty–five, and I'll give the older guy credit. He could sling the lingo with the best of them.

He would have made a hell of a con man if he had really wanted to be one. He'd already conned me some.

We reached the house, and I knew that something was up. The

chief winked at me and said, "I would like to offer you fellers a drink but I got nary a drop on the plantation." I winked back and wondered what he had fathomed from old Walkie Talkie. Old Walkie Talkie had talked about nothing but all the high powered juices sloshing around inside him, up and down and side ways at this time of the year. At least it kept the sinnerkit guy's mind off things like how in the hell we had gotten there in the first place, or what the heck we were doing, walking up through his field to his house and him not even knowing us.

I wondered how the informant had gotten from Durham where he said he lived, to Raleigh.

When we reached the house I asked the farmer if we could get maybe a jar, or at least a drink. He winked again and pointed to the informant. I winked back. I told the con man, Arthur, to wait on the porch. I went into the kitchen with my new friend who advised me that he thought Arthur was to "secky minded." He had some "moon" on hand but was "afraid of Arthur."

I made a mental inventory of the place. It was a one story unpainted dwelling house. It had a galvanized tin roof with rust spots on the south central portion and several on the north upper east gable side. It had a long porch at the rear and a small one at the front. At the bottom side of the house, in red paint, was printed with inverted "N," the word or proclamation, "Nuts." The kitchen was furnished with one table, four chairs, an oilcloth covered orange crate, a pedal type New–Home sewing machine, a kitchen wood stove, a water pail, a country pie safe, four unwashed pans, some dishes, knives, forks, and a kerosene hand lamp.

On the stove was a Mason jar containing milk, a plate with four whole panfish which had been fried and a plate with some biscuits. Behind the stove were several pieces of wood, a dirty white cat, a box containing old newspapers, and some lightwood knots. A rusty Rayo lamp hung overhead from a screw–eye which had been painted green like the ceiling. The rest of the interior had once been painted the same color. The house smelled of fish, woodsmoke and just plain family odor, country style.

I looked out the window and Arthur was walking down the path toward the road. The racketeer walked over to the stove, picked up a fish by the tail and inched it head first with his teeth and tongue down into his gullet. He wiped his hands on his overalls, picked up a biscuit and chomped down on it, and went to work on another fish like he was making for a sandwich down inside. This was luncheon, no fuss, no bother. I could hear noises of people in the front part of the house but the door to that part was closed.

When I saw him go for a third fish, I thought of Leopold Bloom and his mutton kidneys in Joyce's "Ulysses," and I wondered if my friend had cooked the fish or if his wife had. As he eased the fish down his throat, he made a funny sound, wiggled his big belly some, and with his wide stance, it seemed to me that he was rising to meet the fish rather than letting it work down to him by gravity or release. I wondered if the fish had been cleaned. It looked to me as though they were just like they had come from the pond except for a little careless cooking procedure.

Now that his buffet luncheon was over, he reached into his overalls pocket which I figured he'd worn clean through by now. He brought out a pack of cigarettes and a couple of old timey Ho–House matches. He put one match back and picked his teeth with the holding end of the other. I said, "How about a toddy?" He said, "Good."

I didn't know whether he was talking about the fish, or the idea of a drink. Comrade Arthur was well down the road by now, so I said, "He's gone. I'm thirsty, how much a drink?" He struck the sulphur match on his bare sole, lit up a cigarette, looked me straight in the eye and said, "Is fifteen cents too high?"

"Hell no, unless I have to wait all day." He went into the parlor and I followed.

In the parlor there were four kids with long hair and overalls. I couldn't tell if they were boys or girls. Sugar Babe was there too. She was his wife, he explained, of eight or nine years that day. Sugar Babe was about twenty–seven or twenty–eight, skinny, about 5' 6" and 105 pounds. She had sharp but rather attractive features. What messed up my opinion of her was when I noticed that she too was wearing overalls. She did have on a tee–shirt which I attributed to modesty's sake rather than style. I gathered from her that the Chief's name was "Wilbur Honey."

I introduced myself as Nugent Joe Race from Durham County. The parlor had much less furnishing than the kitchen. No doubt it had once been the living room. Now it contained a bed, a mattress on the floor, a trunk in one corner, a pink painted kidney table with an old fashioned mirror nailed to the wall in front of it, and someplace a jar of whiskey I hadn't seen yet.

I was hoping that it wasn't under the covers on the bed, or even inside the mattress. Oh yeah, there was a nutless nutbowl on the dressing table with a sticker on it that said, "Souvenir of Raleigh, N. C."

I saw a three wheeled bicycle through the doorway on the front porch, and I recalled that that was the only form of mechanical transportation I had seen anywhere around the place. This guy sure was taking a lot of pains to baffle the income tax man over his gangland prosperity.

My informant had been telling me falsehoods.

If only Sugar Babe and Wilbur had been involved it might have been funny. But seeing those kids there, real and alive in such an existence, it was pitiful. I'd seen Wilbur take out a pack, and I saw Sugar Babe take out a pack, so somewhere they were getting their money for smokes.

I hadn't seen the moonshine jar yet, but Wilbur dispatched Sugar Babe to get it, I guess on account of the fact that he couldn't get it himself. It was under the bed, and fat like he was, and with his backside sticking out, he would have made quite a retriever.

Sugar Babe had no trouble getting under and out from beneath the bed. She stayed a while longer than she should I thought, and pondered about a trap door under the bed maybe. More likely Old Sugar Babe was sneaking a shooter for herself in concealment. That's how skinny Sugar Babe was. Anyone who can drink from a Mason jar under a standard size bed has to be skinny as hell.

When she came out from under the bed she had a half gallon jar containing what I would officially describe as "one–sixteenth gallon more or less of non–taxpaid distilled spirits without stamps affixed to the container as prescribed by law."

Wilbur went to the kitchen and came back with two jelly glasses from the pie safe. Sugar Babe poured a drink into each glass, and there was just about one more drink remaining. I toasted their anniversary and killed what was in the jar.

For a reaction, I walked over to the porch door and started to fling the empty jar into the yard. Wilbur stopped me and said, "Save that jar, it's worth money in trade." He told me in that way, right then and there, that he was selling moonshine. I handed him the jar and we went into the kitchen to get a chaser from the water pail. I drank straight from the pail.

I gave the kids, Sugar Babe had chased them out before we drank, what change I had and Sugar Babe said, "Thank Uncle Joe," and they did just nice as you please. I wondered where Uncle Arthur was right then, and at the same time I really didn't give a damn.

I gave Wilbur a dollar bill for the drink. I was ready to get out of there but I thought maybe I could get Wilbur to tell me where there was a still, or a transporter hauling, or at least something which wouldn't make the day a total waste.

I asked him if he had another drink, and Sugar Babe said, "In the hidey hole." Wilbur agreed, and Sugar Babe went to the wood range and pulled a half–filled jar out of the oven. I told Wilbur to keep the buck and get him some cigars for his wedding anniversary.

They drank again from the glasses and I drank from the jar. I toasted them for their anniversary, "Eighth or ninth, whatever it is." I didn't drink much but I could hardly taste the moonshine. The rim of the jar tasted like burned biscuits, lard and kerosene oil, and maybe some baby wet too, but what the hell! It was the guy's eighth or ninth wedding anniversary and I couldn't be choosy.

Out of a clear sky, I asked him where I could buy about ten cases of moonshine "on account I had an outlet for it in Durham." It flustered him and he said, "I ain't never seen that much moonshine in one place in my life. Ain't that much in the whole township, and besides," he said, "I don't trust that joker you are with."

I made my point, I said, "Look around, see what you can see, and I'll take care of that joker."

"He been here before, his name then weren't Arthur neither. He's an undercover law." I told Wilbur I had a way of taking care of things like that by finding out the facts and then keeping my mouth shut.

Wilbur came out with some real intelligence then. He said, "That feller Arthur, or whatever his name is, is one of them Horny Heads. I seen 'em before like that at this time of the year, right now when them saps is rising, riling him up. He can tell all kinds of things about a woman if he gets where he can look in her eyes or at her teeth.

I thought to myself, "Ol Wilbur is mixed up on his horses and women," so I changed the subject. I asked him where I could buy a few cases of moonshine at least, on account I had to have them on account of an Irishman friend of mine named Finnegan who died, and they were having his wake that night. I said, "Did you ever hear of Finnegan?"

"Is he the one run the pickle plant at Mount Olive?" I guess he thought I said vinegar.

Wilbur was not at all cooperative. I turned to Sugar Babe who was holding the jar to her chest like it contained a million sunshines and no shadows.

Sugar Babe said that maybe them flirts down the road what sold moonshine and with fancy grapefruit juice to swallow after it––they might have all the likker or anything else a feller might like down there, and even a piccolo and TV set too. It was the next house down the road on the same side.

I thanked them, and when they were all lined up at the door, kids and all, I thought, The guy who sells them overalls sure can sell overalls. It was the uniform of the day and the night too probably for that family.

I went down the road to the next place and my buddy from the tobacco factory was there already. He had his arm around a stout blonde girl about twenty–five or so, and when he saw me come inside he grew bold and dropped his hand down on her fanny. She turned around and slapped him one you could have heard all the way over in Sampkin County.

She called him a cheap sunnavabitch and asked me what the hell I wanted. I told her "a shot with grapefruit juice drink chaser." She set it out and I gave her a quarter. She handed me ten cents change. I looked on the grapefruit can saw the price marked as 15 cents. She was sober sho 'nuff. I gave her the ten cents, "as sort of a tip" I said, and she took it.

My impression was that it was one hell of a way to run a railroad of any kind but I sure wasn't on the Cannonball Limited by any stretch of the imagination. The informer guy was cuddly–duddly with an older woman in the front room by now, and I figured that jackass out. He'd been there before for sport.

I asked him what kind of car he had. He said, "A Buick, but my wife drives it to work." One car for two people? I was undecided about leaving him there and was going to slip off and meet the car without him.

We took him home. A few minutes later his wife pulled up in the yard. She was a nice looking, well groomed woman. She drove a new Buick, and the house was in the $25,000 class with landscaped grounds, and it was well kept. I took it all in at a glance and before his wife approached I said, "How in the hell did you know about such a place as we just came from?" He was brief in his answer but he was truthful. "My girl friend lives down that way." I was terse and truthful too. I said, "Well, I'll be a sunnavabitch." He invited us into the house and we declined. My partner said to me, "Gees, let's go before his old lady thinks we kidnapped him."

In a new voice we hadn't heard before, he addressed his wife with great endearment and introduced us to her as "Richie and Herbie," from the bowling team. I almost laughed too spontaneously when she said to me, "I wish that man of mine wouldn't take his bowling so serious, Richard."

"Did you all have a good score, boys."

I said, "We two didn't but Arthur scored a three hundred."

"I'll have to reward him tonight for that."

She didn't say what the reward would be, but with Arthur all secky and horney–headed, like Wilbur said he was, I could imagine. I wondered what she would reward him with if she knew he'd been hot after country poontang all afternoon, telling lies and drinking moonshine and grapefruit juice.

"Won't you boys come in the house for a coke or glass of lemonade?" Arthur's wife was real cordial and Arthur was playing the role of dutiful husband to the hilt.

"They wanted me to stop and have a beer with them, but I know how you feel about that sort of stuff, so we didn't stop."

I listened and looked aghast. I hope I didn't say "you lying sunnuvabee" too loud. I could see the gleam in his wife's eye. I didn't want to spoil it. I said, "See you at the office, Arthur." My partner said, "Race, you lyin' S. O. B. "

FIFTEEN

THE INFORMERS

If there is one thing for sure in the field of investigation, be it Moonshinewise or otherwise, it is that the good detective will expose himself to informers and cultivate them, and by their information make many sound cases.

I had often thought that if the situation was turned around and an unwary detective was cultivated by a posing informant, then that informant could in a number of ways enrich his coffers.

Unitl not too long ago, I thought that such a thing would naturally incur many hazards for the individual, too many indeed to be overcome, but I did not reckon with the cunning and chicanery, and storybook–plotting ability of such a man as Mr. X in my conclusions.

I was introuduced to Mr. X in a curious manner and in which the secrecy requested in the whole thing nigh approached the ludicrous.

I went to meet Mr. X. wondering who might be so knowledgeable in the bootleg crafts as to warrant such secrecy.

I believed in taking one thing at a time, and when a secret, too secret meeting had taken place and we had gone through the roster of prominent bootleggers and their activities, I let the man do most of the talking.

Every minute or so he would parry his statement with a question as to who is doing what, in what manner, at what time and at what place. He also dropped names of all kinds from prominent bootleggers to the names of bigshots in the government. But he did not tell me anything, and I did not answer his questions, as I had become wary as to whether the man was a B. S. artist or a skilled fisherman.

I did not take his bait. The first whiff sent me into deliberate stupidity which can be effectual and a credit to an alert investigator.

Finally, the guy came up with a location of an alleged large scale illicit distillery. At my insistence he even consented to ride by the place and point it out as an actuality.

After some lengthy discussion of many things we parted company and I set out for my post of duty.

The informant ran a country store which is always a good place for contact for all sorts of things. The coming and going of people is not conspicuous in itself at such an establishment, and the arrival and departure of automobiles is nothing to wonder at if you do not know the ways and means of occupants.

The distillery described by the man and the modus operandi of the alleged operators was just a bit too vague to me. To top it off he had said it was an out–of–state gang. In my mind it all added up to a probably zero score in proof.

I had been dealing with informants for years and each contact always provided some new, refreshing, challenging slant when it came to pondering the whys, wherefores, and whatizzes of it all.

There are ways of fast checkouts in all forms of information if the officer is on his toes, and keeps his think box well oiled and functioning.

In such a position he can't but help think about an informant, how he ticks and why he informs. He knows in the first place that a Sunday School is the last place to look for criminal information. He seeks it elsewhere.

As a law man he knows that a good detective is as good as his information. If he has doubts, he rides out the storm and keeps a cocked eye on the clouds and sky of it all.

He thinks that a good place to begin is with the informant's name. Does it ring any bells from some dark tower from the black beyond? He juggles the name around on his tongue or in his mind. He checks the office files and thinks of the guy's physique, his mannerisms and appearance and of places he frequently mentions. In brief, it is a professional routine all good officers know.

Riding back to the office for my morning report chores that day, I placed the informer in his own locality and let his name bounce around in my mind and on the tip of my tongue. I wasn't half a mile from his place when the name juggling routine came up with red lights in my head and an odd flavor on my tongue.

The last time I had seen or heard of the guy was some years before in a distillery informant role which he was playing. The information was not only late, it was screwy.

When we went to the distillery, some vital and valuable equipment had been removed beforehand by the Lord knows who. Only a carcass remained of the whole operation. It was pure and simple that someone had suspected someone else of reporting the distillery to our office.

Some local law enforcement officers were in on the visit, and since the thing was a violation of State laws, we let them have the whole thing lock, stock, and barrel, insofar as any elements of raid and seizure were concerned.

We tucked the situation indelibly on the file cards of our mind–recording systems for future reference, and it wasn't until the guy's name clicked, a number of years later that morning, that I had to call on my unwritten reference system.

Like so many other times the cybernetic response was accurate. I had the guy pegged years later. I recalled the words of my earlier partner, a man well versed in the ways of the world and its errants.

"This guy is bad medicine," he said. "Keep clear and away from him, pay him no heed, and be wary whenever you hear of that rogue. He's sharp as a tack, twice as pointed and will stick you at every turn."

So secret was my meeting with the man supposed to be, that I had all but pledged to tell no man of where I was going that early morning. Of course I had my obligations to my supervisors and the matter of reports which I could not alter in truth at any cost. I contacted the supervisor in charge on the phone and told him the story.

If I felt that I had been drawn into a hoax, or what I then thought was a worthless, artless, production–minus thing, then I could only feel sorry for the guy who proposed the meeting in the first place. He was a man of impeccable character, a stout–hearted and stout–minded man.

To keep things simple, I retained in the hollow chambers of my mind the continuing echo, the advice of an old and respected friend and co–worker concerning the informant. "That guy is bad medicine."

My next step was to check out the alleged distillery site which was a place at a definite point. It was not at a place in the woods which could be missed in the dark, or misconstrued as to its location.

If I had been pledged to secrecy as to the identity of the informer, the investigation was another thing.

Years before I had been on the witness stand in a case in a Federal District Court, and the defense counsel was crying for the name of the informant to be disclosed. He persisted while I sat mute in the witness box and he parried with the Assistant United States Attorney prosecuting the case.

The judge was silent in the matter, but the prosecutor was vehemently defending the right of the informant to secrecy. He irked the judge somewhat. The opposing counsel was claiming that I was refusing to tell the judge the story of it all, although I made the direct assertions in his court.

I looked toward the judge in one brief, fleeting quiet spell in the courtroom and asked his permission to make a statement.

I said, "Your honor, I will gladly disclose the identity of the informant to you in your chambers if I may."

This seemed to soothe the judge and he dismissed the matter of the informant's identity forthwith.

The informant had long been suspected of divulging secrets by his gang, and they had warned him twice by violent physical reprisals against him. (eg. threw him through a plate glass window on one occasion, and on another––gave him an assist through an open upper story window.)

They really needed to be sure for the final deal though, and while I testified from the witness stand I scanned the courtroom and what I saw made me do some mighty fast thinking. I came up with the idea of telling the judge in private. It was a reflex thought entirely.

What I had seen out in the courtroom were four obviously interested spectators. They would have been delighted to learn the informant's identity who had clobbered their operations with his accuracy in reporting their activities. They were part of the gang concerned and guys who could be nasty with odd sorts of devices for inducing and prolonging physical pain for betrayers.

What I would have told the judge was the man's name, of course as I knew it and his position with the gang.

I really respected that judge for not asking me to go into his chambers with him.

The United States Supreme Court, and State Supreme Courts have in their files much data which relates to the subject of informers and the degree of guarantee for secrecy available to them.

Any Federal Officer is acquainted with what is permissible with informants and what is not. A few areas concerning this are: possibility of entrapment; senseless motives on the part of informants; the informant being on the scene of the crime himself; and the validity and integrity and reliability of the informant––and so forth and so on.

To return to my earlier described storybook informant, Mr. X was an informant whose specialty was not in telling things but in asking things.

What this guy would do almost staggers the imagination.

He would walk into a nest of formidable moonshiners, and by discussing fragments of their operations, insinuate or imply that he knew more, and that he could get state and government informant fees for telling what he knew.

Even further, he made sly references to moonshine personalities and intimated that he was more than friends with a bevy of revenooers of all sorts, which was an outright lie, of course. He did have a hireling or two who wore a badge and whose integrity was more than once phrased as dubious.

He had companions who ranged from hot–rod moonshine runners, airplane pilots to taxi drivers, policemen, lawyers and what have you. He had made vague references as to the source of his apparent wealth.

With practitioners of diverse occupations, he was able to throw up a rather opaque nightshade in every quarter. His friends were gullible but usable, and Mr. X dared not except in rare instances proffer the greenback in turn for information from all quarters. "We are friends, Brother, and friends do all things for friends" was his motto.

The guy practiced the theory of great, helpful, loyal friendship in every quarter. He preached the essence of those great things he would do for a friend, and that in turn he could be expected a little favor, not for himself but for a friend, a friend just like the man he was soliciting for information.

Description in such a case is bland, or boring; typical dialogue would be more on the scene and appropriate. It would go something like this: It takes place in the country store of Homer, the sage of Gallboy Farm.

"Hi, Homer."

"Hi, Virgil, old buddy, buddy, how's the flying game?"

"Great, Homer."

"Beautiful weather for flying, Virgil."

"Sure is."

"Virgil, this here is my very good friend, Diogenes Dinwiddie, I call him Dodge, want you to meet him. Old Dodge is a constable up the county a ways, damn good law man, lock up his own mother."

"Old Dodge" smiles, shakes hands and looks around at Boscoe, the Federal man. Boscoe took in the "lock up his own mother" bit and thinks to himself almost too loud, and his old man too, for a buck.

"And this here is the champion runner, driver, my good friend, Ernie Boscoe. Old Ernie here, he's a Revenooer, the one who caught old "Pumpkins" Eversham.

Boscoe laughs, gets a soft drink out of the cooler box, pays Homer, who makes a great gesture of refusing payment, and wants to act like he is buying something big for a ten cent investment.

Boscoe places his money on the counter and he is sizing up Dinwiddie and Virgil, but he doesn't see them like they are standing there.

He sees Virgil, as a face behind an airplane window over a still.

Virgil the pilot, has no intention of saying in front of the revenooer what he saw. Homer emphasized the word revenooer and also "Pumpkins Eversham" too much.

Constable Diogenes, or old Dodge, comes up with something straight and direct to the point. "Do you see any of them stills while you are flyin' around up there?"

Boscoe catches the sly nudge that Homer gives Virgil, and says to himself, "Crap," and Virgil says, "I sure would love to see one of them things in operation, never have though. Seen 'em while I been huntin'."

Homer takes up, "I wouldn't be seein' too many of them things up there, them moonshiners are dangerous. It's like takin' your life in your hands to tell 'em what you saw."

"About time for one of them old chicken stews or a rock mulley, or a good old Brunswick Stew. Got a batch of fattenin' hens over at my farm, boys, need Brunswick Stewin'." Boscoe figures one thing that is different about old Homer. He believes that the greatest memories come from good eatin' rather than good lovin'. Homer has never mentioned women as bait to be put out to gain unwary confidences.

Boscoe recalls the moonshiners who would complain about old Homer one day and the next day deny it, as though they were afraid of Homer.

Boscoe recalls the times he has talked to newly caught moonshiners and the way things unraveled for old W. Homer Gallboy.

It is simple. What it amounts to is that the moonshiners are making money. Homer wants some, and they give it to him because Homer can suggest violence of the worst sort, and he has gall, plenty of it. A walk into an unknown house late at night, tromping hard on the porch, and to tell the man he wakes up to come outside that he has something to tell him.

Gall is totally what gets Homer by.

"It's Homer Gallboy from down X county way."

"What do you want?"

"Want to talk to you, have some information for you."

"About what?"

"About thirty one barrels of beer over on Buck Creek."

"Don't know nothin' about that, nothin' at all.

"I do. Know they're yours and the ABC found them from a plane yesterday afternoon. Thought it might interest you."

"Let's walk over to the well. Want a drink of water, Homer?"

"No, let's get into my car."

"Feller, you know I'm not here at your house this hour of night for nothing. I got my own racket. You got yours."

"Yeah, I heard about you."

"I hope you heard it all because I want two dollars a barrel to keep from saying what I know about you and your plant."

"Sure Mr. Gallboy, if that's all you want, sixty two dollars, I'll get it for you."

The moonshiner goes into his house and returns with three twenties and two one's.

"Much oblige, Mr. Gallboy."

"You're welcome and you can keep on working your plant. I steered the liquor cops away. Be at my store this same time next week for sixty–two more, that is if you don't add any more barrels in the meantime. I'll be checking."

The moonshiner thinks to himself, you son–of–a–bitch! He smiles while he thinks it, but stops smiling when he realizes that Gallboy has been collecting from bigger guys than him for years.

He concludes that Gallboy must have an in with the local law and the Federal law or otherwise he wouldn't be so bold.

Nothing could be further from the truth. The local law has been after his beer license that he has had for years at the country store. The Feds are hot after him.

They know him for real. They know that he is a storybook character. And they also know that getting the goods on a storybook character that nobody will believe exists is not an easy thing. It would be hard to go into any court for a conviction.

Homer Gallboy has an office of sorts in back of his store. He has a huge old desk that he bought while he was a J.P. a long time ago, when he was finding out a lot of things. Over the desk is a long mirror. Homer Gallboy does most of his thinking in front of the mirror when he wants to think things out, and think of them deeply. He has a habit of pulling at his jaw while he thinks. He does this as he looks in the mirror as a gesture in the same vein as a corporation executive would make before his board of directors with his eyeglass stems.

Homer is more serious, and he looks at himself in the mirror and challenges himself to be honest to himself, by himself, and for himself in all things which he has seen fit to establish for himself. He repeats his personal oath of allegiance to Homer Gallboy at least twice a day before his morning and afternoon dose of Black–Draught medicine.

He promises to be neat and orderly and accurate in his record keeping so that none will affront dear Homer by missing a payment due. Naught except very few taxes will be paid either.

Down the road from his store and off into the woods is a deserted weather beaten rough–hewn cabin with mortar rows between logs. At least it is deserted to everyone but Homer.

The windows are boarded up, the door padlocked and a trash pile which blocks vehicles from approaching close is replenished periodically by a new supply of empty beer cans, potato chip bags, and the usual worthless waste products of a general store operation.

A bushel of corn now and then is good to attract rats, and plenty of rats about do discourage curiosity seekers or interlopers.

In truth, the cabin is the first and only bank of Homer Gallboy, and his deposit box is a patented cement septic tank in the ground. It has an interlocking fireproof removable top. Access to that unique vault is through an unused fireplace hearth.

Homer enters the cabin through a passage tunnel he dug himself, which leads from a trap door beneath the garbage pile untrampled. Grass and weeds all about the cabin attest to its unvisited, unoccupied status from the outside.

At such times as Homer descends into the trash pile, he does so with a feeling he cannot describe. A few times he has at a point considered himself a Pilgrim come to stand before a monumental mountain built and dedicated for the glory and benefit of Homer, the Great Gallboy. He pulls at his jaw violently at such times and finds a sensation he obtains as increasingly pleasant stabbing until he shudders all over. He reaches into his pocket for his flashlight and continues his earthly sojourn. He kneels above the septic altar of his false gods and pays tribute to his coffers.

He fondles the roll of greenbacks from his collections and wonders what the full story of each greenback might be. He thinks what wonderful stories they could tell if they could talk, but only to Homer Gallboy, of course. Nobody else would care or appreciate the sweat, laughter and tears that passed them on to the sweetest of beyonds, of all beyonds, to the sweet–sour hands of Homer Gallboy.

He unscrews the cap from a half–gallon fruit jar half filled with tightly rolled bills of all denominations and drops the next roll inside. He laughs audibly, and he has visions of his wife of another day who has long since left him for a moonshiner. He holds up the jar as a staggering symbol with money as its potency.

He thrusts it violently forward at the center of her naked image before him and says, "Bitch, bitch, bitch," and he laughs and he cries. He laughs again when he thinks of all the moonshiners, transporters, sellers and drinkers who are working to pay tribute to his superior thinking.

He thinks too of what Boscoe the Fed said to him more than a year ago at the store. "Homer, you have more money than you should have by rights, but what gets me, is what in hell do you do with it, and what the hell good does it do you?"

"Yeah, I got it buried all around this place, go take that shovel over there and dig yourself up a new car, if that's what you think."

"You don't mess with the dollies. You don't have a big car. And you hang around this store like it was the New York Stock Exchange. Your pants are baggy, your shirt torn, and your hat looks like a moonshiner threw it away after filtering a pond full of moonshine through it."

"Nuts, Boscoe. Sometimes I want to call you bitch, bitch, bitch! You talk just the way that bitch wife did who left me for a moonshiner."

"You're off your rocker, man, you haven't given me any information worth a darn in a year."

"No, Boscoe, I really don't mean it, Boscoe."

"How about a nice get together real soon that's what we all need, a barbecue. I'll buy a whole pig, have it dressed, and cook it over the coals myself."

"Nuts Homer, if I don't come up with a good case soon, I'll need a barbecue like it's the last thing on earth."

"You work too hard Boscoe."

"I'd bust my tail if I thought I could nail you right."

"Hey Boscoe, what do you hear of so and so and what is whatchamacalit doing these days?"

"Gonna get you some information on some big stuff real soon, Boscoe. Gonna put your hand in the mash. You're rough Boscoe, but I can't help likin' ya."

"Nuts."

"Hey Boscoe, how about droppin' by Monday right after dark?"

"Nuts, if I wanted to hit the jackpot I'd be here tonight with a shovel, like you say, and I got a goddamn good mind to stake out your ass by myself, and catch you doing something or other."

"Now ya know Boscoe, I carry a big roll and a 38 and git skittish off at night, and it wouldn't do any good for you to get plumb on my tail. I'm clean."

"I agree Homer, you're clean all right, clean nervy."

"You better find something better for me to do or I'm gonna spend my time working on you because I think you are hot as a goddamn firecracker, and as full of crap as a Christmas turkey."

Gallboy knew real turkey talk when he heard it. He talked hard and he convinced Boscoe that he should drop by the following Monday after dark. Boscoe did. Homer Gallboy had him a lulu of a distillery lined up and rode with Boscoe to point out from the road its approximate location in the woods.

Homer was right, the distillery was there. Doubt arose in Boscoe's mind and he reclassified Homer in his mind from a Christmas turkey to a loose goose. He didn't tell Homer that he found it.

As things sometimes happen---come forth with those great unexpected breaks which frequently occur in law enforcement; a Federal undercover agent was at work diligently in another area and in full confidence of the gang he was secretly working with. He said of it. What I heard there was enough to "almost give myself away, so great was my surprise."

The message was brief, direct, astounding and disappointing. What the U.C. man learned from one of his cohorts was that Old Homer had sent word to the gang that Boscoe the Federal man had told him he had found the distillery while flying in an airplane. Also the Feds planned to work it to the hilt; that it would be better to drop the whole operation.

This was the same distillery Homer himself had told Boscoe about.

As a token of appreciation for an unknown doublecross it was told that the gang chieftain sent old Homer Gallboy a substantial down payment on a new car.

When word got to Boscoe of the two–handed pitches tossed by Gallboy he didn't rush in and blow up the distillery, but staked out a party of investigators at discreet distances from the plant.

There is always the matter of temptation at hand to remove some valuable and hard–to–get equipment from a distillery. Most operations are valuable.

Boscoe figured that such a thing would be attempted and let the plant sit a while to cause doubt in the mind of the distillery operator as to the reliability of Gallboy's communication.

Boscoe was certain that someone of the gang had seen Virgil's plane in the area. Gangs like that have a way of taking plane numbers and having them identified just like automobile license plates.

It was now Boscoe's turn to swell up the turkey for all it would hold. He slipped by old Homer's place with one of his buddies as a witness and observer.

"Hey, Homer, you Bastard, you did it again."

"Whaddya mean, Boscoe, I told you the still was there, didn't I?"

"Yeah, that's what you said, but it ain't."

"It gotta be there, a man seen it. Said he had his hand in the mash."

"He's goofy as hell. We combed those woods and all we found was a little old twelve barrel plant about two miles from where you said the big one was.

Homer, someone's taking you for a sleigh ride. Come on over there tonight with us and we'll show you or you show us one."

"Hell, no, I don't want to get mixed up with those guys."

"Keep handing us that kind of crap, you're going to get mixed up with us in a big way for giving false information."

"Gees, Boscoe."

"Homer, why in the hell do you want to keep sending old Boscoe out on wild goose chases?"

"Gees, Boscoe, you know I wouldn't do that. Got a big one coming up, no kidding, son–of–a–bitch runs it, got a new twist to it, all electric."

"Nuts, Homer, I'm through playin' cat and mouse. Gonna take a long, hard, narrow look right down my sights at that pussyfoot Virgil's operations. All the Moonies are hep to him, locating their stills and that crooked no good lying Diogenes Dinwiddie, the Constable is treading on soft ground."

"Boscoe, are you SURE that there's no still where I said it was?"

"Why the hell should I lie to you. If we found it you know damned well we'd be working it and I wouldn't be futzing around here."

Homer is pulling at his jaw as though it is a wad of bubble gum, his color is somewhat pale and he is visibly upset.

"Homer, I'm gonna put the squeeze on Virgil. You know damned well he's the guy who told you about that still."

"What difference does it make Boscoe who told me? You want information, don't you?"

"Exactly so, but I don't won't that tail walking, nothin' to it, crap you hand out. You don't have to tell me anything. You are the one who is always sending for me, and asking me to drop by."

"Gotta have a barbecue. Tomorrow night. I'll get a pig, some chickens, and I'll get me a cook to cook it for us. Get everyone here. Have fun, relax."

"Great idea Homer, make it real hot, red hot and saucy, you hear?"

"Yeah Boscoe, a whole pig. Yeah, a whole pig, red hot, you get that Boscoe, red hot?"

"Yeah, Homer. Good and greasy."

"Yeah. Boscoe."

"Yeah, then stick it. So long Homer, you lyin' son–of–a–bitch."

"Hey, Boscoe, don't leave."

Homer rushed to his mirror and tugs at his chin like it was a hind–tit. Somebody gotta blow that damned still up, or things will look bad for Homer if they don't look that way already.

"Bitch Boscoe, bitch, bitch, bitch." This time Homer doesn't shake and shudder all over himself, he stomps, gnaws on his fingers, cusses his ex–wife, and looks at the bars securing the back windows of his store. For the first time in his life he cries. That's because he doesn't know what else to do.

He walks to the window and looks at his brand new car outside. He locks up the store, gets in the car and drives over to his ex–wife's house.

He knows her new husband is in jail, where Homer's information has placed him. He calls her to the yard, and when she approaches his car he speaks softly to her until he can get out of the car.

Uncertain, she stands off a little distance from him, but he lunges at her, slaps her hard across the face and screams, "Bitch, bitch, bitch." He throws a roll of bills on the ground at her as she cowers. He drives to his hideaway tunnel, opens the trap door, and makes his way into the cabin. He spends the night sleeping on the floor.

When he wakes up he can't get up enough nerve to open his cache. He doesn't want to see it. He is sick.

He hears a car drive up outside, and voices close by, and the command to "Come on out, Homer." He freezes where he is, screams, "Bitch, bitch, bitch." Homer takes the '38 from his right pocket, pulls violently at his jaw with his left hand. He opens his mouth, and with his left hand holds it open, and with the revolver barrel against his palate, he shouts something that sounds like "Bllith, bllith." The gun goes off, and Homer too.

Boscoe turns to his associates and motions. They break down the boarded up door and walk inside. Boscoe says to nobody in particular, "It's funny, but Homer's old lady was the best thing he ever knew. He had ordered her to play up to that moonshiner for information and it backfired. He's got a tunnel around here someplace."

They searched and opened the trapdoor, and when Boscoe saw the septic tank cover below he lifted it up. He flashed his light down inside, and whistled.

"Holy Cow, that guy wasn't kiddin' when he said 'Come around with a shovel, dig it up.' What he really meant was a wheelbarrow."

"What are you gonna do now, Boscoe?"

"Make three phone calls. One to the coroner, one to the District Supervisor, and one to the whatchamacallit County Sheriff's office and report in a disguised voice that still Homer was talking about—–to keep the whole shebang guessing."

"Yeah, we gotta keep that gang guessing, Boscoe."

"Get out your pencils and papers, we're gonna count this money down to the very last dime and list every bill and denomination. Uncle Sam will want it for taxes, you bet."

At Homer's funeral parlor there weren't many visitors. A few curious moonshiners were there mostly because they wanted one last look for sure.

A woman with a black eye was there wearing the first new complete outfit that Homer's money had ever bought for her.

She heard a moonshiner say, "Nobody'd believe what that son–of–a–bitch did if you told them."

"Hell no, he'd a been in his grave a long time ago if he tried that stuff twenty years ago."

The woman smiled and walked out. At the door she said, "Evenin' Mister Boscoe." Boscoe tipped his hat, and said, "Evenin' Mrs. Gallboy." He turned to watch her skip sprightly down the steps to the taxi waiting for her at the curb.

Let us deliver all good enforcement men from the attentions of an intoxicated informant who wants to report his whole family, his wife's family and everybody but himself, for breaking the codes of gangsterland, citizenship, and what have you.

If you do not heed him, and he is just high enough to know somewhat of what he is doing you might miss out on something, but the odds do not favor such.

Such a guy can wind up, (a) passing out in the back seat of the car if you bother with him. (b) Messing up the inside of your car by any of several personal biological channels. (c) Get you in trouble in a number of ways such as insulting women encountered in public, challenging strangers for fights, tell everyone nearby that you are carrying a gun, and if he has told you anything of value double back and tell the operators he saw you snooping around their operations the next day.

Once though, I received a call from a guy who was neither high nor drunk, but at best did not have much more thinking capacity than a drunk in a number of areas.

"Hello. Hello. This is Herman Werman."

"How are you Herman?"

"Fine, I got some information. Meet me in Slabover in thirty minutes."

"That's forty–five miles from here."

"Drive a fast car."

"How's so and so's leg doing?"

"Took that cast off last week."

Now I know there is a possibility of something of information, as old so and so did have a cast removed from his leg last week. I arranged to meet him in an hour and a half, or one–thirty a.m. so to speak. We meet at a lonely country intersection at one–thirty some forty–five miles from my home. There is just the two of us. I follow his car up the road and he parks it and joins me in mine. He is going to show me a distillery he found earlier in the evening.

"Gotta long walk to it."

"Okay, where are we going to park the car?"

"About a mile from where the still path takes off from the public road."

"Pull in down here, I gotta say something first."

"Okay."

We pull into the woods path, deep into the woods and I park at a turn around place. We light up cigarettes.

"This is a lovin' up place."

"That's not what you called me down here to tell me at this time of night, is it?"

"Nope. Just familiarizin' you with the territory. Gotta nice gal in here tonight about seven o'clock myself."

"Look, I believe you. I know the territory better than you do, so let's get down to business and go to that still."

"Gotta tell you something."

"Go ahead."

"Bad gang. Got one picked out for me, gotta go, if we run into 'em tonight just lookin' around, I'm gonna kill one with my bare hands."

"Okay, now what gang is operating the plant, how big is it and where is it?"

"Come, I'll show you."

We set off through the woods, sloshed through two branches, and came to an open field.

We crossed the field at the edge of a vehicle path.

"Keep to this side, there's a deep sand quarry on t'other side." I was seized in a bearhug of almost super strength and I finally managed to tear my aggressor loose.

"Lights acomin', save me, them guys will kill me."

"Lights where? Take it easy damnit, you brought me out here."

I looked toward a curve in the road and saw a reflection of lights on some high trees.

"That car is on the road. Now about that gang, they probably will be coming in from the other way, and anyhow that car is a mile away," I said.

The informant pointed out a huge tree top outlined against the sky straight in front of us which no doubt had it's roots in a bottom-land.

"See yonder tree?"

"Yeah."

"The vats are under that."

"Good, I'll take a look. You stay here in the weeds if you want to. Keep down, nobody will see you, and if they do maybe it'll be the one you figure gotta go and you can jump him.

"Don't leave me, don't leave me."

I didn't leave him, something told me not to.

I heard the sound of tires on asphalt some distance away and I looked in the direction of the sound and saw carlights set on high beam. The car was moving fast. My informant followed my gaze and left me forthwith, and literally flew in terror, across the vehicle path. I heard a scream and I didn't know what to think.

My mind went to what he had said of the sand quarry and I set out to find him.

I traced him by his moans from somewhere below.

When I found him he said, "You got me, I didn't tell nuthin', honest I didn't."

As far as he was concerned he was in the clutches of some imaginary gang, and I threw my light on his face and on his clothes. It was apparent that he had bellywhoppered most abrasively from top–to–bottom of the sand bank lining the quarry. It was a good distance down.

I was happy to learn that aside from bruises and blood on his face that he had no broken bones.

"You okay, now? It's me, damnit, stay with me and we'll find that thing."

"No, they're gonna get me, I'm a marked man, and I don't want them to get me down at that still."

"Okay stay here, I'll go down and locate it."

"No, please don't leave me alone."

Something in his voice indicated clearly a strained alto. Too alto for a man as big as he was. I flashed my light into his face, and took my handkerchief and washed the blood from his face. I noticed the long eyelashes, the not too heavy, silky eyebrows, and I involuntarily exclaimed, "Holy Gees."

It was the first time I had seen the informant's face with any kind of light at hand, other than a cigarette match, and I knew I wasn't to go to that still that night. The face I saw was that of a big kid, almost sixteen years old, and a juvenile who had no business out scouting at night for whiskey stills.

I took him back to his car and asked him to tell me the truth, who he was, a few routine things about himself and why he called me.

He said, "I weren't lyin' about that lovin' back there. I had this married gal, says she's forty–five, and she told me her old man doublecrossed her and she wanted to get even, and that she had seen some mash boxes he had, and why didn't I call the Federal man."

"Did you see mash boxes?"

"Not rightly, but she did and we got close to them, had a party down that way just before sundown. Say, can we go into Slabover and have a cup of coffee together?"

"No, here's a buck, go by yourself, you know the all night place."

"Sure do," and he named it.

I flashed the light on his face which had oodles of scratches and some with blood clots from his fall, and I told him, "First place, you don't want anyone seeing you with me because they will figure you for an informant––second place, around there they think I'm rough enough as it is without walking into a place with you the way you look. You look beat up something awful."

"Feel okay?"

"Sure do."

I left the boy at the edge of Slabover, and headed for home. The next morning just before dawn, I checked the place beneath the trees that he had pointed out.

I was glad that I hadn't gone down there poking around in the dark of the night before. I saw the boxes, plenty of them.

I didn't lift the covers to see what was inside. I didn't have to. I could hear those bees buzzing before I got near them.

What that gal had seen was literally and figuratively a beehive of activity, but not the kind I was interested in.

SIXTEEN

POTPOURRI

In some of the reflected moonbeams descending from the moonshine arts, there occur flashing moments of glee, humor, sadness, work and play and all of the things which produce the sparkling broth of life from the heavy potage of it all.

I will tell you of some little images I saw vignetted thusly through the oval center of a specific time and place, and of the sounds and stories echoed there.

One night I had the privilege of not being busy, and of being able to remain at home. I took delight in that and invited some workaday friends to come over after supper.

My telephone rang just as the guests arrived. I excused myself and answered the phone.

"Hello, Mr. Race."

"Hi! Oh, hi, William."

"Hi! I just come from a still. Operatin' and the workers there."

"Great."

"They got a car down there too. I been watching them the past couple of hours."

"Good. Did you get the license number of the car?"

"No. Want me to?"

"Sure. You betcha."

"Okay, I'll get it."

"Where do you want to meet, William?"

"Kuyver's Crossroads, behind the church, in the woods."

Yeah. See you about nine–thirty. Be sure and get that license number——they might finish up in the meantime."

"Yeah, and bring some more help too."

"Yeah, okay."

"Hey?"

"Yeah."

"Bring that car speaking set."

"Yeah, I'll bring the walkie talkies too."

"Attaboy. See you along about nine–thirty. In the meantime while you're driving down, I'll slip on down into the woods and get that license number. You gotta move right smart if you'll be here by nine–thirty. Get the help, too."

"Don't worry, won't have to go far. Got one of the ABC boys, Al, here now with me but he's dressed up like a country preacher."

"Okay. By now."

"So long."

Al didn't say anything when I came out to the living room from the hall where the phone was. Louise, his wife said, "I knew it. I knew it."

I looked sheepish I guess, and forced a smile. "One cooking, plenty of meat there too. Good report too, Constable's a bearcat, and he just came from it. You ready, Al?"

"Yeah, Race. Gotta change my clothes."

"Me to," and I headed for the bedroom closet where I kept my work greens, boots and all my gear.

We kissed the girls goodby and even though they wanted to call us a crazy pair of jokers they said the same words they always said as a last thing, and as a reminder——"Be careful." We said, "You betcha" and left.

We walked out the door and drove over to Al's place. He changed his clothes in sixty seconds flat, and we were on our way to Kuyver's Crossroads Church and an evening spiritual service almost but not quite, all our own. I fanned the Offenhauser Ford but good. We made it by nine–thirty and found William waiting.

William briefed us. The still was next to a swamp. The flush man would have to go in from the backside through the swamp. Might be noisy. Three or four down there. The car had left while William was watching.

"Did you get the license number?"

"Sure did."

I opened the door of William's car to turn the inside light on. I took out my notebook.

"What was the number?"

"Can't remember. Was in too much of a hurry before they might see me. Got it as quick as I could."

"Gees. Okay William, maybe we'll nail it in the stillyard."

"Not that number, no sir."

"Why not?"

"Got it right here under the seat, got it just like you told me to."

William reached under his seat and pulled out the license plate and handed it to me. "Thar tis."

And sure enough it was, and that wasn't all.

William smiled. "Seein' they had no use for them I took the bolts too."

The same night William provided us with another real vignette and showed that he took things truly literally. He was a good worker and willing.

The outfit was in operation when we walked toward it in the dark, down in the woods toward the swamp. We noted that the car was not there just then, so we made our plans for the raid. It went off okay.

I was talking to a prisoner when we heard the car coming through the woods. We had to move fast. It was close.

"Sit tight on this guy, William." I gave him the prisoner whom I had known for some time, and I ran toward the approaching car to intercept the driver.

There was a hullaballoo up on the path when the guy did not want to stop, but he finally did. We walked toward the still. Halfway down the footpath William spoke out. He said, "Mr. Currins, I had no trouble from this fellow, sittin' tight on him like you said."

"Holy Cow," I exclaimed, after I flashed my light downward.

William was sitting on top of the prisoner who was face down, and said, "This feller warn't goin' nowhere with me sittin' right there on top of him. Fool asked me for a cigarette and I been figuring out how he could smoke it anyhow laying squat down like he is."

"Damn," the prisoner almost shouted, "am I glad to see you, Mr. Currins, this feller is pure hell." It didn't help any that William was six feet tall and weighed two hundred and twenty pounds. The prisoner, soaking wet, would be about one hundred and thirty five.

The car carried no license plates. The driver was puzzled when I asked him about it. He said, "Damn, I mighta got caught with that load of liquor I took over to town tonight."

"Yeah, and you would have screwed us out of a nice case too."

"That's the least I got to worry about."

I will tell you now of a situation which I have often pondered as being worthy of being told as a tale, and I certainly think it is. It is something out of farm, forest and fireside.

One day I was talking to a man who lived in the city but had a small farm where he could visit on weekends as a retreat place.

He said, "I have decided to fix up my country place so that it will have all the comforts of home for me on weekends."

I thought it would be nice to have a place like that. The setting was right and it was not too far from town. There was plenty of space for horses, a nice lake for fishing, and plenty of grounds around for hiking; and just about anything a fellow in retreat from the city could wish for, except for one thing maybe.

The farm was situated on the fringe of an area long known for its quantity of moonshiners, but which had actually lost more of its moonshiners than reputation.

He was that kind of a guy who says, "Live and let live," so I did not even imagine him giving any information about moonshiners to me. In fact, he didn't even take a drink. He was a guy who saw real life on any horizon and the moonshine horizon was no different. He told me of a situation after I had observed first hand some introduction to the incident.

"You mentioned about these two guys being up the store for lunch the other day, and what followed."

"Yeah."

"Well, you know I'm having that tobacco barn converted into a small weekend cabin, so to speak. Got two floors, sort of a den on the first floor with a kitchen. On the second floor I have a nice bedroom and bath combination. Using paneling and want to keep the thing rustic."

"Yeah, sounds great, and with a lot of originality too."

"Well, I had this plumber working on the bath upstairs, and that day he went to lunch up at the country store."

"Sure, of course."

"Well, while he was up at the store he saw a couple of

moonshiners whose names you've told me. Don't matter none. But anyhow they asked the plumber what he was doing in those parts. The plumber was truthful and said, "I'm putting a bathtub in a tobacco barn."

I happened to be on the other side of a row of shelves at that time and I had taken it all in. I knew those guys to be anything but timid or docile.

I almost dropped my cola drink and moonpie when one of the guys said to the plumber, "You're a smart S.O.B. If I wanted a stupid answer, I'd have asked a stupid question."

For those who know little of tobacco barn architecture, it is a place where tobacco is cured late in July or early August.

For many years the tobacco barn in the bright–leaf belt of North Carolina has been something of a log cabin of considerable height and narrow longitudinal dimensions. It had a door at opposing ends at ground–level and no windows. Usually there was an upper door too. It had an overlapping sheet metal roof.

A metal flue system and a firebox, both easily removed, completed the tobacco barn with high rafter points from which tobacco was hung. By utilizing the height, a second floor could be installed without great trouble.

Rows of logs grooved at each end were placed on top of each other and mortar chinking was placed between the open spaces to make it air tight and heat–escape proof.

During the curing season, oil fires, wood fires or even coal fires were ignited in the fireboxes and the tobacco was exposed to the heat ascending in the metal flue system.

Today, metal barns, and portable barns on wheels are fast, if not almost completely, replacing the log tobacco barn for the curing process.

The log type barn lent itself with its native and easily procurable materials to the rural, economy–minded situation existing everywhere in the early thirties and forties.

However mirthful, it was easy to see why the moonshiners thought that the plumber was being too smart in the truth. Knowing something about tobacco barns and their utility, it is normally a hell of a place to suggest the installation of a bathtub.

In analyzing the routine situations when it comes to moonshining, sometimes it makes it hard to make something of the whole cloth. In such, I believe there is much which creates the tendency of people to side with prohibition.

For several days a long time ago, I was engaged in an all–out assault on illicit whiskey stills in a prolific area. Everyone in our office from Charlotte to Washington was in full agreement in that it needed drastic attention because of the great production and sale in the area compared to those in other parts of the state. We decided to saturate; to seize and destroy.

As a starter we obtained a Coast Guard airplane and a two–man crew. It was a small plane. The pilot and one of our personnel would fly over known violation.

The plane mechanic stayed on the ground with others from the ATU, ABC men, Constables and Sheriffs too.

They call those planes beer buzzards, and believe me, sometimes I wondered if a plane hadn't gotten some kind of a jag on as we flew over creeks at tree top height and looked down at a violation. It seemed to want to dip right down into every stillyard.

The pilot was usually from a search and rescue crew from Elizabeth City. He would be familiar with the worst antics of the sea and the problems it created for unfortunates at sea in all kinds of craft in all kinds of storms. Gees, those guys could fly, believe me, and they flew slow poke planes too.

Anyhow, to make a long story short, we found ourselves, the two of us up there, looking at stills and signs of stills galore.

We used axes in those days to destroy the moonshine plants and what I saw up there that day looked to me as a full week's hard labor without quitting, in "busting up."

Later that day, I took to the ground with a demolishing crew of two other axe swingers, and we went at it over and over again.

The beer buzzard was using another spotter. It would contact us on those World War II walkie talkies that sounded more like aggravation all the time than intelligence.

It was summertime and after a couple of real busy years my arms were about as big as my waist. My neck, where it joined my shoulders, looked as though it belonged to one of those bull–necked, paunchy characters they always used with the short hair cuts to portray a mean German in the movies.

All of us on the job were skinny waisted, and could put away some kind of meals when lunch or supper time came.

For breakfast though, I had coffee and cigarettes, myself.

Despite being physically fit, I was tired as hell when I got home from that area where we were busting one still after the other.

The locality was not far from a town with a mayor who portrayed himself as being progressive. He had said to me more than once some things which said that he was not a real Southerner, and he wasn't.

What the mayor really said to me that amounted to anything more than all the rest he said was, "You are persecuting my town."

It was almost funny the way he came out with it. I had stopped off with a couple of other guys and had a cup of coffee at the local restaurant. We were pooped. I was driving a car.

We came to an intersection and I was waiting for the stoplight. It was around seven–thirty at night and was not quite dark yet.

The mayor ran over to the car and all but put his head in my lap through the open window.

"Wait!"

I pulled over and invited him to get in the back seat. He did. The guy in the back made room.

"Mr. Currins, you're killing the economy of this town and I don't like it a bit. Washington will hear of this."

"You mean the way we played hell with the moonshiners around here the last few days?"

"Yes. How long do you intend to keep it up?"

"As long as we can find anything which is in violation of the Federal law."

"What's on your mind?"

"You are a government employee you know, and you can't go around doing anything you want to."

"I'm taking the government's money to do it, and that's my job, and if you ask me, you have one hell of a way of interpreting Civics if you went to high school."

"It isn't Civics."

"You wouldn't call it morals, would you?"

"No, not exactly, but things like the churches and people who vote."

"You know how it is."

"No, I don't know, Mr. Mayor. I don't know at all."

"If Washington didn't like it and you were transferred somewhere else you might know."

"Nuts, I've already lived in more places than you have or ever will. Don't push me. I might take it that you are saying that you will have me transferred in reprisal for what I have been doing around here this week."

"Maybe so. Maybe so."

"Well, kiss my foot and goodby, and good luck in Washington, and look for me up in that buzzard about light tomorrow. I'll get every one of them, every single one. Might even write your name on a few."

"Don't get excited," he said, as he was half–in, half–out of the car. "It isn't me. It's the merchants, you know."

"I know damn well it is; merchants like some sugar sellers, like Mason jar dealers, like merchants who depend on prompt payment from credit customers when the stills are at full blast and like merchants who don't get paid when the stills are smashed."

"You said it, I didn't."

"You're doggone tootin' I said it and you didn't. You can tell them I said it, and that I quit blaming prohibition on morals a long time ago."

I dropped him, and took off and went right through the red light at the intersection after I looked to see that nobody was coming.

I was hoping he'd have me arrested for it but he didn't. Civic pride don't have much to do with a lot of people who've got an axe to grind but none to swing.

Legends seemed to be steeped out of the potpourri of those things closest to home. With the moonshiner there are things his opposers had better beware.

They are not difficult things to cope with, particularly in the southern mountains which have lurked in the beyond while other places went ahead in everything except propriety and morals which come from the heart.

Mountain men do not like to be handcuffed. Mountain men consider a word as good as a bond and the mountain revenooers consider it such. The mountain men at least of yesterday, would be obliged to see a man caught forthwith if he violated his word as his bond.

Some mountain men in the past have sincerely believed in the physical and occult powers of a woman at a certain time of the month to be able to destroy mash in even its most vigorous form of fermentation.

High heel marks on the ground, or the scent of perfume or rose sachet, or a real small barefoot imprint in the mud could mean a more vicious challenge at hand than ever met a Revenooer in a stillyard.

The same men felt that horses were clean and that horse manure added to a fine mash would produce great liquors in a hurry. They believed that lye, lime and other things, some with cause and some without, would have good effects upon their manufacturing processes.

Some men believed in things like the moon and the tides, as things to be reckoned with in high–distillation.

A lot of those men too believed that a pig, or a hog, killed in the light of a certain moon would yield almost total fat and no meat.

Some believed in dreams and interpreted them in whatever fashion applied to the next day's events. Whether they were caught or made money, fell in love, or beat up the old woman. That's been from out of the long, long ago, of course.

Once I had a moonshiner tell me that the night before, he had dreamed of money, and that when he looked it up in his dream book it meant "Revenue Officer and poor luck coming," and that he was sitting there waiting for us to come.

He couldn't explain why I had to chase him on foot for a quarter mile before I caught him. I told him that any money he had or dreamed about could be put to better use by paying his fine or spending it.

The worst mess of porridge ever served up to moonshiners or even non–moonshiners was in the nineties. (1890's).

From the records I have read it looked as though nobody was actually ever caught " 'stillin'." I will quote you from a few incidents as charged. I think these are dillies and what's worse than that is that they are true.

I am quoting closely on some items from the records of a United States District Court from the 1890's.

The charges in those records are not much different in their wording than those of today in many instances.

The ways and means of prosecution, the conditions and the words out of mens' mouths meant more; so did the character of some men and the character expected from other men, which tended to establish their guilt in the light and color of any formal proceedings.

It was obvious that then there was plenty of illicit whiskey being made and sold. The advertising media of the day, being mostly word and mouth, had to point directly to those who made it and those who sold it if there was to be any commerce in the product at all.

It is probable that the court took such a view in interpreting the guilt or innocence of a defendant.

It was easy as hell to put a competitor on the spot if he was getting too big for his breeches. Somewhere in all of it, the illumination of it escapes from beneath what seems to be a closed door until one speculates what might lie beyond it.

I quote to ye now from Federal Court records of the 1890's:

Affidavit--9-5-96

U.S. versus William Yates

John M. Pugh, witness stated that in company of Deputy Collector Moffitt Cranford he went to a blockade still which was being operated in Month of March, 1896 near Sandy Branch.

When we came in sight of the still we secreted ourselves about fifty yards from the still. Saw William Yates stirring the beer in the still with a still swab. The still was on the furnace and fire under it. We ran up to the still and captured it. Yates and another party ran off. There were several stands of beer there also.

Sworn to and subscribed before me--9-5-96

Oran Hanner U. S. Commissioner

The violation was described by witnesses in March of 1896. The affidavit was made on September 5, 1896 or close to six months later. The defendant was tried in December of 1897. Apparently the case had been presented at the May term of 1897 and postponed. Court connected fees for the May 1897 term for Yates were as follows:

Clerk's fees--May term--Ent. ret. & filing copies 25
May 26--Entering order for alias capias 15

June 9––Issuing alias capias 1.00
Total 1.40

December Term, 1897

Clerk's fees––Ent. ret. and filing copies ....=.....25
December 7––Entering nolle prosequi 15
Filing final bill of costs 10
Dockets Indexes––no jury trial 1.00
District Attorney Aycock 5.00
Clerks fees ....=................................... 2.40
Marshal 14.84
U.S. Witnesses 7.00
Total 43.74

In light of present day debates, criticisms, decisions and criminal court procedures, let us examine this record from yesterday with a view toward the real facts. My interpretation of the situation is as follows.

For some reason or other, citizen John M. Pugh had knowledge of the distilling operation of William Yates. Pugh could have been a well–meaning citizen, a natural enemy, competitor or customer of Yates. Pugh, for some reason, went to Moffitt, the Internal Revenue Deputy Collector, and reported the operation.

For purposes of expedition and simplicity, Pugh accompanied the Deputy Collector to point out the exact location of the distillery in the woods alongside Sandy Branch.

The two men watched William Yates at his illicit trade from a distance of fifty yards. They saw Yates stirring beer (mash) in the still, and they saw the fire under the still.

From the earliest days of moonshine hidey–go–seek it has been natural in such a situation for one man to place himself surreptitiously on the far side of the operation while the other approached from the opposite direction––and then close in––for at least one capture.

Pugh's affidavit says, "We ran up to the still and captured it. Yates and another party ran off."

The word "capture" in reference to the seizure of the distillery is not at all as incongruous as it may seem, in provincial language of the area, and in its usage at the time.

Annandale's Imperial Dictionary published in 1894 says of the word capture, "The act of making prize of something." The verb form "captured" was in almost universal use in the South in the case of raiding an illicit distillery. Now it is desirable to use the word arrest as to the initial prosecuting action employed upon a prisoner and the word "seize" in relationship to forfeitured distilleries, or contraband.

If Pugh was a competitor of Yates', or even a good citizen fearing reprisal, it is not likely that he would expose himself directly at the time of the raid, so perhaps it was the plan all the while to deliberately run the operators away from the scene.

Too, the transport of a prisoner would be difficult if he had no horse.

It would be natural enough in the course of the six months which followed the raid until the affidavit was signed for a number of things to happen. It is possible that the Deputy Collector, Moffitt, reported the whole matter promptly. There is a lag of some six months before the affidavit was made by witness Pugh, and the first recorded court action is shown in the May, 1897 term of court entries totaling one dollar and forty cents in cost. This was over a year after Moffitt and Pugh watched Yates and another party at work in the woods.

In all of it there is the notable entry in the ledger in the final decision for a nolle prosequi, or no prosecution paper which cost fifteen cents out of the total cost to Yates of forty three dollars and seventy–four cents.

Another affidavit given on June 4, 1896 reveals a bit of old timey woods drama which came to naught except in that the defendant chose to travel to other points to escape penalty, which seems rather severe.

AFFIDAVIT––June 4, 1896

Affiant states––he saw defendant whose house he lives two miles from just before Christmas 1894 at still pouring water into cooking tub–shoving up the fire under the still which was running–saw him toting wood to the still–saw him come there with a wagon. Have seen him carry off a keg of liquor from the still. Henry Perry was the stiller. Defendant lives about three hundred yards from still.

In the charge at the U.S. Court, the defendant denied the charges.

The defendant was convicted.

Costs were set at forty–two dollars and fifty–eight cents and the sentence was four months imprisonment and five hundred dollars fine.

The gem of them all; however, is in the following affidavit given on February 1, 1897 on an alleged offense occurring in September or October of 1895.

"I bought a pint of whiskey off the defendant at my father's corn shucking in September, or October of 1895. Defendant had whiskey at corn shucking for sale. I paid twenty or twenty–five cents per pint."

The next lulu of evidence given in an affidavit was dated March 3, 1897. It is suggestive of entrapment.

"Went to get some brandy for a Mr. Avery who was very sick. Defendant wouldn't take money, but I told him to take it (seventy–five cents) and defendant did but said that he 'wasn't charging anything.' I think it was last April, 1896, and the defendant said that he only had a half gallon but "I beg so hard he let me have one quart."

One unusual and more formal procedure recorded was as follows in another case:

"Went to defendant's house on March 1897 with search warrant. In company of Deputy Collector Troy, and H. F. Bray, Deputy Marshal. Searched premises of defendant and found one box of unstamped manufactured tobacco, and one keg whiskey under counter of defendant's store house. Whiskey and tobacco seized were turned over to Deputy Collector Troy."

An inventory record of one seizure lists the following: One cord wood––1 bushel meal––1 pack of malt––1 gallon cane juice.

I wonder what they did with "one cord seized wood?"

The affidavit in the same case given on May 20, 1897 almost two years after the alleged offense went as follows:

"In February of 1895, saw defendant at blockade still draw off slops and build up fire. In March or last of February 1895, saw him at another blockade still in Durham County near Ben Ellis's. Saw him draw off slops and making mash."

The defendant was convicted and received a six months sentence and one hundred dollars fine.

There is some humor in the commercial tactics attributed to defendant John Jordan in his practice of vending whiskey.

In the lineup of witnesses against Jordan, one witness said:

"I bought a dozen eggs and gave Jordan thirty cents, and Jordan gave me a pint of whiskey. I have also bought a pint of peanuts from Jordan for twenty five cents and he gave me a pint of whiskey. I saw others get peanuts and whiskey from him and pay him for same. He had the peanuts and whiskey in a wagon."

Another witness stated:

"I paid him (Jordan) twenty–five cents for peanuts at two different times and he gave me a pint of whiskey with each pint of peanuts. He sold me a pint of whiskey yesterday for twenty cents without the peanuts."

There was speedy action in that case on the latter charge. A notation at the top of the court page was "May, 1897––121st. year of independence of the United States."

Another blossom from moonshine flowerhood of seventy years ago is blooming in the affidavit given February 9, 1897.

"Bought whiskey by pint several times from defendant and paid twenty five cents a pint about last May or June."

Another witness said:

"I bought one quart whiskey from the defendant two years ago, paid fifty cents or let him have fifty cents worth of meal for the whiskey."

The defendant being sworn said:

"I never sold whiskey but let the witness have a quart two years ago and he let me have the meal. They never paid me for liquor but generally brought me trade for it. I never let George Morrison have any liquor except to pay back what I borrowed. I quit selling liquor about December 1894, and never had a license."

In 1896, the U. S. Deputy Marshals, as witnesses, were given six cents per mile for travel on horseback, and this was included in the costs of court for the defendant. The same rate probably applied to other witnesses. The court clerk and the District Attorney too, were paid fees in United States Courts.

In the Southern Court regions of Federal Courts in the nineties the volume of business was small and consisted of few criminal prosecutions among which were Postal Law Violation, Counterfeiting cases, Admiralty cases, and Land claims.

The Civil War found Southern federal judges resigning, and the Confederate judiciary was never completely organized in North Carolina. The Confederacy failed to organize a Supreme Court, and little attention was paid to Confederate courts.

The transition to federal courts after the War between the States was apparently a slow thing for the Southern population to fully accept.

It is more than likely that smouldering resentments burned to the core in some individuals engaged in law violations; and that because of this, the duties of federal law enforcement officers in the South were extremely hazardous and did not have the sympathy of the people.

When one considers that the first session of the Federal Circuit Court, convening since the beginning of the Civil War, was held at Raleigh in June of 1867, it is readily understandable that its full working level on a wholly acceptable plane would not be reached for many years. I believe that the view I have given through some of the vignettes in this chapter supports this. In no way have I attempted scorn or directed ridicule toward anybody in these pages.

What will one write of things now, seventy years hence?

I really feel that in the punishment dealt to defendants in the nineties, the judges, particularly in moonshine cases, were extremely severe in their sentencing. Fines of one hundred and five hundred dollars in the coin of that realm would indeed be enormous in comparison with the same purchasing amounts in today's currency.

The proximity of people, in all things, in sparsely populated rural areas of the South lent unspoken words to the knowledge of one's neighbors. Travel facilities made one stay at home almost all of the time, or within walking or horseback distance at most.

A judge before sentencing a man could learn of him from his neighbors and so could the man who arrested him.

SEVENTEEN

SOME CUNNING WAYS

There have been a multitude of guiles and examples of cunning, displayed by moonshiners in their operations. At stillside a good deal of such has been used in detecting secret visits by officers to the distilleries. Some things work and some don't.

The primary purpose of the officer is to arrest the violators and seize and destroy the distillery. It is not always possible, however, to arrive at the proper time and place for an arrest procedure.

The conscientious and alert officer will approach carefully the point where a distillery has been reported to him as being in operation. He will, also in seeking distilleries on his own, proceed with caution and carefully avoid being seen by guilty or sympathetic eyes.

Such a procedure requires full use of the senses, and a determination to be quiet and observing.

The sun's position, familiar noises from highway and bog alike and some particular preliminary reconnaisance tactics come into full play. Eyes trained for wide ranges of vision and to detect the slightest of movements on either side or straight ahead, and overhead and downward are needed to detect distillery activities unseen in the outdoors.

In the immediate vicinity of the distillery, or what might be called the stillyard, fancy footwork becomes of the greatest significance in the craft of a diligent officer. He must be exceedingly careful where he places his feet to avoid leaving tracks which a wily moonshiner will readily observe and depart forthwith forevermore. That chore is known as "lettin' 'em have it, but not me too."

"Lettin' 'em have it," however, is a final act with moonshiners and is done only when there is more than reasonable certainty that officers have discovered the plant.

In secret visits to a distillery the investigator is primarily concerned with the state of the mash, and he calls upon his experience to ascertain when the mash will become suitable for distillation. The presence of the operators will follow naturally.

It is amazing how this can be judged repeatedly and accurately. Such accuracy leads to consistent and additional arrests.

The enforcement man who has done this will be in the woods long before daylight and the appointed hour the moonshiners choose to enter the distillery yards for the task of running off the batch.

The officers will conceal themselves in the brush nearby, or behind suitably large trees at hand, and perhaps one will be up the road with a walkie talkie to forewarn of the moonshiner's entrance, either by foot, mule and wagon, or by car. Sometimes they come pushing a wheelbarrow load of one half gallon glass jars in anticipation of bottling the day's run.

Locating the distillery outdoors at night is a tricky business. If the operators are not on hand at that time, a preliminary survey of the immediate area or exploratory investigation is limited.

The best time to locate a distillery with the moonshiners absent is in broad daylight where full care can be taken, signs of foot traffic eliminated, possible escape routes detected, and the best places for concealment noted. One old trick in muddy places is for the officer to walk to the distillery in bare feet as the still hands tread barefoot.

The sight of a fellow officer with his shoes tied by their strings around his neck is something like this. He is playing skip–jack slowly, standing still at times, listening. His pants are rolled to his knees and his feet sloshing in oozing, stinking mud. He is putting one foot carefully before the other in the soggiest places to let watery action efface the pattern of his foot tracks.

Thoughts of one's self and that you are no different on the approach from the other side as you pause, listen for the right and wrong kind of noises, and look dead ahead for that first glimpse of the stillyard. You are sensing delicately the upper part of your legs so that you can feel the slightest resistance of a fine, weak thread which may be there, and strung out across all possible pathways leading to the distillery. The thread is an alarm system.

If you feel the thread against your leg you back–off, locate the thread and step over it. If you break the thread you search the ground for the broken ends. You squat and reach sometimes agonizingly outward to gather the ends without moving, to avoid imprinting the story of your activity on the muddy ground. You make a nice little knot and conceal it by tugging just a wee bit and easing the knot over into the foliage away from the open path. It works beautifully.

It is amazing how much the mind responds to sensitizing certain areas of the body so that it will respond with a forewarning. I have detected truly fine threads which seemed cobweb–like. I have done that on cold winter days and nights, with my leg areas while wearing long drawers and heavy corduroy trousers.

When an officer detects such symbols of guile it can be similar to hitting a home run in a baseball game. The operator tends to get a bit cocky and overconfident and gets taken in by his own guile. He becomes careless and is caught when a fast curve is tossed his way.

One wintry day I went into a general merchandise store in a small town in an area well known for moonshining. I had just fixed a flat tire down the road, and almost froze my hands while doing it. My gloves were worn, so I went into the store to buy a pair of cheap cloth gloves to wear in finishing my day's work.

The owner was waiting on a customer whose voice was familiar. The man had his back turned toward me and had not seen me. He was standing before a wooden box on the counter and with a hinged glass cover which was open. He held a spool of black thread aloft in the light.

"Gotta have it the thinnest littlest fellers of all. You know what I want it for. Fooled ol' Constable Jones ten times with them fellers."

I walked out of the store before the man turned around. Bought my gloves elsewhere. I headed straight for the branch in back of the man's house and found the still.

At dawn three mornings later, I almost chuckled aloud as I watched the same man at work at the distillery. I stepped out of the foliage when he had his back turned. I touched him lightly on the shoulder and said, "Tough luck Ol' Boy, Federal Officers, you're under arrest."

After the distillery was completely destroyed I walked in front of the moonshiner on purpose. My companion was behind the man and his son who we had caught too. I deliberately plowed through gossamer–like thread strung across the path about knee height. I had a mash smaple bottle in one hand and I stopped and turned to my partner and said real casually, "Reckon the commissioner's out of bed yet?" I eyed the moonshiner as he surveyed the ground and the broken thread.

"Let's go," I said, and we continued walking up the path, and through two more inconspicuous Clark's No. 20 telegraph lines strung uselessly across our route.

I never mentioned the thread to the moonshiner at all and at Federal Court he pleaded guilty. In the hall he said, "You caught me fair and square and I pleaded guilty like I was charged, now maybe you can tell me one thing now that it's over."

I said, "Sure, if I can."

"How did you fellers get down to that stillyard without bein' seen?"

"Just walked up the branch, that's all. You saw the hunting waders we had on, didn't you?"

"Well, I'll be doggoned. Fellers, you sure outsmarted me. I had three of the quietest little fellers watchin' that path all the time, and you slipped up the branch."

"You had young'uns out there looking out for you?"

"Well, I wouldn't exactly call 'em young'uns. Much oblige. I know who reported my outfit. Drop around my house about Thursday night along about eleven–twelve, and I probably will have something on him for you."

I did as he requested, and he told me of another man's still, and before I departed he said, "Watch out all around that place, he ties fine black thread all around it, even across the branch. Don't break none of it or he can tell if you been there."

"Well, I'll be damned, a feller learns new things all the time."

"You bet," he said jovially and probably in anticipation that his competitor would be caught despite his precautions of using fine black thread. He was right, too.

Often little actions are observed during an investigation and are seemingly unwarranted or unexplainable at the time. At later times they either clear themselves up or someone who has changed their ways long since will volunteer a solution.

Many years ago I heard of a moonshiner who had grown old with the reputation that he was uncatchable at a still by any of the local officers who also had the duties of serving legal papers, enforcing gambling laws and prostitution laws and other laws. They perhaps operated a farm as a chief source of income.

The moonshiner was not a big operator but maintained what might be known as a community nuisance. He made fiery stuff that was to be distributed in the toughest quarters. It was a great assist in keeping disturbances, cuttings and violence at a maximum.

He was truthfully a thorn in the side of the Sheriff, his deputies, and the constable from his area. The prohibition "feds" were busy stumbling over outfits such as this enroute to much larger violations. In their parlance they called such little outfits "piss pots." They had no time for small operators.

It was not so with Constable Jones or whatever his name was. Jones could not go anywhere without someone asking, "When are you going to catch ol' Charley Slard?" Jonesy had the stock reply to all, "Got plenty of his outfits, didn't I?"

"Sure, when somebody reported them to you, and practically led you to them like a blind man."

The constable was a proud man and rather honest too, and he fancied himself as a miniature FBI in his community.

He was no law man though, despite the pictures of himself in his uniform, which was a pair of overalls adorned with a huge badge proclaiming only, "Constable" scattered on the family piano, and all over the house.

In the language he had come to know from hanging around the county courthouse or being there on business, he did not seize a distillery, but he "captured" a still.

Whenever he "captured" a still, he would smash it with an axe, and drape the fire smudged copper utensil over his shoulder while spent mash dripped down his back. The county rewarded him with ten dollars for each captured still. With a thirty gallon copper still, smashed and slung over his shoulder, Jonesy projected an image which suggested an "on duty" consciousness within.

It was a feeling of anticipation for him on the ride back to town in his touring car with the top down, and the smelly captured still sitting square on the front seat beside him for all to see.

In the back of the car he had an additional remuneration in his official calling. This was whatever he could salvage as his own. Things like an axe or two, a grubbing hoe, short lengths of copper pipe and tubing, an oil burner here and there, and a battered and broken copper condenser coil. Sometimes he would take empty mash barrels, too.

The copper he could keep for himself as salvage, excluding the still. The county folks piled the still copper up in the basement of the courthouse, where it stank and grew to impressive size, in what used to be the judge's stable area.

Every six months the copper was weighed and sold "as is, where 'tis." Jonesy sold his personal loot once a year in an old cowshed on his farm where he stored it. The same man, Sam Jinks bought both piles and carried them to his junkyard.

Jonesy's favorite joke to visitors at his house was to take them out to the shed where he stored his loot and point out a series of seized hoes and say, "I never thought of it before but it do look like I'm a runnin' a ho house sho 'nuff." Glibb Williams said he'd heard Jonesy tell the story at least five times.

Jonesy never caught anyone when he captured a still and nobody cared. Ten dollars for the still, and five dollars for a piece of meat captured alive didn't provide any incentive for arrests.

Jonesy didn't consider that; his philosophy was "folks have a bad enough time of it these days without me making it any worse for them."

Jonesy did have a rough time with the town wags who chided him about a "one legged man who ran away from him on crutches." Whether it was true or not nobody really knew, but they wouldn't be surprised if one had.

Jonesy did want to get one man, and he tried hard to catch him. That was Charley Slard. The "nuisance apparater" as Jonesy termed him.

When I talked with Charley Slard years later he explained away all of Constable Jonesy's dilemma rather simply. "Shucks, 'twarn't nothin'—all I did was leave a bright shiny fifty–cent piece or two lyin' on the path like I lost it. I'd leave maybe a shiny brace and bit or a new hammer, and it got too much for old Jonesy. He'd pick it up, look around, take out his handkerchief and wipe whatever he'd picked up, and head for the still like a young 'un with a newfound toy."

Other variations on the black thread theme, to detect the visits of officers to distilleries, extended to battery operated, longwire controlled buzzing or bell systems. These were triggered by stepping on a board or device concealed underground.

Once in a New York garage used as a "front" or blind for an alky plant, the alarm system for a raid was to be triggered by a mechanic who completed the circuit of electricity at two terminal nails driven into the top of a wooden bench. The mechanic merely approached suspected visitors in a casual way, laid a wrench down so that it bridged the terminal gap and inconspicously sounded the alarm upstairs. On the occasion whence I saw it, it didn't work. The guy had to walk too far and made his motions obvious and he had no wrench or steel object in his hand.

We had the place surrounded. It made it easier without an advance alarm. The new nail heads were a bit too shiny on top of the grease smeared bench. We looked up into the underside of the bench and saw the wires and dry cell batteries. We told the man he was under arrest and he accompanied us upstairs where we put on the "flush" for a perfect score.

Another time I saw a whole wall swing outward on a pivot to reveal an alky plant in full swing. The blind was a laundry, and the transporter trucks were marked "laundry." They backed inside, and the outside overhead door was lowered, the inside wall was swung aside and the truck loaded or unloaded. Exit was made with the wall in structural position and for all that an innocent passerby could ascertain, it was just another laundry truck with a load of soiled or clean clothing. We caught five or six there.

The wall was a good job but was too new in appearance to be completely deceptive. We had some men enter through another door leading through an apartment upstairs and flushed that way. The thing was too easy to trace, and probably it wasn't put there to keep us out but to permit loading and unloading from a platform. It could have worked as a deceptive device though under other circumstances.

A well–trained dog is in theory a fine thing to have at hand to give alarm against intruders we all know. I have encountered many dogs who were supposed to be just that. I guess that it might be said that we encountered all kinds of dogs, but the lonely participation they had in the operation of the distillery seemed to make them lonesome for some attentive human companionship.

A soft voice, a kind word, and finally a friendly pat with a soft touch can do wonders to puzzle a dog. I have used that approach time and time again, and I have never been bitten while on duty. I believe it is about the only area of occupational hazard I have not experienced.

If you know dogs, you know that each dog is just about a distinctive little personality in itself. A little persuasion along the right lines is great, but alas if an intruder sets out with the wrong form of persuasion.

I will tell you of several incidents which I experienced while dealing with dogs on raids. In New York there was a violator with a great deal of cunning and a fondness for huge German Shepherds. It was natural enough for him to eventually think of these dogs in terms of still–security, and he did. He confined one in his distillery apartment as a guarantee against all intruders.

I visited the place with a policeman who really had a way with dogs. We had been tipped off about the dog in advance by our informant.

The cop said to me, "I'll bet you ten to five that I can have that dog either eating out of my hand or else he'll be hell and gone clean over to Third Avenue before he takes time out to bite. I've seen a couple of loose bitches in heat along the block the last couple of days and I'm sure that the dog will be more aware of it than I am."

I declined the bet because I knew of the cop's reputation for not considering dogs to be anything other than pets to be played with.

As it happened, the owner of the dog was in the violation premises. He was not engaged in active distilling, however, he merely had gone there to feed the dog. Ironic, wasn't it?

I went down the fire escape to flush or get inside if I could, and the cop stayed at the door. I saw the man and the dog inside and watched the man break for the door. I couldn't get in as the back windows were secured with stout and bolted iron bars.

I went back up the fire escape to the roof and then down the stairs to the top floor landing. The apartment door was wide open. The cop had his nightstick pointed straight out at the dog's nose and was speaking softly to the dog who was between the cop and its owner.

To the dog, "Nice doggie. Come here boy, easy, that's it."

To the owner, "You son–of–a–bitch you think you're smart. Call this dog off, you moonshiner, or I'll bust your nose when I get around this dog."

Me to the dog owner, "You better do what he says Mister, or else." Then the dog broke toward me and past me, downstairs and away to the queen dog of the block who was not far away.

The owner cussed out one dog and all dogs, and returned to civility at a prodding from the end of the cop's nightstick. I couldn't help laughing the way the cop had his nightstick in the moonshiner's face just like he held it in the dog's face, and he said, "One phoney move out of you Rover and I'll pop you good."

The cop laughed himself and the violator had to smile half–heartedly, and when the cop said, "I'll be a sunnavabitch; he keeps the dog here to guard the still, and he gets caught feeding him yet, and the doggone bow–wow runs away to tear off a piece and leaves him."

"I put the bars on the window too to keep you from coming in, the owner lamented and they only helped to keep me from getting out. No, today is not my day," the man said.

I guess that the best dog tale of all sort of takes a bite out of my own rear end as far as vanity goes. My partner and I had a nice still located in a house in New York. We had a consent from the moonshiner to search, and noticed as we entered the place a vicious looking bull dog. We seized the violation and arrested the guy, and he was to have his court, but good. He claimed illegal entry. His lawyer instituted a motion to suppress.

The assistant D.A. brought out the fact that if the man had chosen not to admit us he could have readily done so. All he would have had to do was to sic the dog on us which he did not do. The D.A. made much of the dog issue. Actually there was everything to support our case, observations, etc. and somehow I felt that the D.A. was off on a tangent with the dog testimony, but he was prosecuting and directing the questions. I was only a witness.

The defense counsel made much of the fact that the dog was described as a bull dog. He concluded, "Was it an American Bull, Italian Bull, or was it just plain bull?" He had his client produce a dog which appeared to be an undergrown chihuahua who quite intelligently or accidentally ran direct to the Ass't. D.A. and licked his hand when he patted it. Laughter was general throughout the courtroom.

I took a second look at the dog and I knew well indeed that I had seen the dog before. I knew where I had seen it too. It was in a suspected speakeasy just about twenty miles away from the premises in question and I recognized the dog as the property of the speakeasy owner. I tried to get the word to the D.A. but he had had enough of dogs for one day and my message went astray.

Later, in the courtroom hallway I saw the dog held on a leash by a woman. I bent over, patted the dog on the head, and read the identification tag on the collar. It was imprinted with the owner's name and the address of the speakeasy, and even included the apartment number.

The woman saw my half smile and offered, "Oh, that's where he (the defendant) used to live and she half smiled too. I went on to my next case.

The prize dog of them all, as far as I was concerned and the one which evoked the most mirth was an animal which had been described as a vicious thing, a dog to be feared alike by man and beast. His owner lived on the Carolina countryside.

It was the fondest hope of its owner that the animal would one day prevent his distillery from being raided, or even better yet, assist him in eluding capture.

As so many times the plans of mice and men go aft aglee, so do those of dogs and men. It might be better said that the plans which the man had for his dog did worse than that. They backfired completely. I first saw the brute as I was working my way toward the distillery through a particularly nauseous swamp which was over-endowed with briars and potholes to make foot progress slow.

I could see the man working about the distillery and the dog there too and it looked in my direction and spotted me. I stood stock–still. The dog who probably had wearied of trying to gain attention from his owner, came bounding off to where I was trying to move in the slop without making that sucking tell–tale noise of deep swamp travel.

I patted my thigh in a gesture of welcome while I was watching its owner through the foliage. The dog was wagging his tail a mile a minute and accepted my petting wholesomely, and he made not a sound.

One at a time I pulled my feet slowly from the mire and put them down with a careful motion until I was about twenty–five yards from the man whence he turned and saw me. He ran immediately and his dog after him and then me.

I came out of that swamp onto high ground in what I thought was fine fashion and set out in pursuit of the man. He was a racer, that was for sure, and he had gained on me considerably from his solid ground start.

I kept after him and I saw the dog bounding beside him and then cut across in front of the man putting a perfect block in his path. The two tumbled around and the man was having trouble scrambling to his feet. Before he reached full height I was upon him and placed him under arrest.

The dog showed a more impressive friendliness toward me than his master. The man looked down at my muddy shoes and my muddy pants legs and said, "You're a good 'un, gettin' a fast start in that swamp, but I'd a had you beat if that dog hadn't tripped me up." I acknowledged the likelihood of the fact in his statement.

He turned toward the dog and said, "Got beat by my own goddamn dog." He lashed out at the dog with his foot, and the dog went tearing away.

"Paid a hundred dollars for that animal and he messes me up. You want 'im you can have him." I declined the offer and when we drove away from the still, I saw the dog in the rear view mirror and the dog was running behind my car. I speeded up because his owner might want to get out and beat him.

We stopped up the road at a store for a soft drink, and the man told his story to the proprietor. "My own damdog," he kept saying. "I gotta give him away, or kill him one. You wanna dog?"

"Sure do."

"Then put up my bond for this case and I'll give you the damdog in payment."

I said, "That's a good deal, fellers."

The store owner allowed that it was. My prisoner looked at his soft drink bottle held at arms length straight in front of him. He appraised the bottle intently, and as if from far away, and said, "I ought to get something for my hundred dollars out of that damdog."

Dogs are not the only creatures beside man who can serve as alarming devices. Geese, mules, guinea hens, crows, goats and other things can serve well in the fashion of an alarm.

Some farmers say that guinea hens are the best. Others say that a mule is good, but a mule doesn't always fit the scenery of a time and place, in a house or a garage or other place. One farmer I know said that he could have a cat and a dog in his living room and that nothing could approach his place without him receiving some sign from one animal or the other.

He said that he watches the cat's ears and his movements and that the cat can pick off the noise of a car coming into the dirt road more than a mile from his house. "The dog," he said, "will pick the sound up much later and the dog will make more of what it's all about, so that you can figure it out for yourself by being alert to something stranger."

A cat–dog combination that must be watched all the time are not at all suitable in combination in many places, and certainly not at a moonshine still.

Once, I recall an amusing incident which took place near a fair sized outfit in the woods. It had just gotten dark when we approached the distillery area and fanned out. It was our third visit there.

One of our men was wearing a white hat. He laid it beside the distillery path a good distance from the stillyard.

I heard a harness jingling and a man issuing commands to a horse or mule and they were coming down the path to the distillery.

I squatted down low in some foliage not far from the path. A wagon load of moonshine was piled up in the stillyard and we had planned to arrest the violators just as they started moving the moonshine.

Another man who was concealed not too far from me eased over and joined me. Right then something went wrong with the flush man coming into the distillery from the other side. There was a hell of a commotion and all hands set out toward the distillery.

A mule in frenzied terror, rushed by me so that I felt a piece of flying harness strike me on the chest. I set out in pursuit of the man who had been guiding the mule. I could hear him beating the brush up ahead of me and I pointed my powerful flashlight in that direction. I waved it back and forth to cause a pattern of jumping shadows in front of him to slow him down. It did, and I was upon him.

I was escorting him to the distillery when the officer who had been near me emerged from the brush and asked, "You got him?"

"Yeah."

"Thought I had one too. I started to jump what I thought was the biggest sunnavabitch coming at me through the brush in the dark and I nearly tackled him before I found out that it was a mule or horse. It scared the hell out of me. Better go up along the path and get my hat."

"A white hat mister?" The moonshiner said.

"Yeah."

"Hell, that there's the thing scared the plumb fool outen my mule and me too in the first place."

"I hadn't thought about mules when I put that hat there. I left it there so it wouldn't give us away."

Some things work as planned and some work in devious ways which the best of planning cannot foresee, but any moonshiner worth his shadow in the moonlight is more than willing to take his chance on that.

One of the cagiest operators I have ever met operated a distillery for twenty–two years without detection. I first saw him as I was shopping for an alarm clock which were becoming scarce shortly after the advent of World War II.

As I left the store I looked across the street and saw a man placing a hundred pound bag of sugar into the trunk of a car. He went from the car to a nondescript store at hand and came out with another hundred pound bag and loaded that.

I went up the street a short distance to where my official car was parked and waited for the sugar car to pass me. I tailed the car from about one p.m. until eight p.m. over a circuitous route through the city.

The guy was an old man. He would stop every few blocks and enter a bar and remain a while, but not long enough to drink a beer. I figured that he was belting down short gulps of whiskey at each stop.

By four o'clock I was concerned that the man would pass out or have a wreck so I moved up closer to observe his equilibrium. He looked fully sober to me, so I decided that if he stopped again I would follow him into the bar and see what he was doing. He still had that car trunk loaded with sugar. Maybe he was peddling moonshine to legitimate bars, I thought, but I dismissed that idea too. A guy just can't corral the owner about something like that and do business that quickly in so many places.

I walked into the bar behind the man. The place had only a few customers, and my man walked straight toward the back of the bar and went into the men's room. I ordered a short beer, and when the guy came out of the rest room I gulped the brew and gave him a chance to get ahead of me.

I followed him, and had to stick pretty close with the late afternoon and evening traffic. He continued to stop at bars all along the way.

About eight o'clock that night when it was dark, the man pulled up to a brownstone private dwelling house uptown and drove the car into a garage under the house. I waited some thirty minutes and he did not come out.

I went to a house a couple of doors away, went upstairs and on to a fire escape ladder and through an escape hatch to the roof. I crossed over and tread lightly all the way. It was easy to hear someone overhead in those places and I didn't want to arouse any neighbors.

I paused before the chimney flue and took a good whiff. I smelled fermenting mash good and strong. Once more I had that good old feeling of holing up the mouse after playing cat and mouse all day long.

We watched the place, did some tailing, and wound up with a nice alky stache and the distillery too. It was a one man operation. From the looks of it, it had been there a long, long time.

I talked with the man I had followed and who was the only prisoner in the distillery seizure. He talked freely.

"How long have you had this still?"

"Twenty–two years."

"What?" I looked about the still room. "You didn't operate it all the time did you?"

"Oh no, sir, just when I needed some money."

"You went way back into prohibiton time then."

"Yes sir. Oh, I made plenty of money in those days, bought this house, always had a nice car."

"Didn't you ever think of getting caught?"

"All the time, and sometimes it seemed like the day would never come."

"How did you keep bouncing in and out of the alky market, and what was the longest period during which you did not operate?"

"About three years there for a while."

"I'll be dammed, if this don't take the cake. Have you ever seen me before?"

"Don't believe I have. I don't get out much, and stay by myself practically all the time. Oh, I had contacts from the old days, and I just seemed to know where to go."

I looked him over but good.

"Do you drink?"

"Quit twenty years ago."

"What?"

"Why in hell do you always stop at a bar every few blocks while you're out riding?"

"You been following me?"

"Bet your life I have."

"Oh, that, well I can't hold my water. I have a bag harnessed around me. Can't stand that for long at all, so when I see a bar and grill, I go to the men's room and sort of adjust things for a while."

"What caused that?"

"Got beat up bad by a couple of hoboes back in '22 when I was riding the rails from California to Texas and they pure beat the pie out of me."

The guy wasn't kidding either, they had.

EIGHTEEN

MULES I HAVE MET

With farms getting bigger and mechanized agriculture being the order of today in America, one of her stalwart creatures is fast becoming a mere legend memory, namely the mule.

If you have never been around mules perhaps you think that men are the contrariest creatures on earth. You have heard of the profanity of the "mule–skinner," that poor soul in army uniform of pre–World War II days. Those men were charged with the care and feeding of military mules, and their profession was recognized as the cussingest one in the history of mankind. The mule was the cause of it all.

The intensity of the profanity on the part of a mule–skinner was equal to the square of behavioral patterns displayed by the animal.

The condemnation of the mule has been opposed by the moonshiners of yore who valued it as a telltale watchdog with hearing far superior to any canine.

The mule is a hybrid "IT" which cannot reproduce.

Some mules I know for fact can have their sex, as well as women can who have had hysterectomies; as one gal I know put it, "They took the baby carriage, but left the playpen in."

I had always heard that the mule could not participate in sex until I saw it the first time. Hell it was the white chicken lays the white egg and the brown hen lays the brown egg thing all over again for me, being born and reared a city boy for all practical purposes.

I once heard a moonshiner say of one of his mules that she was a regular hussy when it came to some of the buck horses around his place.

The old time moonshiner found the mule to be company in lonely places where he fired up his stills and worked hard 'astillin' all day long. If anyone came around, friend or foe, the mule was sure to make a noisy signal of their approach, and many a man has escaped the clutches of the law because a mule "done told him that they were around."

I guess that in most places up North, the mule is practically non–existent. Their ranks are thinning rapidly in the South, but here and there remain some kind farmers or retired moonshiners who still love them and keep them as pets of nostalgic servitude days.

The mule was, and still is with us. I will tell you of some mule personalities I have known in my revenooer circuit years.

I have ridden mules, and my city ways predominate in my opinions about them. They try to plant their feet into the ground when they walk, like they were trying to stamp out cigarette butts or imitate a burlesque stripper's bump and grind promenade across a stage.

It hurts your rump to ride a mule if you are not used to it.

Once, speaking of mule riding, I told a guy about Lady Godiva and her horseback ride. It interested him and he said, "Hot damn, how long ago was that?" Talking of mules can end up with some peculiar subjects.

When I was out working on whiskey stills in the South, I dreaded the times when I would have to seize a mule as an item of forfeiture; to be later auctioned off by government order.

I had some unhappy experiences along that line, and so has every other revenooer who found himself on the leading end of a mule. I once heard a moonshiner say of a revenooer who got stuck with a seized mule and didn't know what to do with him, "We boys wouldn't take a gold silver dollar for that."

"He come around my place just before dark, and called me "Mister Dude," instead of "Dude" which was what he usually called me."

"Hello there, Mister Dude. Mighty fine day we're havin'. How's the crops? I trust that you and yours are doing nicely and tolable."

"What you got there on the end of that rope, Mr. Williams?"

"Isn't this here mule a pretty thang? Got beautiful eyes and nice big ears, she has. How'd you like to keep her and use her for free until the government sells her?"

"Nope. That ain't no mare mule nohow. That thang is a hoss–mule and a had–been IT."

"Just caught this animal over a liquor still. Takin' her in for the government."

"Whar' did you cotch that thang?"

"Well, if you caught her, dangit, IT, over at that place then I know those folks will be mad. You won't get nobody within ten mile of here to touch that flea bitten, blind, walkin' glue factory. Better climb up thar and ride IT back to town or carry it one."

What old "Dude" really didn't know was the trials and tribulations the revenooer would have before he could make the mule a part of his case, advertise it for sale, and then sell it.

It seemed to me that on all but one occasion that I was dealing with the more spirited type of mule. They would run away at my approach. I guess it was because when I was on the flush that I liked to whoop and holler and get the moonshine boys on the run in whatever direction they were looking. I could put life and spirit into the deadest of mules that way.

One moonshiner said that the smartest mule he had ever seen had gotten away from me and one of my buddies.

"That plumb smart mule untied hisself from the tree where I'd put him, right while those revenooers was a'raidin' and a'cotchin' us."

The one mule who didn't get away was really a beast of a burden to me. That poor thang didn't ever have anything at all, I don't believe. When I got up with it only a few teeth remained in the mouth cavity. It was blind, deaf and unfeeling. A young boy who was working at the still looked at me and smiled and said, "You gonna aress that mule too, Mister?"

That boy was going to make sure that we had to. It was tied with a long rope which had been twisted and knotted around a sturdy swamp oak.

"Can you ride that mule, Mister?"

"Look, I already told you that you didn't have to say anything, so keep quiet, will you?"

I unhitched the mule and tied it loosely, a good distance up the stillpath.

We set the dynamite for blasting the distillery. We lit the fuses and ran up to where the mule was tied and waited for the explosions. I counted the shots as they went off as I always did to make sure that no unexploded dynamite would be left. As I counted I watched the mule. That critter didn't even give one sign of hearing the noise which was in about twelve to fourteen separate set–offs.

My partner had more seniority than I had, so he said, "You look after the mule. Get someone to take him in and I'll take the prisoners over for arraignment."

"The hell you say."

I leaned on the mule with a lighted cigarette in my hand.

"I smell hair burning."

"I don't smell a thing."

"Mister you got your cigarette against that mule's hide. That's what's burning."

"What's this mule's name, boy?"

"Tell him Paw, tell 'em what you call it."

"Don't know son, never saw that mule, or that still either, before these revenooers came along."

"Paw, you know you call it "Motherhuggin' sunnavabee" all day long."

"Okay, okay. Now I'd like to make a bargain, fellers. I know how much of a job you fellers got on your hands gettin' rid of that mule, and I'm in sympathy with you on one condition."

"What's that?"

"Let me go, and I'll take that motherhuggin' sunnavabee with me."

"I reckon you would."

"Do it your way then. That's a killer mule, and the nearest gluepot is clean up Rocky Mount way. Have to pay to get 'em down here and take it away."

I said, "Take these jokers over and arraign them, and I'll get someone to house this mule if it takes me a week."

I took the mule by the rope and we started our bucolic oddyssey. I walked off singing, "Go long mule, don't you roll them eyes. You can change a fool, but a doggone mule, is a mule until he dies."

"Sure would like to accommodate you, Mr. Race, but you know how it is with them moonshiners. They're liable to burn down my barn if they know I got one of them revenoo–seized mules."

I did get the mule something to eat at about the fifth place, but that outfit wasn't at all anxious to have overnight mules, especially when they came from "Over Yonder" which we both knew the meaning of.

I remembered a forestry agency of one of the government branches. I knew there were several barns there and horses and mules too. I would make the official approach. I climbed on the mule and headed south wishing I had a camel saddle or at least a bicycle seat under me. It was dark when I reached the caretaker's house. I pulled out my badge and slipped my sidearm around where he wouldn't fail to see it. I knew that any rapport we had would necessarily be official.

"Good evening sir. I'm a Federal officer, and I have an officially seized mule I would like to lodge for the moment (the next three months would be more accurate) in your official stables."

"Glad to meetcha. You're the one they call Race. Is that one of them moonshine still mules?"

"It's a seized mule, seized for a violation of Federal Laws."

"That's one of them moonshiner's mules. I kin smell him."

"That is me sir, that you smell. I have been at a whiskey still."

I could see that his final decision was going to be, "And screw you too, sir, officially, unofficially and unsociably."

"I'm sorry. We can't take any chances with one of them moonshine mules."

"He's not gonna bite you, look."

I practically stuck my arm all the way up inside the mule's mouth cavity. He coughed when I took it out. I said, "See."

"Hell, I ain't afraid of any mule. It's the moonshiners. They'll set fire to all the woods around here over me keepin' that mule. Right now they're takin' bets all over the community that you will and you won't get rid of that mule."

"Lemme use your phone. I want to make an official call, long distance."

I called Regional headquarters. Somebody was still there. It was one of my old buddies working out of the district territorial office.

"You seized a what and can't get rid of it."

"A mule."

"Do I hear right, a M–U–L–E. Holy Cow! Couldn't the damthing hear, see, smell, feel or taste?"

"No, and there isn't a thing funny about it."

"Why didn't you hit him with a rock? Maybe you can make him

run away."

"Look, I have reasons why I'm seizing this mule. I'm gonna make a report on the wholething, so don't give me any smart answers."

"You want to put something in the report?" he said.

"Yeah."

"Put in there that I told you to blow smoke up his ass."

He hung up, and I had to laugh. I wondered why I called in the first place. I guess it was because I needed to talk to someone who might understand.

About nine o'clock that night I stopped at the house of the last guy anywhere who I felt would take the mule off my hands. He was notorious for his misdeeds and bad temper. He greeted me very cordially and asked me to stay to dinner. He volunteered to let me lodge the mule in his barn. I started to ask him what the hell it was all about, but I was afraid he might change his mind.

We put the mule to bed in the same barn with some of his prize breeding horses. I felt sad when I left the mule. I had always thought that no matter what on earth a person or thing was, that someone, someplace, loved he, she or it; and it looked like that ol' critter just didn't have any nice feelings at all directed toward him, her or itself.

I started to leave, and told the man that I would be back in a few days and see how the mule was doing and how he was making out with it. He made me promise him that I wouldn't tell anyone, anywhere, not even my wife, where the mule was stored, He even said, "I know it will take a couple of months to have him auctioned off, but just rest at ease. I'm the goldangest mule lovin' sunnavabitch in the whole world."

He kept the mule for almost three months and never complained.

I used most of a Saturday to auction the mule, and had to sell it to a drunk for seven dollars and fifty cents and throw in my favorite wrecking axe with it. As a bonus I told the drunk he could make a lamp of the axe if he was really handy.

It was only a few years ago that I learned positively that Sam Slard, my mule hospitality man had won over a hundred bucks betting that I would find someone who would house the moonshinin' mule.

I recall vividly a bout I once had with a mule and its owner. It happened on one of those balmy, spring afternoons which makes the sap rise, the appetite keen, and all the personal goodies aware that they are there for the purpose and satisfaction of the man creature.

It was one of those many times on beautiful days that I felt sorry for anyone having to work inside. It was the kind of a day that I wanted to share my world of birds and bees and flowers, and playing cops and robbers and getting paid for it.

It was the kind of day that revenooers want to cuss only blue jays, crows, and mules for snitching on them while they work. They are the watchdogs of any man's woods.

On that kind of day every creature in the forest works overtime toward the night time. During the big moons anything is liable to happen––to man or beast, and the whiskey stills squeeze their red hot innards to push out more moonshine.

The moonshiner thinks that the revenooer is out there somewhere far away. Maybe he is, and maybe he isn't. If he's there he is not thinking exactly the way the moonshiner thinks he is––spending every second of every minute of every waking hour figuring ways to capture him.

Hell, things being the way they are, the revenooer knows that he will catch the moonshiner sooner or later.

"Keep your ears and eyes open," the revenooer says, "and that's enough to catch the moonshiner, providing you have two fast feet and can run clear to Baltimore."

"Damn," he says. "That was a good looking babe over at the barbecue place yesterday lunchtime. Built like a brick outhouse, and no wedding ring. Lucky married guys on welfare, got all the time in the world. Can't mess with her though. She's a moonshiner's gal, and we just wouldn't be a good combination. Gees, the sap's risin' high in these woods." Fresh air is an aphrodiasiac. "Gees, if I ever am reincarnated I'm going to be a stud show dog and live in these woods around here. Right here in the country, taking nourishment and warm sunshine with every breath of fresh clean air and tall, straight pines havin' more sap than they know what to do with."

"There goes a fruggin' mule. Whinnying to beat hell. They must be coming in to take the moonshine out."

"Points one, two, and three, alert. Toddy time."

"Roger one."

"Roger two."

"Roger three."

"Okay Race."

"I'm gonna flush from the path. They have a mule and wagon on the way in for the moonshine. Give me eight minutes and I'll hit."

"Ten–four, one."

"Ten–four, two."

"Ten–four, three."

"Gonnagetsumass."

"Over and out."

I left my cozy place against the tree that I'd known most of the afternoon and walked across the swamp to the service road for the distillery and met head on the biggest mule I'd ever seen. It was pulling a wagon stacked high with cases of moonshine, and big John Ivytree was driving it.

"Whoa! You sunnofabitch."

I grabbed the reins near the bit.

"Giddyap, H'aaaaar, you sonofabitch. Giddyap."

John Ivytree slapped the reins hard down on the mule's rump.

A fellow who heard Big John describing the scene in the country store put it this way.

"There I was on a purty afternoon with the purtiest moonshine I'd ever made. Everything was working for me that day down in the swamp, and here come that big, crazy goddamrevenooer. The one they call Race. I was so close out of the swamp that I was counting my profits, and my mind was kind of cattycorner what with thinkin' of all the women I knew, and how it was the kind of day to slip away to a barn, or a motel, or leastways someplace quiet with a woman.

Man, my manhood was just a'sloshin' until I could get outen them woods, and here come that big sunnavabitchin' revenooer grabbin' my mule, and me tryin' to picture the better things in life."

"It warn't no fair cotch at all."

"You can say that again, feller."

"When do them revenooers find time to cotch up with their womanwork?"

"Damn if I know. They're always in the woods, day and night."

"Must kind of slip up, unnoticed like, on their women, they been so used to slippin' around on everybody else."

"You can say that again."

"You reckon they ever get any lovin' at all like the widder Flannergain passes out?"

"Seen one down at the barbecue diner last week was eyin' your gal Mincie like he'd know what to do with her."

"Anyway down there in them woods it wouldn't have been so bad as far as I was concerned, if he'd jumped up on the wagon with me so I'd had a chance to push him off. Hell, no. He wouldn't do like a normal revenooer. He had to grab that doggone "Surcharlie" mule right at the mouth. Got bit too."

"That was a mistake he made."

"Say that again. I'm whompin' Surcharlie with them reins and everything I got. I layed it on that mule, and he stood straight up and rubbed his feet all over that revenooer. He pulled Surcharlie down and give him a push sideways and that was when I went off the wagon."

"What happened then?"

"When I woke up there was that damrevenooer talkin' to Surcharlie, and whisperin' in his ear. Surcharlie fixed him though, broke loose and ran away later when everything else was busted up. He plumb tore the shaft and harness to pieces gettin' away. He plumb shied when they set off that dynamite."

"That Race, he still got a scar under his chin where ol' Surcharlie dragged his feet."

"What'd he say about that?"

"Nothin' except 'You ought to be ashamed of yourself hittin' a poor mule that way.' "

"Crazy damrevenooers, I don't know whether I'd turn my gal loose with one of them or not. She might get ruint or worse than that."

"You can say that again."

"Surcharlie was one mule they didn't get."

"That's for a might certain. I'd bet my ass on that."

The most helpful mule I ever knew I met one morning just before daybreak.

We had maintained an all night stake–out on a distillery up in Sampkin County. I was driving the radio car, and my job was to come in at the right time and block anything on wheels coming out from the distillery.

I had a nice piece of machinery beneath me, and I spent most of the night listening to the transistor radio I had stached in the glove compartment.

I had a sitting down buffet lunch in my field jacket pockets. I had a wooden box full of canned goods in the trunk. Things like peaches, sardines, potted meats, cold baked beans, fruit juices and soft drinks. The kind of things revenooers and moonshiners dine on in the field.

About four a.m. I slipped over to Vancetown and had a couple of hamburgers at the all night drive in. I didn't radio the others that I was easing out, and I didn't put my lights on until I was a mile from my parking place in the woods. They called it "Fornification Hill." You know the kind of place; empty beer cans all around, whiskey bottles, handkerchiefs, kleenex, used prophylactics, and all the human scents.

I felt sorry for a few couples who had driven in there during the night with a car load of sap and left cold when they saw my car in there. It was a hell of a place at the far end to turn around in. I said "Howdy" real friendly like and wanted to tell them about another place down the road.

I couldn't give myself away, and so the man just tugged on the wheel, rode a little forward and backward, and tugged at the wheel and finally got the hell out of there no doubt cussing me up and down. Gees, there was no telling what kind of plans they had made, and how much guys spent to get the gals there.

Maybe they were afraid to register in a motel or hotel the way they should, and add a little class and comfort that way. Anyhow, I had to do what I did where I was, and when the call came in about six a.m., I put that Cadillac powered Ford through it's paces and hit the road in a wide turn barrelassing it for God knows what.

I wasn't ready for what I saw when I wheeled into the still path from the road.

There wasn't a car or truck around in motion. A '59 Chevvy sedan was parked unoccupied on my left. A dark green '54 Ford pickup was parked next to it. A mule was rearing on its hind legs on the path when I came up. It was pulling a slat type of wooden sled with a load of whiskey moonshine cases on it.

Our men were buzzing around and a couple of footraces were going. They had jumped the moonshiners taking the liquor out.

I got out of the car and tried to soothe the mule. He, she, or it, snapped at my hand. I said a few four and five letter words, and let go of his bridle. He took off like a turpentined boar hog.

I caught a glimpse of a guy running across a long plowed up field. It was about a half mile across. One of our boys was running about fifty feet in back of him. I jumped into the car to head him off at the woods at the other end of the field.

I passed the mule on the road and had to drive between cases of moonshine spilled all over the road. I had a clear view of the footrace in the field.

I bailed out of the car at the end of the woods, and took my time heading the fleeing moonshiner off. His pursuer had quit, and he was looking back at him when I said, "Hi!" and offered him a cigarette.

Naturally he got sick, at that thought, winded as he was, so I sat down beside him and told him what tough luck he had, and that he ought not to run unless he knew how. Things like that, to sort of establish rapport.

"Where in hell did you come from?"

"I passed you in the field. Didn't you see me?"

"Gees, where'd you learn how to run?"

"I played on the track team at college."

"Man, I was going so hard at it I didn't see you pass me."

I couldn't keep a face somehow. The poor guy was caught and I didn't want to make it any harder on him than I had to. The mule had quit his foolishness and was grazing by the roadside in full view.

"See that mule over there?"

"Yeah."

"I rode that jackass down the road and headed you off."

"That sunnofabitch, gettin' me caught like that."

"He couldn't help it. I've been riding mules for twenty years. Know how to make him run."

"You sure know how to make that plug mule run."

"Nothin' to it. I just told him not to put his feet down too hard. That was all."

I wanted to tell him how I jumped out a helicopter and caught a guy once, just to cheer him up, but I didn't.

As far as I know he still thinks I rode that mule. I walked him back through the field and one of my buddies slipped down and got the car unnoticed when I told him the story.

He came back and said that the mule ran away.

The moonshiner shook his head more than once and said, "A mule, a goddammule he gets me caught and runs away himself. I thought the government was full of jackasses and now I know it."

NINETEEN

NATURE UNLOVED

One phase of the revenooer's life which bespeaks of the world of the birds and bees and flowers also bespeaks of things which sometimes are almost unmentionables in their consequences. They can be laughable too——as well as disconcerting. They can even be tragic.

In the woods, as hunters and fishermen know, there are things to plague mankind. Some are chiggers, ticks, poison ivy, snakes, all sorts of fauna, flora, and insect life.

I will tell you of a few recollections I have which concern some uncozy little bouts I have had with those forms in the raw.

I will start with the wood tick since I have only this day removed one from my leg. It got there during a very brief stroll which I took in the woods.

The tick is an ugly thing. It is described in the Harcourt, Brace Standard College Dictionary as follows:

Tick (tik) n. 1. One of numerous flat, leathery, bloodsucking arachnids (order acarina) that attack the skin of man and other animals; especially, the cattle tick (Margaropus annulatus), carrier of Texas fever.

Material supplied to the author by Dr. Herbert F. Schoof, U.S. Public Health Service Biologist at Savannah, Georgia, says of the tick:

"Wood ticks feed on the blood of animals and may bite people. Their bites are painful and some of them carry diseases. They cause economic losses among farm animals and are serious pests of dogs. The ticks infest wooded or brushy areas and grassy fields. They are an annoyance and a health hazard to farmers, woodsmen, and military personnel; to campers, picnickers, vacationers, hunters and hikers; and to persons who live in rural and suburban areas.

The more common species of wood ticks are the Rocky Mountain wood tick, the American dog tick, the long star tick, and the black–legged tick.

The Rocky Mountain wood tick and the American dog tick transmit Rocky Mountain Spotted fever and tularemia, rabbit fever which are diseases of man, and anaplamosis, a disease of cattle.

Adults of these ticks can also cause a form of paralysis in animals and people in rare instances when they attach over the spinal cord or at the base of the skull.

The lone star tick can transmit Rocky Mountain Spotted fever, tularemia, and Bullis fever. The black legged tick transmits piroplasmosis, a disease of dogs, and anaplasmosis."

The wood tick is not to be taken lightly if it has attached itself to the body.

The tick can irritate, embarass, incommode, and hospitalize you too if the situation permits.

I have pulled them from my neck, ears, head, frontside, backside, and butt and belly included. The boldest little warrior of them all dug deep into my scrotum, buried its head in the flesh, and had swelled himself to an impressive size before I discovered him. Such belated discovery of a tick on the body is not at all unusual. Generally though, I have detected them about the time they start to crawl.

Now comes the delicate part of it all. Through my mind flashed all those little gems for tick removal that I had heard. The main and oft–repeated stand–by was, "Put a lighted cigarette to his tail, and he will back out."

That suggestion was fallacy number one.

Now if you want to vision something ridiculous just picture a grown man, about two hundred pounds, six feet tall or so, as bare as Adam, sitting on the edge of a bath tub. He fires up a cigarette, puffs it until it is glowing red–white at the tip. He holds it out and looks at it. It is hot enough. He applies the hot end of the cigarette to that personal lace wherein lies the tick, making certain that he has made contact with the tail of the tick.

He looks closely at the rascal and detects some movement.

Aloud he says, "What the hell, the scoundrel is digging in deeper."

That particular tick must have been spawned in an asbestos pile. His only reaction to the heated barb was to put himself in a position to afford the torch bearer a neat little personal blister for his efforts.

From somewhere out of my recollections from the past I had thought that olive oil would, if applied copiously to the offender, cause the pest to ease out from its fortified position. I tried that. Fallacy number two.

Before I go further I will enlighten you, reader, as to why a proper method for extracting an imbedded tick must be used.

The head of the tick is attached to its body by a slender and easily severed anatomical construction. When pressure is applied to remove the buried head of the tick from human flesh it can easily separate itself and remain buried. It becomes a source for infection, and possibly the dreaded Rocky Mountain fever if conditions are right.

It is imperative then to have the invading tick remove itself, if possible, from the flesh. Extreme lubrication assists in making the tick slide out when persuaded gently with tweezers.

I know that now. I didn't know it then.

I called a nurse friend of ours who had long experience in administering medication and observing medical techniques, and I hoped that she had some knowledge of tick removal methods.

The phone call was a beaut, and went like this. (It was awful in my New York accent complete with tremors of personal distress.)

"Hi Honeychile. This is Jack. I have a problem."

"What's wrong Sugar?"

"A tick is buried in my flesh. It won't back out."

"Good Heavens to Betsy. Where is he?"

I knew that one was coming, and I half said, half cried, "On my scrotum."

"On your what?"

"On my codsack, or whatever nickname doctor's call it."

"Oh dear me. You poor boy. Let me think what you can do."

Pause.

"Oh yes, now I know. Put a lighted cigarette to its tail and it will back out. That's all there is to it."

"That does not work. I have tried it."

"Ticks can be infections. I had a tick fever case once and it was terrible."

"Thanks. Now what else should I do?"

"Let me think."

Laughter in background over my voice.

"What is Myrtle laughing at?"

"My predicament."

"It really isn't a laughing matter. It can be serious."

"She doesn't think so. Says its funny as hell."

"Gosh."

"She thinks that I'm some picture here draped in a towel and making full scale war on a teeny–weeny tick."

"That can be bad."

"Yeah. How do I get him out?"

"He won't back out? You say you tried the cigarette trick on the tail."

"Yeah. His and mine and it does not work."

"How about turpentine?"

"Not on me I won't. I've seen it happen to a hog. I don't want any part of it."

"Call the hospital. The emergency room. They should know."

"Okay thanks. If they can't think of anything then I'll try the sure fire method."

"What's that?"

"Ha. Hit him with a sledgehammer."

"Hey, are you kidding or are you serious. I've never heard anything happening to people like what happens to you."

"I'm not a people. I'm a revenooer."

"Be careful now, and if there is anything I can do just let me know."

That's the way nice people are, but its just like being dead and people wanting to know from the family what they can do. Some things you've got to do by yourself, and getting a tick to back out from someplace is one of them. I called the hospital and was referred to State College and the Department of Agriculture. At best I had a hell of a lot of tick talk.

Before I got through calling around for advice forty people had told me to try a lighted cigarette. The only one who was orginial suggested a cigar or pipe if the cigarette didn't work.

One thing in my favor was that the tick was readily accessible. I pondered a while and thought of a number of formerly amusing incidents I had heard about and which had involved ticks and their personal ostrich–like habits.

I remember one rollicking occasion when one of my erstwhile colleagues described his own situation with a tick:

"Of all places, smack dab on the tip of my pecker. My old lady had a fit of laughing and set to making vulgar rhymes about it. She called one of the neighbor ladies over and all but had me show it to her."

"I tried salt, iodine, tobacco juice, and lemon juice."

"My wife thought it would be nice if I tried Worcestershire sauce. She asked me what in hell kind of a cake I was going to bake. I gave up and took a pair of pliers and pulled the thing in two with the head still inside me. I got a nice infection. I don't know if it really came from the tick or from all the mess that I put on it."

I didn't get much kick out of recalling that conversation. The milkman rang the doorbell and I thought it was some neighbor.

He suggested buttermilk and sold my wife a quart. No good there.

I thought about the times I had poison ivy and that was not a soothing thought at all. I thought about the slight case of Rocky Mountain fever that I had gotten a few years before. I made a decision. I would proceed on my own theory. I would make the rascal so slippery with olive oil that he wouldn't have chance to resist tugging. He might even choke or drown. I felt better. I moved from the edge of the tub to the comfort of the Johnny cover.

I obtained some vaseline and made a circular dam around the imbedded tick. It was deep enough to hold plenty of olive oil for one tick retreat. I poured the olive oil into the dry dock I had made. I sat there while I smoked three or maybe four cigarettes. Every once in a while I would observe to note the tick's progress and to see if he was drowning, choking, or backing out. Again I tried the hot cigarette end but it didn't work, and maybe the rascal was sneaking a smoke while I was at it. I don't know, but what I was doing certainly was not meant for hospitality toward that tick.

I took my wife's eyebrow tweezers. I took a nice easy grip on them and eased them over the body of the tick. I pulled firmly, but gently, and pulled him out as nicely as one would please. That wasn't half as bad as the poison ivy seige I experienced.

That shiny green, three–leaf plant they call poison ivy can mess up a body, but good. Believe me. The first time I had P.I. was when I was a kid. I took the direct method of exposure. I shinnied bare-legged up a tree covered with the stuff. Considering all things, I did not do too bad as the allergy restricted itself to my legs. I learned to respect poison ivy though for all time.

My next encounter was a beaut. I had a poison ivy rash break out on my face after playing golf and seeking a lost ball in an evil vale of poison ivy. I wanted to get the mess over with in a hurry so I went to a doctor. I wound up in the hospital from the sulfa drug cure. The whole thing only cost a few hundred bucks and I learned that I was allegic to sulfa drugs.

The time of poison ivy exposure which I remember most vividly was downright indecent and improper. It was a mess too. I was working up in New York State at the time I contracted that blistering poison. We were working an alky plant tucked in an impressive residence dwelling some fifty miles up from the city.

A dirt road led from the state road to the manor. The lane was lined with foliage on both sides, and it wound from the state road for about a half mile to the house.

On a Wednesday night about the first of July, I was with another investigator walking the lane in secret fashion.

It was a truly dark night and the whole countryside was quiet as we dropped off from an official car which was to be gone from the area for the next twenty–four hours.

Our mission was to confirm or deny an allegation that an alcohol distillery was going full blast in the house which had been described to use merely by appearance and location.

About half way to the house we heard a car turn from the state road onto our road. In a minute or so we saw the approaching lights. We stepped from the road into a maze of foliage. We went down for some six feet and felt the scraping restraint of leafy, tangling vines. I reached bottom just before my partner put his feet into my stomach. I wasn't hurt though. We joked about it. I said, "It would be real funny if this was poison ivy." We laughed and let it go at that. We went about the chore of taking a community leak while we were there, as men are wont to do in private places like that.

We scrambled up to the road. That was on Wednesday. I was not to leave the area until the following Monday. We didn't know that then.

We made a nice seizure and I had the dubious distinction of having a cop take a pot shot at me during the raid. He thought I was a moonshiner. He was a lousy shot and missed. I almost knocked him on his tail when he said, "I thought sure I had that last bastard going and away." What he had thought was that a moonshiner I was chasing and I were a pair making an escape.

To return to the garden of ivy, which I later learned had been thriving at the point where my buddy and I paused for physical relief; it messed me up but good. It began to be mine own verily when I placed my hands for defense while falling. My hands took it from there on.

I stayed on at the violation premises for a while. I was to guard it while it was ascertained whether or not the place would be suitable for a movie for public relations purposes. It was not. An abandoned dairy in New Jersey was.

While I was on guard duty I had two visitors. Two babes painted up to all get–out. I had already been there a couple of days when they arrived and I welcomed company.

They drove up in an old car. When I saw it approaching I did not know who it might be so I ducked behind the house until it stopped. Then I stepped out.

"Hi. Where's Louie and Mike and the rest of the guys?"

"Ain't here. I'm Johnny from Chi."

"Hi, Johnny."

"Yeah, Whatinell you doing here?"

"Had an appointment with the boys. You the boss?"

"Yeah."

"I'm Tillie."

"I'm Lizzie."

"Where are the guys?"

"Gone. We're taking over."

"Anything we can do for you, Johnny?"

"Nah."

The girls were grinning and shifting around. Tillie chewed gum at ninety miles an hour. She was the younger of the two. She was about twenty–five. Lizzie was about thirty–five. They both were nicely built. If either one had anything else on besides a dress I couldn't tell it.

"Hey Tony, we didn't come here for nothing, did we?"

"Depends on what you call nothing."

"You look like a nice guy, Johnny. Let's all take a drink together."

"Got no whiskey."

"Don't make us laugh. We saw tubs of it in the house last week."

"That was last week."

"How about a bottle of soda pop, then. We're thirsty."

"Okay. Let's go up to the porch. Gimme ya car keys."

"Sure Johnny."

Lizzie handed me the keys and said, "We ain't got a thing in it. Go take a look."

I looked in the car. It was empty.

"Anything ya want Johnny, anything?"

"Nah. What do I need? I'm brushing dames away now like flies. I need two more floosies like I need a hole in the head."

"You're not friendly are you?"

"Can't afford to be. Got too many enemies. Do you know what it takes to run a bunch of places like this all over the country?"

"A bunch of places like this?"

"Yeah. What's your story. Give it to me fast and nice."

"We just come here for a social visit with the boys."

"What boys? I want their names."

Lizzie rattled off five first names. She said that she didn't know their last names. I figured that she was telling pretty much the truth and that she had nothing to do with the alky plant. I tossed her the car keys and broke out into a grin.

"What the hell is this?"

"Either one of you married to anyone working here?"

"Nah. Tillie here is married. She just goes along with me sometimes for the sport and to make a few bucks. Her old man don't know abou it."

"How long have you been in the racket, Lizzie?"

"What racket?"

"You just told me that you were a prossie."

"That's no racket. That's damned hard work."

"It's not legit."

"Hell no. I've been doing what I'm doing for the past fifteen years. Got plenty of experience too. Ya wanna see?"

"Tillie, you're not a regular prossie?"

"Whaddya mean prossie? I'm a fun kid. Ya wanna have some fun?"

"I can't."

"You can't. Whaddya mean? You a married guy or something?"

"Yeah. More than that. I got the P.I. too."

"Thanks for telling us about the P.I. Some guys wouldn't. We gotta be going."

They left, all smiles, and with a determination to get gone from that place. I don't think that they ever figured out what I meant by the P.I.

I was scheduled to take a trip to the Midwest. I drove and it was a long hot trip. The P.I. got worse and so did the heat and the discomfort of it. I stopped off to see a doctor on my route. He must have been a poison ivy expert. He said that if I did what he told me to do that I would be in good shape in a few days.

"Gottem coming in all the time." He went out of his office and came back in a minute. He had with him what I thought was a prepared kit for cases such as mine.

"You see these sacks? There's a dozen of'em. Ain't nothing to 'em except that they're big Bull–Durham sacks lined with cotton. This brown soap and baking soda are all that's needed. Wash in mild water and the brown soap quite a few times a day. Then make a paste with the soap and soda. Put your bonnet on and you can ride all day without trouble."

I thanked him and paid him. I still had a good ways to go, but I sure was a lot more comfortable after I left that doctor than before I saw him.

I had a few more bouts with poison ivy in later years. I learned to know the stuff as soon as I saw it. Sometimes that was no help at all, like when I was working at night in the woods. We hardly ever used lights walking through the woods; unless it was absolutely necessary.

It's a good thing that Adam wore a fig leaf. If he'd chosen a poison leaf there's no telling what might have happened.

The chiggers or redbugs as they are known are true pests to be dealt with in the woods in the summertime. They are spider mites and are practically invisible. They are prevalent in the Southeast and trespassers upon the person in the worst sort of way. The redbug is usually accompanied by a multitude of relatives when he visits.

Short bush growths are their favorite roosting grounds. When some unsuspecting individual walks close to the bush the chigger rubs off on his clothes or flesh.

Blackberry pickers are choice and ready victims of chiggers. Woodsmen of all sorts are vulnerable too, particularly loggers, revenooers and moonshiners.

The chigger socks itself into the human skin and torments it with an itching as it has never known before.

The chigger itch is more annoying than the itch of poison ivy. The wound does not usually fester or blister, but it leaves a telltale tiny, red mark or welt at the point of puncture or entry.

If anyone should seek the ultimate in personal discomfort, in all the scratching phases, then let them seek the chigger and it will do the job.

During the days of World War II, a great number of Northern soldiers, new to the woodland ways of the South, were annoyed tremendously by the chigger.

Like the tick, the chigger is no respecter of personal anatomical geography. A guy with a good work load of chiggers in the wrong place can almost go daffy at their teasing.

The marvelous preventions or repellent salves and solutions which are available in this wonderful age of chemistry dispell the assaults and pugnaciousness of the chigger.

I have used myself as a guinea pig for the cause of relief from the torments of the chigger family. I have put solutions and salves on one leg and left the other leg unprotected. I have switched applications to the other leg and at loose clothing openings.

Those repellents work and are a boon to mankind.

Before such repellents became available on the open market, on the Federal courthouse steps in almost any southern city, in the summertime terms of court, there would be moonshiners and revenooers about. You could tell them by their scratching ways.

While some people are immune to chiggers, for some reason or other, most people are not. Some people say that heavy smokers and pipe smokers are immune. I was not that way in my heaviest smoking days. I can lay a pretty reliable claim to having had upset many ashtrays, burned umpteen holes in my clothing, and almost every fabric, wherever I was smoking, but nary a claim could I declare for chigger bite immunity, even on a three–pack–a–day smoking diet.

One memorable experience I had which was related to chigger attacks, occurred when I heard that household ammonia and heat from a light bulb or infrared bulb would do much to soothe chigger bites.

At that time some insistent chiggers had managed to get through my clothing to some of my most personal areas. I got out the ammonia and the infrared lamp and went to doctoring. I felt relief and repeated the operation.

One morning shortly thereafter I stepped out of the shower and commenced to dry myself. What ho! I looked down at the manner of secret redhead that I had become. It seems that the process was obvious to beauty operators, but me, never.

One of the questions most often asked revenooers of their contacts with creatures in the woods concerns the prevalence of snakes. Many people ask on learning your profession, "Do you see many snakes?"

Area and ground conditions of course, control snakes in population numbers as they do most forms of earthly life. Climate is important in that too.

My answer would be in the regions that I have worked, that unless someone were to look a good distance ahead while traveling through woods and swamps, that not too many snakes would be seen.

It is a good policy to remain as far from a snake as possible if you have a fear of them. Everyone, fear or none, should beware of the poisonous reptile.

Inasmuch as the revenooer is compelled to trod forest and field, hill and dale, when the matter at hand does not distinguish between night and day, I always put my best foot forward and let it fall where it may, be it day or night. I saved myself a lot of worrying. Oddly enough I did get bitten by a copperhead. It was in broad daylight and I was bitten on the hand. I had bent over to tie my shoe lace and I didn't see the brown saddle back markings until they were slithering away, and the damage was done. I did not miss any work on account of it. I was pretty sick and my hand was swollen to the size of a baseball glove.

I recovered without any ill effects. I guess that my snake's poison pouch had been emptied not too long before as a meal ticket. Some men work the southern woods all their lives and are never bitten by a snake. Here and there a revenooer gets bit and so does a moonshiner.

One moonshiner we arrested was working at the distillery with a swollen foot. He said that a snake had bitten him a couple of nights before. He would not let us get medical treatment for him. He preferred his own way about the situation. A few weeks later we saw him and he said, "Do you remember that snake that bit me at the still?"

"Yeah."

"Well I got that all squared away now."

"Good. How did you do that."

"I killed that there fool snake."

TWENTY

MARSHAL LAW

If there's one thing for sure in the routine of a Federal Revenooer, that thing is in that if he sets out on a journey on official business he is liable to find plenty of detours along the way. He may wind up far from his destination too. One thing near sometimes leads to something afar. It has happened to me many times.

In the spring of 1961, with Friday of the week at hand, revenuers from a great portion of the Southeast were planning to attend a retirement party at North Wilkesboro, North Carolina in the foothills of the Blue Ridges. The man who was retiring was with great respect known as the Dean of Revenuers.

Charlie Felts had reached a ripe old age in his profession as a remarkably well preserved man approaching seventy years of age. A big party was planned for Charlie at North Wilkesboro on Saturday night.

Friday was a real nice day and sometime during the afternoon an alert for all enforcement personnel came from headquarters. No one was to leave their post of duty until further notice. At Raleigh where I was stationed there was much speculation going on as no explanation was given as to the cause of the alert.

Friday afternoon, several of us withdrew from the office for a coffee break at a nearby drugstore. As investigators are wont to do whenever they find something, some knowledge incomplete at hand, we speculated, old hand and new.

It was something big. It had to be big for a regional cancellation of leaves, orders to return to posts of duty, and a command for one and all to remain at stations.

It was something far beyond any shipment of whiskey, or the run of any size distillery.

Whatever it was would no doubt be something of front page newspaper material. It had to be in the Southeast.

We procured a newspaper, and the rest was easy. We had the answer by our own fathoming. Of course there was nothing official either by word or by mouth, but for us it might just as well have been. Attorney General Kennedy was hinting strongly about Federal intervention.

We knew that what we had sensed was far more than a strong suspicion, and that we were not dealing in angles or clues; we were dealing with a way of life we all knew. We were going to Montgomery, Alabama. Our duties would be in the nature of civil rights. Our only remaining question was when.

We were permitted to go to North Wilkesboro for the party however, and since we would all be grouped together, that was no difficult concession to make.

The next morning, Saturday, with my wife in our car, I drove to North Wilkesboro and registered at the hotel there. We met old acquaintances and friends. We shook hands, patted backs, and swapped tales like people anywhere will with a common bond and little opportunity to be together at one place at one time.

Some of the men were hard to convince that our alert was because of a civil rights assignment. There was a great deal of talk about it. "After all, we are Tax Investigators" some said in the fashion in which they had been reminded by lawyers for the defense in criminal cases.

"They can't switch us to that type of duty. After all, there is such a thing as appropriations for specific duties and official functions."

"You lucky jokers from up North, people down in Alabama expect that of you, but us poor jackasses from the deep South will catch hell down there if the going gets rough."

"Hey, you Southern guys wanna get in on a good thing; I'm holdin' special tutoring classes this afternoon in my suite on how to speak Brooklynese Correckeredly at twenty–five bucks an hour, an' the price going up tomorrow."

"Charlie Felts, you lucky guy, retired and out of all this."

"Gees, my family lives right at Montgomery, and they're liable not to speak to me."

"All I know is that they must have one hell of a big hotel down there in Montgomery to hold all the whole Southeast region."

"Let's wait and see what happens. What the hell else ya gonna do; make out like ya got the ipi or something?"

"I sure hope that we can get Charlie fixed up with a real fond farewell before they sound that alert gong."

"No beer, highballs or intoxicating beverages."

"Hell no, you ain't catching me going down there with brew on my breath and wind up in the Alabama clink."

"What a discouraging way to hold a party."

"Tell it to the Attorney General, not me."

"Dern moonshiners will go crazy while we're gone."

"We're not gone yet; you ought to know how to wait and see by now."

"Don't be stupid, they can't send us to Montgomery."

"Of course they can't, stupid."

"Hell, that's the FBI's job, stupid."

"They're sending us down there as a tactical maneuver since we are so accustomed to meeting the public with fine manners and the latest fashions for men in woodswear."

And so it went in the hotel lobby halls and rooms.

"Gees, look what the cat dragged in. Last time I saw you, you were doing your damnedest to catch a fat man on crutches carrying his dear pappy away from the still. You shoulda caught that guy, you could have made it two for one."

"How ya been lardass?"

"Glad to see ya."

"Hey, we're gonna eat soon, ya know what we're gonna have?"

"Sure, potted meat and saltines, with a moonpie and an R.C. Cola."

"Hey skinny, show 'em your badge. Maybe they'll let you in for nothing."

"No crap, we're gonna have quail on toast for supper."

"What, no champagne?"

"My old lady ain't seen me in so long she thinks we're on our honeymoon being in a hotel together. Its been so long I won't know how to act."

"Give it hell, fatty."

"Yeah, this guy was running away from the stillyard and his pants belt broke, he went on his tail and he damn near got away. I had to stop and laugh so hard."

"Believe me Myrt, I'm gonna marry a shoe clerk with nine to five hours, five days a week, next time. It's a good thing there's no kitchen handy or all those Revenuers would be roosting there by themselves."

"You can say that again. We leave the kids with momma, check in a hotel for the weekend we hope, and it looks like Papa and I are gonna spend our time with the doors open all up and down the hall."

"I wonder what it is to be a moonshiner's wife."

"Can't be any worse than this."

"I hope I don't have to drive back by myself."

"You probably will, Honeychile."

"Hey, they can't send me, I haven't got an Alabama driver's license."

"I didn't even know you had a North Carolina driver's license."

"Hell, I can make you eat my dust on any road in North Carolina."

"Ya might if you could find your way back without having some-one have to read the signs to you."

"No crap, you really think we're going to Alabama?"

"I been there. Did I ever tell you about that show I saw in Phoenix City?"

"No."

"That place was wide open, and this gal she gets up there on the platform and she has two tassels, one on her left and one on her right, and she just stands there and makes those tassels go one way and then the other."

"Shh' here comes my old lady."

"Hi, Doll Baby."

"Old Charlie, he sure put a heap of mileage on his walkin' boots in his time."

"Been at it about forty years."

"I've got four more to go to hit the half–hundred retirement age."

"Gonna take it, Race?"

"You bet."

"Me too, in twenty seven more years Race. Yep, I'll take it too.

I'm gonna sit down and write a book about guys like us, and tell it just how it happens."

"Yeah, tell it just the way it happens, and then nobody will believe you."

"At least if they read it they'll think they've been there with me and not a million miles away. Anyhow that's the way I want it."

"Hell, you'll wait until you're too old to write a book and then retire like just about all the others Race."

"Wait and see. I'll be fifty at the end of August 1965 and watch my smoke just along about the first of September, 1965. I'll drop by the office once in a while and have lunch with you guys and give you the ol' taxpayers lament."

"Don't put too much in that book about yourself or you're liable to get us all in trouble with the censors."

"You ought to be glad I'm not joining the Inspection Service, I'd have you all jugged for not paying any attention to your wives and children."

"Gees, I hope we can stay here overnight. It'll be a pleasure to spend the night in a hotel room with someone who don't snore and cuss out loud in his sleep."

"If you came up here for a good night's sleep, bub, you ought to go on back home, because I have a hunch you will be touring the sunny South by car in a pourin' down rainstorm, the way those clouds look yonder by the big brushies."

"You mountaineers are too damn hill conscious."

"Is it true that Charlie and all those old timers up here got one leg shorter than the others from walking across the ridges?"

"Sure, they have a hell of a time backing up if they're turned in the wrong direction."

"Is it true that all you guys from down the Eastern part of the state got webbed toes on accounta bein' in the swamps all the time?"

"Damright, got rings around their shins too. We get ten percent predisability on accounta that too. Ya wanna see?"

"No thanks."

"Hey Race, show'em where that snake bit ya."

"I will if old Buck'll show us where the bear clawed him."

"Whaddya supposed to do when a bear comes after you? I forget whether you're not supposed to run down a hill or up a hill."

"Naw Suh, it's the old b'ar what's supposed not to run while you just sort of ease away slick–like, and mind your manners too."

"That's a fact too, son."

"Yeah, I know, Pappy, a bear fact."

All in all, it was a somber, sober bunch to a certain degree, until the old, "What the hell" attitude set in with jokes and comments being made about the situation. It had to with that bunch sooner or later.

Late in the afternoon we were called to the banquet room and it was announced that the party would continue. The meal would be served without any rush. After the ceremonies were over we were to return to our official posts of duty. There we were to obtain our working gear and government cars. We were then to drive to Montgomery, Alabama. We were to report at the A&TTD office in the Montgomery Post Office on Sunday. No exceptions.

Our North Wilkesboro hotel rooms were paid for, and with all forms of disappointment for husbands and wives, what otherwise could have been a carefree weekend turned into a series of changing plans.

There was some comment such as "The Revenooers Ride Tonight. Not the way they figured though."

"How far is Montgomery from here?"

"Figure it about around one thousand miles to home and there."

"What a hell of a way to spend a second honeymoon."

"Practically shot out of the saddle."

Myrtle set out by herself about ten o'clock over the hills in our five year old Chevvy for Charlotte, North Carolina, with a tricky bit of night driving ahead in the rain. Four of us from Raleigh went back home about one hundred and eighty miles away.

About three a.m. we were all in one of our post–of–duty cars and hit the road southward from Raleigh in one of the heaviest, continuous rainfalls I've ever seen. We figured that we had an eight hundred mile drive ahead. We wondered, each of us, if we had brought the right kind and sufficiency of clothes. We were joined at Raleigh by another investigator who had been away.

One thing we didn't worry about was about the car and drivers. We had a nice Oldsmobile to ride in. One man had driven us from North Wilkesboro to Raleigh. Another was at the wheel when we left Raleigh. He drove southward for about one hundred miles, and the heavy rain and headlights reflecting on the road surface in front of him made him begin to feel drowsy so I got behind the wheel.

It kept on raining heavily through the night, and I drove on with the others talking to me at intervals, asking me if I was tired, and remarking on this and that and keeping me wide awake. It helped, but I was not fatigued.

By daylight the rains had slacked a good bit, and the driving was easier, and I began to think of breakfast and I was hoping like hell all the while that Myrtle didn't have too rough a drive from North Wilkesboro to Charlotte, but I knew that it wasn't an easy drive. It wasn't easy for a woman from flat country to take winding, climbing, and descending curves alone at night in strange territory in a bad storm over an entirely new route to her. (She made it okay though except for making a slight detour just as she reached Charlotte.)

At Columbia, South Carolina, we stopped at a restaurant for breakfast. One of the guys had eaten supper there the night before and when the waitress came over she spoke to him familiarly which amazed us. Here he was in Columbia from Raleigh, and the night before he was in Columbia from Raleigh. We laughed at that, and he shrugged and said, "What the hell, it's just a four hundred mile round trip."

I said, "It's worth it to be in such fine looking, well dressed, mannerable company as us on the return drive." His retort was not at all complimentary.

With a good mess of country ham, a settin' of hen eggs and a double order of good old South Carolina grits, ordered in Bronxese under my belt, I was ready for the next stretch.

While we were at the restaurant one of our cars from Wilmington, North Carolina joined us and we took off in tandem fashion.

Another car from the Raleigh post of duty picked us up at another stop along the way, and so it went down the line until we reached Talledega, and we had five cars moving along together.

We kept the broadcast radio turned on along the way, and we were picking up last minute reports of what we might expect on reaching Montgomery.

The Governor of Alabama was being freely quoted, and from the reports we thought that there wouldn't be much doubt about the bridge leading to Montgomery from the north being barricaded.

We hoped they wouldn't be using National Guard tanks as a

barrier. We stopped a short distance from the bridge, and held a conference beside the road over what procedure we would take. It was shortly before five p.m. and still daylight.

I was driving the lead car and since we had orders to go on into Montgomery, and from what the radio reports said, "would be arrested," there would be no choice but to run a roadblock. It was a hell of a way to spend a nice Sunday afternoon.

All of the cars had North Carolina license plates. Some were green 1961 Fords of the same model used by Georgia and Alabama A&TT Investigators with high shortwave radio aerials, and so for one reason or the other we received stares from people along the highway and in passing cars. We felt that they knew what we were up to. Country folks have a way of knowing things when they really want to.

We were working under orders, and no matter what the personal sentiment of any individual in the group might be, it was agreed one hundred percent by all that we had to go through.

Maybe it would have to be a "hair–parting" moonshiner–style roadblock penetration with the first car moving the obstacle and clearing a path for the others. I did not at all underrate the probable skill of the Alabama Highway Patrol in their ability to put up an effective block.

I was hoping that none of them would act the fool and stand in front of, or near any barrier if we had to go through it. I didn't think they would. I had always heard that the Alabama Highway Patrol and A&TT had been mutually helping friends, and we had in our group some Alabamians. We had one in our car so that if I was doing any praying right then it was in the cause of wanting an empty unblocked bridge leading to Montgomery.

The last news report didn't help a bit. It had white helmeted marshals all over Montgomery and depicted a scene of visible turmoil and scuffling all over the main street.

I think I said something about hoping that the bridge was clear, "because if it wasn't that we would all be writing reports for the next fifty years." Zowie!!!

And then we saw the whole thing right there in front of us. It was the bridge. It was the most beautiful bridge in the world that moment and it was wide open from end to end. I don't believe I saw any state officer anywhere near it. It was almost a simultaneous chorus when we all said, "What the hell is this?"

We halfway had the impression that it was too easy, but it was not long before we knew that some vocal newsman had been making a recital of what he thought was happening right then. He sure as hell didn't know.

At exactly five p.m. we heard the very latest broadcast and it was the same as before.

From where I sat driving the lead car into Montgomery I saw signs only of it being a warm Sunday afternoon in a city called Montgomery, in a state called Alabama. It looked like any other town I'd seen on a late hot Sunday afternoon. Not many on the streets and activity centered on people strolling and perhaps a few more around the movie area than any other place. Stores were closed.

We passed down the main street, and began looking for the telltale American flag which would locate the post office building for us. That, by the way, is a great sign if you are ever in a strange place looking for a post office. That doesn't hold true though for all Federal Offices because so much of their office space is leased from individuals without requirements to raise the flag.

We found the post office building, and I pulled straight into the curb across the street. The others parked alongside. Our front bumpers were parallel to the curbstone.

I volunteered to stay with the cars while the others went up to the A&TT office for further instructions. An investigator from Raleigh, who until a short time before was a native and resident Floridian, remained with me. It was hot, and we were tired and thirsty.

He went into a combination soft drink store and pool room directly in front of where the cars were parked. He ordered a coke with an unmistakable southern accent. The man behind the counter gave him the coke, and pushed his money aside and muttered something uncomplimentary.

When he came out he told me about it. I went into the store and ordered a coke and while the man was all business and accepted my dime, he did not say anything. I drank my coke in the store and kept an eye on the outside. I watched a pool game in progress on the inside.

No one said anything to me, nor did I speak other than in ordering my coke. I ordered a pack of cigarettes and still I did not perceive anything openly hostile toward me, and I knew why that was so. I was a damyankee at work, on a job.

The pure resentment against my buddy was in that he was a Southerner returned to the South to dispute what had been Southern way of life. As for me, my accent, is non cum laude Bronxitis.

They probably figured first that I didn't know any better. Second, I didn't come there all on my own, and third, I was getting paid to do a job, and I was doing it.

I went back out to the cars and joined my friend in the Oldsmobile and we talked it over. For the first time in a couple of days we strapped on our guns. Maybe there would be some action.

The others came out of the Federal Building and told us of instructions. We were to proceed to Maxwell Field at Montgomery. It was west of downtown, just a short drive away.

The base was all so nice looking as we drove on to it with the ranking officers' names on signs beside neat little houses, and we joked about what type of a neat little house would be our immediate abode for our latest assignment.

We would soon know. Very soon.

Our neat little house was not exactly little. The doorway was open and we peeped into our boudoir. It wasn't fancy at all but it had the airs of an expensive set up and we were pleased. Tired as we were we drove inside and parked our cars at the head of our beds and stretched out full length on the iron but comfortable beds, and waited for them to bring our dinner from the Officers' mess. We were in a mammoth aircraft hangar.

"Roast turkey, or a fine medium broiled sirloin would be fitting," someone said.

We remarked to each other how lovely it was to have an assignment in the healthy outdoor air where you had no redbugs (chiggers), poison ivy, or all those underprivileged conditions afforded a revenooer spending the night without a roof over his head on his home grounds.

We had a roof and we had doors we could close if we knew how to manipulate the hydraulic operating system.

Our only complaint was that the assignment to that sunny Southern climate had not been in the winter time. We thought that it was highly probable that some homing–pigeon pilot who had taxied a B–29 or a C–80 cargo plane out of our bedroom the day before might decide to zero in on us unknowingly, of course, but still distressing enough.

The people next door were awfully noisy fixing airplanes in our companion hangar. The G.I.'s who kept putting more beds up must have been recruited from the plumbing detail, and every other detail on any Army post for miles around.

A rather portly and older Special Investigator had already commenced what he had called his "regular Sunday afternoon nap, for my condition" and was asleep on the last syllable.

"Good man, good conscience," somebody said.

Three of us set out to find some sort of washing–up facilities and we found a gentlemen's room.

We had a former Air Force sergeant in our group, and he struck up a conversation with a sergeant at the latrine next to him. They, as old soldiers will, discussed the best manner of procedure in establishing a comfortable location and all the domesticities at a home away from home. I believe that someone has more than once referred to such endeavors as "scrounging," and even "midnight requisitioning."

As it was the sergeant said, "It so happens that there is such a place as you are seeking, but I would advise you to go about your probing in a quiet orderly way, and do not confide in anyone other than your immediate and true dear friends. It would be better that you wait until tomorrow night, though, as things are really moving fast and furious around here."

"We will see to it that you are personally commended by the Secretary of the Treasury Department, Sergeant."

We went back to our master bedroom, and turned the car around so that the trunk with all our effects was right at the back of the beds. We took out our shaving equipment, towels, etc., and a clean change of clothing. We showered enthusiastically and shaved in communal style. We walked in fine fettle back to our light and airy room.

One of our keen eyed neighbors noted our fresh appearance and the gleam in our eyes, and he jumped up from his bed and said to everybody, "Them sunnavabitches know something." He reached under his bed and pulled out a duffle bag and came up with his shaving stuff and a towel. He went in the direction from which we had come. He was on the ball.

The four of us set out for the Officers' mess and walked in like we owned the joint. It was not yet late, and being a Sunday, we had a good selection of food, and we dined heartily.

After dinner we walked around seeking our future domicile, that is if all went well, and we decided on an unoccupied billet building. I wet my index finger and held it aloft. Yes, the wind was blowing so that it would have the most effect upon the front windows. Yes, I had decided upon what exposure I would have in my new quarters. After all, was not our boss the Attorney General, the brother of the President of the United States?

Were we not to be sworn in as deputy marshals in his service? Why then, why not the best for his men? We must be refreshed, alert, well groomed and well fed at all times, for mayhap of nightfall we would be marching someplace or other wearing white helmets and being sunnavabitched from one end of the South to the other.

We sauntered by the headquarters office for the detail. We saw some semi–supervisors there and a short wave radio communications set up. There were guys from Hellangone and back wanting to know what they had to do next.

We shook hands around with old cronies, "for crying out loud, they've got the whole dampostoffice and the border patrol too in on this thing." In the yet to be written language of the practiced investigator that means that "there are more here than they can immediately do with," and I can thereby lend the greatest of assistance in the matter by fading away to some more quiet, more desirable, more relaxing place.

Thence we walked back home to our combination carport and bedroom, and we wrote short letters home to our loved ones and said, "Trip okay, busy as hell, will write later. Have to go."––and we went to bed.

It seemed that I had just dozed off when I heard loud and uproarious laughter around me. One of our more robust investigators was lying in bed, snoring and grunting, and he had erected himself a tent with his bedsheet while asleep. The guy went on sleeping oblivious to perhaps all in the world but some bawdy place where he was cavorting in his subconscious.

It was three thirty a.m., and a bunch of Texas border patrolmen were tearing in and out of the place in cars, which is a hell of a way to act in a feller's bedroom. The border patrolmen were setting up camp on the other side of our cars. Some of them came over on hearing the laughter. They laughed and shook their heads.

Another bunch of Texas border guys came in later on cargo planes and I met an old buddy who used to work with the A&TT at Raleigh.

A loudspeaker now and then was requesting volunteers, and once our group went up, but they had so many hanging around that headquarters through the night we didn't get out. It happened that way quite a few times so that we were beginning to feel like land–locked salmon as far as getting off the base was concerned.

We obtained privileges at the officers' mess and for the hell of it we called each other Colonel and Major and as far as I know we didn't have anything less than that. It was a serious business, and we were itching to get into town, but we had to remain on the base until called.

Some of the marshals were there before us and explained the stand–by system and the planned procedures for eventual strategy and action.

For a change of pace from the waiting, we visited the exchange stores and watched the WAF's drifting in and out. We couldn't buy from the exchange store, but we could look all we wanted to, and some guys did buy some small items there.

The truth of it was that we had years of moving around and were practically our own bosses, and our work spelled ACTION. The change to the confining, semi–regimented life of military posts was boring to us and we were frothing for action. Naturally, we realized that the more peaceful things were all around that we would be less active, and we were not what a layman would call unhappy, just restless.

We hung around headquarters, and once we got into the back of the post office truck, and there were some tear gas bombs in a box on the floor.

We sat there for a good while on the alert. A marshal from up North showed us the proper way to use the tear gas and cautioned us not to pick one up after it was made operable. He said that they get hot as hell, and "could burn your fingers or hand."

That marshal had an accent similar to mine, except faster.

One guy asked him if we were brothers. Later, the marshal slipped me a nightstick, a scarce item, and said, "Ya might need 'dis to protect yourself."

I said, "Ank thay, ooyay."

We were parked behind a radio car and a yankee voice was going and coming and a guy said, "Who in the hell is that?" I was wondering about it myself, and then another voice spoke up and said, "That's the Chief Marshal, McShane." A wag popped out with, "We have something in common, I once was a chief marshal myself in a debutante ball."

We had high hopes being parked right in back of the head–knocker's radio wagon. We had high hopes of some action until some jackass said with a tone of authority, "Men, the alert has been terminated, disembark."

A guy said, "Yeah, you strawbossin' bastard, what in hell do you think we are, a bunch of flakkin' sailors on a battleship? I'm gonna get outta this damned special delivery wagon, but I'll be damned if I'm gonna disembark even if the damned alert was terminated or adulterated. I had enough of that crap in the Navy." He was truly disappointed.

As we were getting out of the truck another guy said, "I thought you had to embark before you disembarked. That joker couldn't embark in a canoe on a two foot creek." I surmised that the requestor was not only unpopular in certain quarters, but that he had as well chosen a most unsuitable form of speech to say "false alarm."

McShane kept in contact though, and another yankee on the transmitting end was moiderin' the names of the streets in Montgomery, but at least he was out there somewhere right with it; and here I was grounded with the post office, Air Force, and dead–letter artillery unit. The mail carrier driver (who knew streets, etc.) said, "I'll bump you guys out wherever you say" as though we were a load of potatoes. A joker said, "Good, dump me out at a cathouse."

To witness the expedience with which the whole operation was organized was indeed a great experience. Red tape was slashed, with great and direct dispatch, probably more so than at any other time in the history of modern peacetime democratic government.

The Justice Department, Treasury Department, Post Office Department and the Air Force all cast aside regulations to accomplish an almost impossible task in not much more than twenty–four hours. Preparations were made for the worst if such were to come. That is the way it should be if such a thing is undertaken at all.

I did not see anybody who could gripe because something original was not tried. The government was throwing everything it had in a first line defense for what had been interpreted as the laws of the land.

I thought particularly that the use of Southern A&TT officers was a most ingenious idea. These men are well schooled in personal emergency tactics, and in meeting people almost daily who are chagrined by their activities. They manage to keep open a reasonable line of communication.

The Southern A&TT men have worked closely and conscientiously with state and local law enforcement officers on every level of authority, and they have participated together in many common pursuits. Both federal and state officers, with such an understanding, assume a tolerance and respect for each other when they are doing their jobs as commanded.

A&TT men in all sorts of predicaments, alone and in a group, learn early that their job is one of patience, tolerance, consideration and determination in a final hour or what might even be a final moment of decision.

While we were at Montgomery, an A&TT man was hit with a brick at the Baptist Church Sunday night demonstration.

An A&TT man let go with a tear gas bomb at what was later noted many times to be the exact psychological and most effective time. What otherwise may have been a major catastrophe dispersed a mob of angry people, gave them time to reconsider, and to feel that what they had been confronted with in the name of law and order had not been a bluff from even the remotest standpoint.

The mob had the opportunity of confronting men at hand who were not strangers to personal violence in many forms in their daily routines.

The mob had the opportunity to see men who could laugh with them, if they chose to laugh, and men who could cry with them, cuss with them and fight with them too if that was the way it had to be. The mob had the opportunity to see men in green woodsman's shirts and pants, some in civilian work khaki's without helmets and some were even without hats. A few had sticks, and all had the badge, "U.S. Treasury Department, Investigator" in their pocket. They had the black and yellow armbands identifying one and all as "U.S. Marshal."

It's for sure that they didn't see these guys with any fancy dress uniforms, suits and ties, shined shoes and neat soft hats, worn in the fashion of men or less rigorous official duties.

In these guys the mob didn't see any boys trying to do a man's job.

On that March Sunday night at the Montgomery Negro Baptist Church and events there led by Rev. Martin Luther King, there was violence and protest, a car or two overturned and burned in the streets, and some sore heads and tails––but that was not much in comparison with what might have been if those treasury agents weren't there right with it––mostly Southerners themselves. They did their job in the tradition of a job that calls for manly behavior, and manhood no matter what, in all phases of their job.

They later said around there that the moonshine stills were fired high and long and bright, in those days at Montgomery, and that the A&TT men would be furious. They didn't think that A&TT men might know something else besides moonshine and moonshiners. They didn't stop to think that an A&TT man was human, that he had a home and a family, and had taxes to pay. That he knew sickness and health, and that he had spent long hours in school to get his job. They didn't know how he felt apprehensive about his first raid or two until he caught the fever for action that his companions had. That he couldn't understand their patience to wait long hours sometimes until just the right moment to release their action. They didn't understand that it was hard for a new A&TT man to catch on, and that the game he was playing couldn't be one hundred percent gentle, or one hundred percent rough either because he was dealing with people, different and unpredictable.

The old bucks in the job said that it wasn't always summer in the heart or head, and it wasn't winter either because some days are hot and cold at the same time in the revenooering climate.

When you have a bridge to cross wait until you get to it and see what gives, but if you know that you have to cross it, if it is open or blocked, you think about it one hell of a lot. You know you might be saying hello or goodby but you'll say something.

That's when you either cry or you laugh, or you write a zillion reports about it later, or you drive on across and six months later you have to think before you can name the river the bridge was strung across or the name of the town northward before Montgomery.

You never forget though what the north side of that bridge looked like, or what you had thought it might be like.

More than four guys along on most any moonshine raid is a crowd you feel, and when you feel that way it takes one hell of a big mob to impress you when you've got about five hundred of your own at hand. That's the way we felt in Montgomery, and that's another reason why somebody was using their head when they suggested, "Let's get the treasury agents in on this, just to be sure."

At Montgomery, the days came and they went. We read the papers forward and backwards and we were eager to learn of any news from the outside which might concern our own situation.

I remained at Montgomery until it was obvious that things had quieted down considerably in the way that only time can quiet things down. The following Sunday there was an announcement made that volunteers could remain for another week and that the others could depart Wednesday morning.

My group departed on Wednesday morning enroute to Raleigh. We had breakfast at the air base, and packed our gear, and left for Raleigh at about eleven a.m. It was a warm and sunny day. As we drove back through the main street of Montgomery, I saw a traffic policeman with his foot on the rear bumper of a car parked in violation and he was writing out a ticket. To me it was an especially symbolic thing, as though the dove of peace had swooped down on a troubled scene, with the biggest headache for all at hand right then belonging to the driver of the offending car.

There were four of us in the car and someone said, "Well, let's take two days driving back." We laughed and headed for our supper stop to spend the night.

EPILOGUE

Gone for me now are those nights of moonshine in lonely places, some near, and some so far away. Yet from all of them I can look back and recall some places, some incidents, some persons, and some times which have shaped my way of life.

I can think back on a thousand vital hours that seem to have come from one day at Manhattan's Battery Park a hundred years ago when I saw that big black boat.

I can still see Dutch, and Red, and Swede standing there. I can see all the things about them that day. I can recall the city noises there and the sounds of the battery shore, and I hear the voices of the gulls trailing the red ferryboats. I can smell the salt from one of yesterday's seas, and I can reach up for that sailor cap that wasn't there when I really needed it one day.

I can do all those things but I can't bring that day back, and I can't bring back Dutch, and Red and Swede.

Maybe up there where they are, beyond the highest moon, they have sent me some of their light which they've gathered from the good years on earth. They are up there I know.

The three of them said that they wouldn't have my job for anything. Too many revenooers died with their boots on, they said.

Now here in Raleigh, North Carolina, where I traded my gun and badge for a typewriter and eraser two years ago, revenooering ended for me, I am about to wind up a book.

Since you have come this far in reading this book, I think that you will know why I began it, and why I stayed with it. My theme is of life in the times and places I have known it. The plot is how I have known it, or came to know it, and how it is ending too.

I'm a pretty lucky guy. I've worked and played with the best gangs that I could gather at hand. I've trod the long, and mostly happy, road of the revenooer with a song in my heart wherever it was possible.

I'm lucky in that I never wanted to reach for a gun to impress anybody in the same way that I once wanted to reach for a sailor cap that wasn't there with me in Battery Park when I needed it to really impress.

I worked with great men alongside me in difficult places, and in happy places; and in final places for them, while the echoes of their laughter in life was still loud in my ears.

I've seen plenty of moonshiners with many fine qualities. Their troubles arose from being born and reared where they were––in places where moonshine was the king, and the bread–and–butter too, and warm clothing, and a tight roof overhead. They had to be sharp aplenty to remain out of jail, and they acknowledged it when the chips were down for them. In that, they laid aside their curses, their guns, their heavy foot upon a gas pedal and played the game for real––and more of us went home those nights that way.

I am lucky to be on the retirement side of revenooering because of my years of enforcement service rather than to be on disability that has touched so many revenooers.

The ones who were rocked crazily around inside tumbling cars with the new noises of it all not helping a bit. The ones with lead in them, and missing limbs, and unseeing eyes, and secret, deadly pains that announce themselves in a foggy recollection of one night upon a mountain or in a swamp or tenement cellar––the night they should have taken leave or stayed in bed.

I am lucky that I have had good doctors and nurses when I needed them.

I am a lucky guy too, that in all of the high speed races I've been with, and all the crazy driving I had to do, that I never had a chargeable accident.

They permit us to retire at age fifty if the number of years in service is sufficient. It is a good thing too. I wanted to retire at midnight on my fiftieth birthday. I was disappointed. I had to wait two more weeks because of paper work involved and such. I don't think that I did much work during those two weeks, but I did work up until the five of the o'clock, p.m., that day.

The government has things figured for revenooers the same way the insurance companies did when they put those high–risk rates on our policies.

Even though I am lucky I am not rich or anything like it. My wife, Myrtle, worked full time while I've been writing this book. We have a small house but a convenient one with trees in the yard and some nice azaleas and camellias. We have a branch down at the back of the house. Sometimes it dries up, but it's a good place for me to go some nights when I get a hankering for the outdoor night life. I can sit there with my back to a tree and listen to old night friends and night sounds.

In some ways, this now, as I write becomes the loneliest of all writing hours. This final parting from you once imaginary readers is like separating from old, unseen friends of many months.

As I close now I see another old friend up beyond the pinetops at the back of my house. It is a friend from many times and places. Keep shining up there old feller, and say "Howdy" to all the revenooers up there for old "Racer," and give my best to Dutch, and Red, and Swede.

On special nights, old Moon, if I get the yearning to be out there under your light some more, I'll just stroll out my door and down to the branch. I'll put my back to a sturdy pine and sit there and look up and say, "Shine, Moon, shine."